HAIL TO THE CHIEF

ALSO BY ROBERT DALLEK

Lone Star Rising: Lyndon Johnson and His Times, 1908–1960

Ronald Reagan: The Politics of Symbolism

The American Style of Foreign Policy:
Cultural Politics and Foreign Affairs

Franklin D. Roosevelt and American Foreign Policy, 1932–1945

Democrat and Diplomat: The Life of William E. Dodd

HAIL TO THE CHIEF

The Making and Unmaking of American Presidents

ROBERT DALLEK

OXFORD
UNIVERSITY PRESS

OXFORD
UNIVERSITY PRESS

Oxford   New York

Athens   Auckland   Bangkok   Bogotá   Buenos Aires
Cape Town   Chennai   Dar es Salaam   Delhi   Florence   Hong Kong   Istanbul
Karachi   Kolkata   Kuala Lumpur   Madrid   Melbourne   Mexico City   Mumbai
Nairobi   Paris   São Paulo   Shanghai   Singapore   Taipei   Tokyo   Toronto   Warsaw

and associated companies in

Berlin   Ibadan

First published by Hyperion, 1996
114 Fifth Avenue, New York, NY 10011

First issued as an Oxford University Press paperback, 2001
198 Madison Avenue, New York, New York 10016

Oxford is a registered trademark of Oxford University Press

Library of Congress Cataloging-in-Publication Data
Dallek, Robert.
Hail to the chief : the making and unmaking of American presidents / Robert Dallek.
p. cm.
Originally published : New York : Hyperion, c1996.
Includes bibliographical references and index.
ISBN 0-19-514582-8 (Pbk.)
1. Presidents--United States--History. 2. United States--Politics and government. I.
Title.

E176.I.D34 2001
973'.09'9--dc21   00-069878

3 5 7 9 10 8 6 4
Printed in the United States of America

For
Edward A. Goldstein
Lorris Gosman
Minna Gosman
in Friendship

ACKNOWLEDGMENTS

This book grows out of exchanges with students and colleagues about the presidency. A class I taught at the UCLA Honors College on the modern presidency provided an opportunity to discuss my ideas with thoughtful undergraduates who helped me refine my thinking.

My agent, John Wright, not only arranged the details of publication but also gave enthusiastic encouragement for which I am most grateful.

Steve Gillon, Stephen Hopgood, and Byron Shafer, three of my colleagues at Oxford University, provided valuable suggestions for the opening chapter. Geraldine R. Dallek, Edward A. Goldstein, Lewis L. Gould, Max Holland, Stanley I. Kutler, and Bruce J. Schulman gave me the benefit of their wise counsel on the whole manuscript. They saved me from factual errors and added to my belief that historical understanding always profits from collaborative scholarship.

Richard P. Kot, the talented executive editor at Hyperion, made suggestions about content and form that helped clarify my prose and arguments.

CONTENTS

INTRODUCTION

There are three "impossible" professions, Sigmund Freud said: education, psychoanalysis, and government. America's history is a vivid affirmation of this principle, considering the problems that the nation's educators and public officials have confronted in trying to make its schools and government work. The latter, especially, has often been viewed by Americans with suspicion and hostility. "The government that governs least governs best," Jefferson told us at the start of the Republic. "Government is not the solution; government is the problem," Ronald Reagan declared almost two hundred years later.

Occasionally the country has witnessed a surge of confidence in the federal authority's ability to sustain national institutions and solve economic and social problems. But while the first years of the Republic under the leadership of Washington, Adams, Jefferson, Madison, and Monroe were a "Golden Age of American Government," they offered little preparation for the ordeals of the Civil War, Reconstruction, and the dislocations of a rapidly industrializing nation. While the twenty years of progressivism dominated by the presidencies of Theodore Roosevelt and Woodrow Wilson were a welcome change from the stumbling administrations of the nameless, faceless presidents who occupied the White House for thirty-five years after Lincoln's assassination, the return to the doldrums in the 1920s, when Harding, Coolidge, and Hoover presided over caretaker administrations, was more the norm. The success of Franklin Roosevelt's twelve-year presidency gave hope that we were entering a new era in which chief executives would provide effective leadership both for an ever larger, more complicated domestic society and a nuclear-armed world endangered by national passions and apocalyptic ideologies. The fifty years after World War II, however, saw a reversion to form; by the 1990s

Americans had less faith in the capacity of Congress, the courts, and the executive to govern effectively than at almost any time in their history.

An anecdote about an argument between a physician, engineer, and politician is emblematic of current attitudes toward politics. "My profession is the most important," the physician asserts. "The Lord created Eve from Adam's rib; it was a surgical procedure; we physicians were there at creation." "No, no," the engineer responds. "Take one step back. The Lord created the universe from chaos. It was the greatest engineering feat in history. My profession was there at creation." "Fair enough," the politician replies. "But who do you think created the chaos?"

Throughout the country's history, the presidency has been a consistent focus of antigovernment feelings. To be sure, as one historian has said, Americans "have a profound longing to believe in and admire" their presidents. But at the same time they seem to take as much satisfaction from presidential shortcomings: animus toward national chiefs has been a mainstay of national public sentiment. Of the forty-one men who have held the office only fourteen have been elected more than once and only eleven have served two full terms, with FDR serving a little more than three.

To most presidents themselves, service in the office was, as Jefferson said, "a splendid misery." Andrew Jackson called the job "a situation of dignified slavery," a description echoed by Wilson's comment that "The President is a superior kind of slave." Along with the exhilaration of reaching the zenith of political ambition came the burden of an abusive press and public all too ready to declare its chosen leader a fool and a knave.

As John Steinbeck remarked: "We give the President more work than a man can do, more responsibility than a man should take, more pressure than a man can bear. . . . We wear him out, use him up, eat him up. . . . He is ours and we exercise the right to destroy him."

"I greatly apprehend that my Countrymen will expect too much from me," George Washington wrote shortly after entering the presidency. "I fear, if the issue of public measures should not correspond with their sanguine expectations, they will turn the extravagant (and I may say undue) praises, which they are heaping upon me at this moment, into equally extravagant (though I would fondly hope unmerited) censures." By the end of his term, Washington "was beset by 'unmerited censures' of the vilest kind."

The press berated Abraham Lincoln, the greatest of our presidents, with what the historian David H. Donald has called "virulent obscenity." He was abused as a "half-witted usurper," a "mole-eyed" monster with "soul . . . of leather," "the present turtle at the head of the government," "the head ghoul at Washington." An 1864 editorial in the New York *Herald* said: "Lincoln is a joke incarnated. . . . The idea that such a man as he should be President of such a country as this is a very ridiculous joke. . . . His inaugural address was a joke. . . . His Cabinet is and always has been a standing joke. All his State papers are jokes. . . . His intrigues to secure a renomination and the hopes he appears to entertain of a re-election are, however, the most laughable jokes of all." Democratic and Republican politicians were no more charitable to Lincoln, comparing him to the "original gorilla" and describing him as "pitiable," "shattered, dazed, utterly foolish," and "an awful, woeful ass."

Washington's and Lincoln's experiences with the public proved to be all too typical. The evolution of the presidency from Washington to Ulysses S. Grant, Henry Adams said, was by itself evidence enough to refute Darwin's theory of evolution. "My God! What is there in this place that a man should ever want to get into it?" James A. Garfield asked a few months after entering office. Publicity about an illegitimate child he had fathered subjected Grover Cleveland to vilification as a "moral leper" and "a man stained with disgusting infamy." Cleveland saw his time in the White House "as a dreadful self-inflicted penance for the good of my country." Woodrow Wilson believed that "Men of ordinary physique and discretion cannot be Presidents and live, if the strain be not somehow relieved." For Herbert Hoover the office was "a compound hell."

Toward the end of his term, Jefferson looked forward to relief "from a drudgery to which I am no longer equal." While in office Wilson suffered a stroke; Harding walked the floors of the White House at night. The Great Depression made Hoover so dour that critics complained "a rose would wilt in his hand." Harry Truman kept his sanity by writing scathing letters in response to attacks, although he rarely sent them. Reading what Vietnam war opponents wrote about him and hearing pickets chanting, "Hey, hey LBJ, how many kids did you kill today?" so upset Lyndon Johnson that one aide considered calling publicly for a psychiatric evaluation. Richard Nixon reportedly left office psychologically broken, unable to sleep and talking to the portraits of past presidents. After three years in office, Jimmy Carter looked a decade older in photographs. Bill Clinton complained that he was "subjected to more assaults than any previous president based on the evidence."

Is the office of the presidency, then, an unmanageable institution that invites failure? In the 1970s, in the aftermath of Vietnam, which had driven Lyndon Johnson from power, and Watergate, which had compelled Richard Nixon's resignation, "a theory arose," Arthur Schlesinger, Jr., explained, "about the fragility of the American Presidency. . . . Columnists wrote of 'the Presidency in decline.' Scholars mobilized their colleagues to join in producing books under such titles as *The Tethered Presidency, The Post-Imperial Presidency, The Impossible Presidency.* Pundits confidently predicted an age of one-term Presidents. The impression arose . . . of a beleaguered and pathetic fellow sitting forlornly in the Oval Office, assailed by unprecedentedly intractable problems, paralyzed by the constitutional separation of powers, hemmed in by congressional and bureaucratic constraints, pushed one way and another by exigent interest groups, seduced, betrayed, and abandoned by the mass media. . . . In 1980 ex-President [Gerald] Ford said to general applause, 'We have not an imperial presidency but an imperiled presidency.' "

The pundits and political scientists have not been without reason for concern. Constitutional checks on the presidency have always made life difficult for incumbents. Congress's power of the purse, approval of executive appointments, freedom to override presidential vetoes, declare war, and investigate and legislate against executive abuses have combined with the power of the courts over economic and social policy to restrict greatly presidential freedoms. Add to these inhibitions the constraints imposed on presidents by undisciplined political parties, an ever more critical press, and a fickle public impatient for quick and painless solutions to complex problems, and one marvels at how much the country's successful presidents have been able to achieve.

Writing in 1980, the English journalist Godfrey Hodgson argued that traditional legal and political restraints combined with current circumstance consigned future presidents to certain failure. He believed the five presidents from John F. Kennedy to Jimmy Carter were all unsuccessful in their operation of the office, and since their tasks were getting "progressively more difficult with the passing of time, then the fault can hardly be in the individuals," he asserted. "It must be in the institution."

Presidents have added to their grief by encouraging public inclinations to view them as capable of performing miracles. *New York Times* columnist Tom Wicker has written: "Americans like to think—and a history insufficiently studied or understood persuades them—that for everything that's wrong there's bound to be a solution, only needing to be found; and the quicker the fix the better. . . . So it tends to be with our presidents. If we just elect the right . . . person, we can get this country moving again. Throw the rascals out, vote in the miracle man, and we can all stand tall; it'll be morning again in America." William Howard Taft stated his predicament perfectly when he complained that his countrymen assigned the president responsibility "for all the sins of omission and of commission of society at large." But, Taft cautioned, "the President cannot make clouds to rain, he cannot make the corn to grow, he cannot make business to be good."

True, party platforms and presidential campaigns have by their very nature been exercises in hyperbole. Who wants to vote for someone who will do less for the country than his opponent? But while campaign rhetoric, like economic forecasts, is largely forgotten and forgiven the day after the polls close, an incumbent's ambitious commitments are held to a higher standard. Americans expect their presidents not to speak idly about weighty matters of prosperity, taxes, race relations, war, and peace. Promises to end war permanently, turn depression into economic well-being, roll back Communism, abolish poverty, assure racial harmony, balance budgets while cutting taxes and then not raise taxes again have all been miracles presidents could not perform, and many have found themselves losers for having failed to fulfill such pledges.

How, then, can we account for the considerable achievements of our most respected presidents? Though George Washington, Abraham Lincoln, and Franklin Roosevelt had limitations, all three made exceptional marks on history. Washington's initiation of the constitutional system that has lasted longer and been more effective than any system of modern governance remains a great presidential success story. Likewise, Lincoln's determination to hold the Union together and his leadership in the worst crisis in the country's history will probably be regarded as the greatest presidential accomplishment for as long as there is an American nation. Franklin Roosevelt's ability to rally the country against the worst economic crisis in our history, to prevent a repetition of such suffering through far-reaching domestic reforms, and to meet the challenge of Nazism, fascism, and Japanese militarism will, to borrow from Winston Churchill, always stand as one of America's finest hours.

Surely, great achievements have partly been brilliant responses to great crises. Would Washington, Lincoln, or FDR be remembered so well if he had served in the 1850s, as the nation drifted into civil war, or the 1870s and 1880s, the Gilded Age of business expansion and declining moral standards, or the 1920s, an era of the triumph of private over public solutions, or the 1950s and 1980s, when the governmental activism of the New Deal and Great Society eras had lost some of its appeal?

Similarly, luck and circumstances beyond any individual's reach also help account for presidential victories and defeats. President Lincoln was always mindful of how much public affairs depended on conditions he did not shape: "Now, at the end of three years' struggle," he said, "the nation's condition is not what either party, or any man, devised, or expected. God alone can claim it." Would Theodore Roosevelt, Harry Truman, or Lyndon Johnson ever have made it to the White House without the deaths of McKinley, FDR, and JFK? Would Wilson have gained the presidency without the 1912 split in the Republican party? Didn't the onset of the Great Depression give Hoover, an intelligent and competent executive, a claim to being the unluckiest president in American history? Would FDR have won third and fourth terms without the outbreak of the European and then Pacific wars? Could Truman have carried off his 1948 upset without the "do-nothing, good-for-nothing" Eightieth Congress? Wasn't LBJ entitled to curse the fates for leaving him with responsibility for the Vietnam war? Imagine how much more successful Jimmy Carter might have been without the oil crunch and Iranian hostage crisis, or if the U.S. rescue mission had managed to bring the hostages out of Teheran. Isn't there much to the assertion that Ronald Reagan's popularity was in some measure made possible by the relatively benign circumstances he faced as president? Would Bill Clinton be president without Ross Perot? Can't at least part of what accounts for presidential success and failure be ascribed to Ralph Waldo Emerson's belief that events are often "in the saddle and ride mankind?"

No one can deny that challenges to the nation's economic and political survival have presented opportunities for presidential greatness and that circumstances beyond human control have caused some presidents considerable grief. Yet if the effectiveness of the presidency depended solely on its reactions to crises, the office would never have stood at the center of American politics, as it has for much of our history. A number of presidents have managed to leave honorable legacies without having faced tasks as daunting as those met by our three greatest leaders. Indeed, some of our most successful presidents were those who converted relatively lesser dangers into political capital. Moreover, they did not allow themselves to be overwhelmed by unanticipated problems, but rather seized upon them as opportunities to lead the nation through a time of troubles.

There have been no dearth of difficulties confronting political leaders throughout our history, and it seems reasonable to argue that the least effective of our chief executives simply did not rise to the demands of their day. Were the issues of slavery and sectionalism of such small consequence that John Tyler, Zachary Taylor, Millard Fillmore, Franklin Pierce, and James Buchanan were entitled to see themselves as presiding over an era in which no president could have made a great mark? Were the upheavals of Reconstruction so negligible that Andrew Johnson and Ulysses S. Grant could rationalize their stumbling performances by regarding themselves as chief executives in an unheroic time? Were the class tensions, economic dislocations, and conflicts between established and newly arriving Americans in the 1870s, 1880s, and 1890s so transitory that Hayes, Garfield, Arthur, Cleveland, the second Harrison, and McKinley were justified in not formulating major policies that could address the anguish of their day? Similar questions can be posed against Taft, Harding, Coolidge, Hoover, Ford, Carter, Bush, and now Clinton in the twentieth century.

Among the presidents who did elevate the standing of the office by confronting the difficulties of their eras with intelligent statecraft that continues to resonate through American history is Jefferson, who, in spite of constitutional scruples, decided to purchase the Louisiana Territory. With this act he created an "empire of liberty" where opportunities for self-supporting middle-class Americans were greatly expanded. Madison's leadership in the War of 1812, by which he turned aside domestic divisions and reestablished American independence from European strife, was exceptional. "Notwithstanding a thousand faults and blunders," John Adams wrote Jefferson in 1817, Madison's administration had "acquired more glory, and established more Union than all his three predecessors, Washington, Adams, Jefferson." James Monroe's doctrine forbidding European intervention in the New World, combined with the acquisition of the "Floridas" in the (John Quincy) Adams-Onis Treaty of 1819, helped further insulate America from European turmoil and advanced continental development. Andrew Jackson's presidency gave both symbolic and substantive support to the democratization of American politics and the supremacy of the federal union over the states. His administration marked the beginning of modern American party politics and helped establish the country as a standing example of popular sovereignty under the rule of law.

In the twentieth century, Theodore Roosevelt's Square Deal, his invocation of federal authority as an arbiter between competing interests, and his use of the executive office as a "bully pulpit" set the government on the modern path toward the constructive solution of national problems. Wilson's progressive policies restored a measure of economic and social justice at home and encouraged peoples everywhere to make cooperation and harmony standards of international affairs. Truman's containment of Soviet ambitions assured what historian John L. Gaddis has called "The Long Peace" and the ultimate demise of Soviet Communism. Eisenhower's general restraint in dealing with overseas difficulties gave the United States a decade of peace.

JFK's effective handling of the Cuban missile crisis and negotiation of a nuclear test ban in the atmosphere greatly reduced the chances of a nuclear war. LBJ's comparable mastery assured an end to the southern system of racial apartheid, the opening of greater opportunities to minorities and women, and the introduction of guaranteed health care for the elderly. Nixon's opening to China and détente toward the Soviet Union significantly shortened the Cold War. Carter's mediation of Egyptian-Israeli differences resulted in the Camp David accords and signaled a breakthrough in Middle East peace talks. And in the eighties, after the traumas of Vietnam and Watergate, Reagan's skills in communicating with the mass of Americans temporarily restored faith in the federal government generally and the presidency in particular.

How, then, can we account for the variability of presidential performance, and the variations within presidential terms themselves? Wilson's domestic gains and stewardship of victory in World War I outstripped his failed peacemaking at the end of the fighting. Truman's largely unfulfilled Fair Deal was no match for his achievement in building a restrained, coherent response to the Communist threat. Eisenhower's foreign policy record was significantly better than his domestic one, which was dominated by three recessions and general passivity toward the struggle for black rights in the South. Johnson's failure in Vietnam has little resemblance to his inspired leadership toward a Great Society at home. Nixon's erratic record in extending the Vietnam war for four years while at the same time creating a general framework for peace with the Communist superpowers is a particularly striking example of an uneven presidential performance. Reagan's handling of the Congress in winning tax cuts and adroit dealings with Mikhail Gorbachev do not square with the massive deficits and huge debt he left his successors or with his unproductive intervention in Nicaragua.

In a compelling essay on the presidency published in 1986, Arthur Schlesinger, Jr., argued against structural changes in the office. He wisely declared the institution sound, pointing out that "structure is an alibi for policy failure. Let us not be beguiled by constitutional reform from the real tasks of statecraft," he counseled. "In the end, politics is the high and serious art of solving substantive problems. . . . The salvation of the Presidency lies in the realm of politics, not of constitutional reform."

Hail to the Chief is an attempt to explain precisely how such political practice has been the key element in presidential success and failure, national advance and public loss. It is one historian's view of how fallible, well-meaning men have used the presidency to good and poor effect. Nevertheless, no one should ignore the importance of circumstances beyond the control of any man or institution in shaping the outcome of a presidential term.

Two hundred years of our country's history suggest that five qualities have been constants in the men who have most effectively fulfilled the oath of office. First, every successful president has had vision, insight, or understanding: a clear idea of where he wished to lead the nation in its quest for a better future. However illusory some of these dreams have been, whether for a harmonious nation or for America's Manifest Destiny to expand across the continent and out into the Caribbean and the Pacific, a clear and comprehensible grand design has been central to every significant presidential advance. Second, the most successful of our chiefs have also been great realists or pragmatists—politicians who understood that politics was the art of the possible or that the road to proficient leadership was through a sensible opportunism or flexible response to changing conditions at home and abroad.

Third, presidential gains have depended on the consent of the governed: presidents without a national consensus for major policies touching people's everyday lives are politicians courting defeat. Fourth, the best of our presidents have always recognized that leadership required a personal connection between the president and the people, or that the power of the Oval Office rests to a great degree on the affection of the country for its chief. From Washington to Lincoln to the two Roosevelts and, most recently, Reagan, the force of presidential personality has been a major factor in determining a president's fate. And fifth, a corollary to conditions three and four, presidents need credibility—presidents who are unable to earn the trust of their countrymen are governors who cannot govern and lead.

While vision, pragmatism, consensus-building, charisma, and trustworthiness may be considered discrete categories, they are in fact inextricably linked: each of these political practices connects to and builds upon the other. No president has distinguished himself simply by being a visionary, or a good practical politician, or a charming, trustworthy reflector of national views. Though the chapters that follow elaborate on how the presence and absence of each of these elements in various administrations has made a difference in advancing the national well-being, it would be reductionist to suggest that any of them stand alone. Can there be consensus without vision or political compromise? Can there be trust without popular appeal or vice versa? Like history itself the elements of presidential effectiveness form a seamless web. And like the scientist in his laboratory, we isolate each of them only for the sake of closer study. Taken as a whole, I hope they will demonstrate why and how past presidents have served the nation well and ill and how a fresh attempt at understanding them can advance the cause of enlightened leadership in the years ahead.

The White House at the end of the twentieth century is as removed from Washington's day as the jet plane is from the horse and buggy. The global responsibilities a chief executive faces today dwarf those his counterpart encountered in the 1790s, as does his impact on the economic and social life of the nation. Nuclear weapons, electronic communications, and national and international responsibilities compel presidents to think and act differently from their early predecessors in the office. But, as the examples in the following chapters demonstrate, the elements of compelling leadership have largely remained unchanged. Washington and Jefferson, Jackson and Lincoln, TR and Wilson, FDR and Reagan, are continuing models for effective performance in the White House. Future presidents will not find a formula for greatness in their actions, but they will gain some wisdom from remembering the accomplishments of their most effective antecedents. History offers no surefire solutions to current dilemmas, but it can provide guidelines that future chiefs ignore at their peril.

CHAPTER 1

"THE VISION THING"

The Bible tells us (Proverbs 29:18): "Where there is no vision, the people perish." The United States has been as subject to this principle as any other nation. Like citizens everywhere, Americans have wanted leaders who have had the capacity to imagine a better future. This desire has remained a constant in our history despite the fact that the country has at the same time regarded itself as an expression of national perfection. Likewise, it has remained central to the country's political values even though some politicians have decried grandiose statements of national purpose as more salesmanship than viable prescriptions for change. George Bush, for example, had little patience with what he called "the vision thing." Yet no candidate has been able to attain high office in the United States without some expression of faith in a greater America, and nowhere has this proven to be more true than in the case of presidential aspirants.

Nevertheless, once in office many of our presidents have been notable more for drift than mastery, for passive, ill-defined administrations than for activist ones leading to significant gains. How does this happen in a country that has consistently been most enamored of its preaching presidents, of those who have urged us to "pay any price, meet any challenge" in the service of national advance? Some key factors have been America's equally strong affinity

1

for laissez-faire, its distrust of government intrusion into private lives, and its suspicion of overseas involvements—all of which have served as counterweights to bold designs promising federal assertiveness at home and abroad.

Like so much else in American politics, presidential vision has required a balancing act, an ability to sell the country on a grand purpose—a Square Deal, a New Frontier, a Reagan Revolution—that would not carry it too far toward presidential control, national planning, or bold foreign commitments. While vision has been an essential ingredient of presidential history, its content has been as varied as the problems that have confronted the forty-one men who have served in the White House.

I

Whatever his record in history, every American president has entered office holding a long-term view of where he wished to lead the nation. Whether this meant restoring earlier values or forging new means of meeting current problems, presidents right, left, and center have won popular support by inspiring hope that they had a sensible design for improving the national well-being.

In and of itself, however, vision has not been a sufficient guarantee of securing access to the highest office. On the contrary, the least successful presidential candidates have been third-party aspirants who separated themselves from the established political organizations because of a compelling idea or program that neither major party would embrace. In 1912 Theodore Roosevelt organized the Progressive party out of frustration with conservative dominance of the Republicans. He also believed himself and the New Nationalism, his program of federal activism, as preferable to Wilson and the New Freedom's restoration of greater economic competition. Though TR ran ahead of the Republican incumbent, Taft, he split the Republican vote and thus enabled the Democrats to return to the White House after a sixteen-year absence.

In 1948 Strom Thurmond's Dixiecrats, who opposed civil rights, and Henry Wallace's Progressives, who espoused domestic advance toward greater economic equality and Soviet-American

friendship, garnered only 2.3 million out of 48 million p
votes and allowed Harry Truman to stay in office. In 1992 R
Perot announced, "We owe it to the American people to explain
to them in plain language where we are, where we are going, and
what we have to do." Though Perot acted on his convictions,
promising to balance the budget and eliminate Washington red
tape, only 19 percent of the electorate gave him their votes.

Similarly, the least successful major-party candidates in this century—Republicans Taft in 1912, Alf Landon in 1936, and Barry
Goldwater in 1964, and Democrats George McGovern in 1972
and Walter Mondale in 1984—took markedly strong stands on
major issues. But the pronounced conservatism of Taft, Landon,
and Goldwater in periods of liberal reform, and the single-minded
liberalism of McGovern and Mondale during years of triumphant
conservatism, left them victims of electoral landslides.

These examples are not offered to suggest that victorious candidates reached the promised land simply by adopting bland
mixtures of competing ideas, all-purpose ideologies that threatened
little offense to majorities. However inattentive Americans are to
politics, they do insist on knowing a candidate's general aims. In
the late nineteenth century, for instance, Grant, Hayes, Garfield,
Arthur, Cleveland, and Harrison, none of whom ultimately made
much of a mark on the country, nevertheless all stood for the ideal
of a harmonious, prosperous America. Their presidential campaigns
offered no remedies for continuing North-South divisions, or for
economic and social ills besetting farmers, laborers, and recently
arrived immigrants. Yet voters who put these men in the White
House saw them as symbols of national unity and reflections of the
ethos of the self-made man, an ethos that promised eventually to
overcome national problems. These Gilded Age presidents were
emblematic of the nationalistic, entrepreneurial spirit that encouraged visions of one America, where hard work, frugality, and a little
luck assured individual gain.

The most persuasive cases of how important vision is to a presidential candidate are those of challengers running against unpopular incumbents: Harding in 1920, FDR in 1932, Eisenhower in
1952, and Carter in 1976 offered themselves as alternatives to the
stumbling administrations of Wilson, Hoover, Truman, and Ford.
(While Harding and Ike were actually running against James Cox

ı, respectively, for all practical purposes they
against the current incumbents than the Dem-
In these campaigns the electorate was so fed up
cemaking, Hoover's Depression, HST's Korean
xon-Ford transgressions that a constant drumbeat
t administration's failings seemed sufficient to give
Harding, velt, Eisenhower, and Carter electoral victories. Yet
each of them felt compelled to give some general idea of where he
intended to lead the nation.

Harding's 1920 campaign is particularly instructive in this regard.
After twenty years of progressive appeals for civic-mindedness and
sermons on the need for personal commitment to public change,
Americans wanted a respite from political crusades. Wilson's inability to turn the sacrifices of the Great War into a democratic,
peaceful world confirmed the country's desire to put private concerns above public activism. Given that climate all Harding had to
do, one Republican strategist advised, was to stay on his front
porch in Ohio and preach "Americanism." Asked what the word
meant, one party boss declared: "Damned if I know, but it's going
to get a lot of votes." Keep Warren at home, another Republican
leader counseled: "If he goes out on the hustings, he's the sort of
damned fool who will try to answer questions."

But even the most confident Republican wheelhorses in 1920
knew that their candidate would have to take some position that
spoke to the current mood. In a number of dreary speeches, which
one critic described as a series of pompous phrases wandering over
the landscape in search of an idea, Harding nevertheless successfully expressed the national yearning for a return to presidential
passivity and less government regulation. In his most famous expression of this idea, Harding said: "America's present need is not
heroics, but healing; not nostrums, but normalcy; not revolution
but restoration; not agitation, but adjustment; not surgery, but
serenity."

Calvin Coolidge, Harding's running mate, added to the conviction that the Republicans would make the future look a lot like
the past. The taciturn, undynamic Coolidge, who impressed TR's
daughter as having been weaned on a pickle, epitomized the old-

school New England virtues in which he had been reared. Frugality, honesty, hard work, faith in God and country, and small-town family values were the conventional wisdoms for which Harding and Coolidge and much of the nation stood in the 1920s. Despite one of the least dynamic campaigns in presidential history, the Republicans turned their symbolic appeal to tradition into the largest popular majority for a presidential candidate to that point in U.S. history.

Franklin Roosevelt's 1932 campaign had some similarities to that of Harding in 1920. Like Harding, FDR, the challenger, seemed assured of a victory. After four years in which Republican prosperity had become an economic disaster, with about a quarter of the work force unemployed, business nearly at a standstill, and a large minority of Americans ill-fed, ill-housed, and ill-clad, Hoover was an easy mark for the Democrats.

The White House took on the atmosphere of a funeral parlor, and hostility toward the president was rife. "Lend me a nickel; I want to call a friend," Hoover was reported as telling a cabinet member. "Here's a dime," the man replied. "Call all your friends." According to another joke, Hoover was the world's greatest engineer: "In a little more than two years he has drained, ditched, and damned the United States." When told that business was improving, vaudeville comedians asked, "Is Hoover dead?"

Roosevelt understood that his surest route to the White House was through calling attention to Hoover's failings and not by offering specific details of a Democratic program to end the Depression. "Lack of leadership in Washington has brought our country face to face with serious questions of unemployment and financial depression," FDR emphasized throughout his campaign. He blamed Hoover and the Republicans for sitting on their hands, declaring, "Nothing happened but words." But he was careful not to say exactly what he would do instead. Though he sharply attacked high Republican tariffs, for example, he refused to take his own clear stand on the issue. Asked by a member of his "brain trust" to choose between a high-tariff and a low-tariff speech, Roosevelt told him to "weave the two together." The columnist Walter Lippmann called FDR the master of "the balanced antithesis," a member of the "school of politicians who do not believe in stating their views unless and until there is no avoiding it."

In 1932 Roosevelt took ambiguous positions on farm policy, federal spending, and government power. He promised to rescue impoverished farmers without keeping the government in the agricultural business, to appropriate funds to prevent starvation and dire need while proposing to cut federal spending by 25 percent, and to reduce Washington's control over industry despite plans for government regulation of utilities and Wall Street, public power development, and expanded federal conservation programs.

Though Roosevelt saw the advantage to his platform from straddling controversial issues, he also felt compelled to give people hope that a Roosevelt administration would take bold steps to relieve suffering and restore the nation's economic health. A master of symbolic politics, he made his campaign, as he would his presidency, a vivid illustration that his very presence on the national scene signaled a better day. As soon as he was nominated, he took an airplane from New York to Chicago, and thus became the first candidate ever to fly to his party's convention and deliver his own acceptance speech. By so doing, he told fellow Democrats, he was consciously breaking an absurd tradition, and declared it "from now on the task of our Party to break foolish traditions"—a declaration in line with his earlier statement that "the country needs, and unless I mistake its temper, the country demands bold, persistent experimentation." In his acceptance address that day, he boldly promised a "new deal" for the American people. When an astute journalist underscored FDR's commitment to a New Deal, Roosevelt's campaign and administration seized on that concept as a historic label that encapsulated a vision of what he intended to do for the nation.

Like FDR, Dwight Eisenhower was in a strong position to take the White House in 1952 simply by running against the incumbent's—in this case, Truman's—faltering policies. A military hero with an infectious smile and winning personality, "Ike," an architect of Allied victory in World War II, seemed an ideal leader to meet the challenges of the Cold War. A nonpolitician who had never identified himself with either party, Eisenhower also seemed to promise a respite from the bitter McCarthyist partisanship that had engulfed the nation in the early fifties.

Korea, Communism, and corruption, "K1–C2," were particularly troublesome burdens carried by Truman; Adlai Stevenson, his preferred successor; and the Democrats during the campaign. The deadlock in the Korean fighting, where the United States had sustained more than twenty thousand casualties and faced a Chinese Communist army apparently willing and able to fight a long war of attrition, drove Truman's approval ratings down to 25 percent. Furthermore, accusations of Communist infiltration of the government, especially the state department, where "fellow travelers" were supposed to have abandoned China to Communist control and passed atomic secrets to Moscow, made Democrats vulnerable to charges of insufficient determination to meet the Soviet-Communist threat. Democratic nominee Stevenson was mocked as having a Ph.D. from Secretary of State Dean Acheson's "cowardly college of Communist containment," in a characteristic formulation of Republican vice-presidential candidate Richard Nixon. Wisconsin Senator Joseph McCarthy assailed the "twenty years of treason" by which FDR and Truman had betrayed Eastern Europe and China to Communism. The Democrats were further compromised by charges of influence peddling, which led to their being attacked as a corrupt party that had to be driven from office.

Though Stevenson gamely belittled Republican charges that "two great decades of progress in peace, victory in war, and bold leadership in this anxious hour were the misbegotten spawn of socialism, bungling, [and] corruption," he could not convince the country to ignore the shortfall in recent Democratic policies and return the party of Truman to the White House. After twenty years during which the country had passed through revolutionary changes at home and abroad, Americans were eager for another period of relative quiet in public affairs, which the GOP, with its conservative antigovernment pronouncements, seemed more likely to provide.

Despite the assets of his personality and the vulnerability of the Democratic record, which seemed sufficient to assure an electoral victory, Eisenhower felt compelled to announce his own program. Distressed by a 1952 Truman budget $14 billion in the red and a right-wing drift in the Republican party toward abandoning military commitments in Europe, Ike was determined to run against bankruptcy at home and isolationism abroad. With his invitation to Nixon to join him on the ticket, he effectively declared his intention to make his campaign a crusade for beliefs he and the country shared.

Although the excesses of the anti-Communist Republican right troubled him, Eisenhower was content to make the Truman record on combating Communism a major element of his own platform. This strategy ensured not only that the Republican right would remain loyal to the party but also that a majority of voters did not drift back to their natural home in the Democratic camp. Just as significant to Eisenhower, however, was his conviction that the Democrats had in fact been too passive in countering internal subversion and opposing Communist domination of Eastern Europe. Throughout the campaign he declared his determination to root out disloyal Americans in the government and to initiate a policy that fostered some hope "of obtaining by peaceful means freedom for the people now behind the Iron Curtain." He promised sustained "aid" to "enslaved" peoples until their countries were free.

Eisenhower's anti-Communist rhetoric heartened Americans to believe that he would function as a president who knew how to assure the national security against a powerful adversary. He promised to put an end to "stop-and-start planning" in foreign affairs; we would not "demobilize and then hurriedly remobilize, or swing from optimism to panic." Best of all, he vowed to end the war in Korea by establishing a just and lasting peace. And though he offered no concrete details of how he would achieve this beyond making a personal trip to the war zone, his declaration of intent electrified the country, confirming the impression that Ike had firm views on the most important issues of the day and knew how to put them into effect.

Like Harding, FDR, and Eisenhower, Jimmy Carter entered the presidential campaign with a decided advantage over his opponent, the incumbent Gerald Ford. Not only had Ford's pardon of Nixon tainted him with the very corruption that had driven Nixon from office, but a stumbling economy plagued by stagflation—high unemployment and inflation—made Ford especially vulnerable to

Carter's particular and apparent virtues. A one-term Georgia governor with a reputation for strong religious convictions, high ethical standards, and no ties to a Washington establishment notable for arrogance and wrongdoing, Carter entered the campaign with a thirty-point lead over Ford. As political scientist James MacGregor Burns characterized him, Carter "appeared religious but not pious, compassionate but not sentimental, moral but not moralistic." As a nuclear engineer, a naval officer, a successful southern politician and peanut farmer, he also gave off an aura, Burns added, "of proved competence—competence at running a business and a state, a submarine and a tractor" and at difficult primary campaigns against better-known Democratic opponents.

After the 1974 traumas of an unprecedented presidential resignation and Ford's succession as the country's first unelected chief of state, Americans wanted a reliable leader who would be consistent and effective. Instead of encouraging a view of himself as having clear ideas that he would put into practice in the White House, however, Carter undermined his appeal by trying to be all things to all people. In spite of that, Ford seemed so devoid of vision and so unsuited to the nation's highest office that Carter became an acceptable alternative. After Ford gave both symbolic and substantive demonstrations of his ineptness by tripping as he left an airplane and by declaring in a debate with Carter before a national audience that "there is no Soviet domination of Eastern Europe," voters gave Carter the narrowest victory in the electoral college since 1916.

One commentator on the election complained that he never did "hear what the candidates had to say about the campaign issues." While this vagueness was partly the result of the media's inclination to avoid policy questions that bored a mass audience, it also reflected the largely visionless campaigns run by both men. Though Carter certainly had an edge on Ford when it came to standing for some larger national purpose with which the public could identify, he was no TR, Wilson, or FDR. His aversion to defining grand designs that could expand and solidify his hold on the country was a foretaste of what was to come during his presidency.

II

There is something almost magical in the mass appeal of presidents who are devoted to a high-minded, broad-gauged purpose. The first requirement of presidential leadership, Arthur Schlesinger, Jr., argues, "is to point the republic in one or another direction. This can be done only if the man in the White House possesses, or is possessed by, a vision of the ideal America." The president must be like the "commander of a ship at sea," Henry Adams said. "He must have a helm to grasp, a course to steer, a port to seek."

Presidential vision is especially compelling when it proves itself to be realizable, as has most notably been true of Washington's efforts to create a working national government, or Lincoln's determination to preserve the Union, or FDR's promise to destroy Axis power, or LBJ's commitment to end southern segregation and guarantee affordable health care for the elderly, or Reagan's determination to reduce the power and influence of government.

As the country's first president, George Washington faced the daunting task of making a new Constitution work by convincing the representatives of thirteen states, who jealousy guarded the prerogatives of local rule, to cooperate on behalf of an untested national government optimistically called the United States of America. His job was made easier by memories of failed efforts under the Articles of Confederation to combat European trade barriers with a unified American response, and by the excesses of state legislatures enacting arbitrary laws that jeopardized republican rule. Even with such advantages, however, putting the government on a stable footing remained a challenge requiring exceptional political skills.

Washington's standing as commander-in-chief of the victorious revolutionary armies gave the new government, and the presidency in particular, instant credibility. In a world convinced that the differences separating the diverse peoples and regions of the United States made governance by a central authority impossible, Washington's presence as a unifying force was essential. It gave Americans a renewed sense of shared purpose, which had waned in the six years since the end of the Revolutionary war.

With competing selfish interests plaguing the country in badly needed a symbolic expression of national selflessness as fying ideal. It was part of Washington's hold on the nation tha was just such an "incorruptible" gentleman "whose principles wei more perfectly free from the contamination of . . . selfish and un-worthy passions" than any actor on the public stage in history. The hagiography portraying Washington as "the father of our country," as a man who could not tell a lie, and as a patriot who ascended di-rectly to heaven on his death became an essential national myth. In death as in life Washington served as a model of American ideals: the moral man who left the comfort of his Virginia home at the age of fifty-seven to assume new public burdens became a paradigm for a moral people sacrificing selfish interests to the larger national good. The first president served as a permanent exemplar toward which the country would aspire throughout its history.

Washington was mindful of what his presidency represented to the nation and acted accordingly. "Many things which appear of little importance in themselves and at the beginning," he wrote, "may have great durable consequences from their having been es-tablished at the commencement of a new general government. It will be much easier to commence the administration, upon a well adjusted system, built on tenable grounds, than to correct errors or alter inconveniences after they shall have been confirmed by habit." (His expression of opinion on this matter was more the exception in his statecraft than the rule. "With me, it has always been a maxim rather to let my designs appear from my works than by my expressions," he said in 1797, at the end of his presidency.)

Washington understood that his every action as the country's first president would set a precedent and bespeak a vision of how the government would administer national affairs for the foresee-able future. He shunned indecision, ambiguity, and vacillation as undermining popular confidence in the government's competence, and he aimed to show his countrymen that, in the words of one commentator, "the head of a state can be powerful without en-dangering liberty. In his daily administrative tasks," this historian adds, "he was systematic, orderly, energetic, solicitous of the opin-ions of others but independent in his own judgment, insistent on facts and deliberation but decisive, intent upon general goals and the consistency of particular actions with them." Though he fal-

...ing stricter attention to the divisions of opin-
...tes, which he feared would lead to the rise
...the same sort of public strife that had beset
...e succeeded in planting "in the minds of
...he model of a government which com-
...y reason of its integrity, energy, and compe-

As the record of his achievements so well demonstrates, Washington was not only "first in war, first in peace, and first in the hearts of his countrymen," but also first in understanding that successful presidential leadership greatly depended on a vision of purpose, which was necessary to inspire and unify a newly formed country divided by competing impulses that could have torn it apart.

Abraham Lincoln was the other great visionary president of the nineteenth century. While Jefferson, Madison, Monroe, and Jackson were all more than capable ideologues, none were as dependent on a single-minded purpose as the Rail-Splitter from Kentucky and Illinois. Lincoln's presidency was a travail unlike any other in the country's history. A four-year civil war that consumed 620,000 lives and wounded hundreds of thousands more presented a challenge that would have tested the leadership skills of even the most astute politician.

As it happened, Lincoln barely clung to power. Having won less than 40 percent of the popular vote in the 1860 election, suffered repeated military defeats during the first two years of the war, and announced a policy of slave emancipation that troubled many in the Union, Lincoln almost lost control of Congress in the 1862 elections. Although by 1864 he had begun to achieve greater success on the battlefields, the war's mounting casualties, lack of any discernible end to the fighting, resentment over arbitrary executive actions, and assertions that Lincoln had converted the war from a struggle for the Union into one for emancipation put his reelection in doubt. Just a few weeks before the 1864 election, Lincoln predicted that his Democratic opponent, General George B. McClellan, was likely to win. But the capture of Atlanta by General William T. Sherman at the beginning of September broke an ap-

parent stalemate in the fighting and gave the president enoug.
momentum in the closing days of the campaign to win 55 percent
of the popular vote.

Yet Lincoln's triumph and greatness as a president rested principally on a clear confidence in the beliefs for which he stood.
Throughout the four-year ordeal of the war, which extracted a
personal toll on him as great as that suffered by families who lost
loved ones in the fighting, Lincoln never lost sight of his fundamental aim: to preserve the Union and secure its existence as one
nation. Seeing the United States as a test case in self-government,
"the last, best hope of earth," Lincoln believed that its preservation
was a crusade to save democracy for the world. In his first war
message to Congress he declared the struggle "essentially a people's contest. On the side of the Union it is a struggle for maintaining in the world that form and substance of a government
whose leading object is to elevate the condition of men." The war
was a fight to assure "that government of the people, by the people, for the people shall not perish from the earth." Likewise, in
his Second Inaugural Address, when he urged "malice toward
none and charity for all" as the country's postwar policy, it was to
be in the service of binding up national wounds and fulfilling the
United States' God-given destiny.

In 1962 the historian Allan Nevins and the novelist Irving Stone
edited a volume of essays entitled *Lincoln: A Contemporary Portrait,* with contributions from twelve authors of vastly different
backgrounds. Though the essayists—professional historians, journalists, television and radio writers, an artist, a businessman, a jurist, and a poet—did not consult one another "on the character,
tone, mood, or conclusions" of their pieces, what emerged was a
portrait of "a man unified in mind, spirit, and action; we were
tempted to title the book: *United He Stands,*" the editors explained. The result would have gratified Lincoln, who declared
himself "determined to be so clear that no honest man can mis-
understand me, and no dishonest one can successfully misrepresent
me." (Once, when misquoted, he objected to "a specious and fantastic arrangement of words, by which a man can prove a horse-
chestnut to be a chestnut horse.")

*   *   *

t visionary among the country's twentieth-century
eodore Roosevelt. Because he confronted no crisis
that of the Civil War, and faced a variety of prob-
momentous than the grand clash of sectional interests in
Lincoln's time, Roosevelt's definition of the future was never as
grand and single-minded as Lincoln's. To some extent, TR had to
manufacture his greatness as a leader. In 1910, fourteen months
after he had left the White House, he declared that "a man has to
take advantage of his opportunities, but the opportunities have to
come. If there is not the war, you don't get the great general; if
there is not the great occasion, you don't get the great statesman;
if Lincoln had lived in times of peace, no one would have known
his name now."

But even without the burden of a civil or foreign war, turn-of-
the-century challenges at home and abroad gave TR all the opportunity he needed to make his presidency a memorable moment
in national history. Increasing divisions in society between the
wealthy and the poor, and the suffering of those at the bottom of
the country's industrial system, provided TR with potent issues for
his administration to address. Calling on Americans to abandon
national habits of self-indulgence for "the strenuous life," Roosevelt issued broadsides against corporate monopolies clogging the
arteries of national commerce and enriching themselves at the expense of middle-class and working-class Americans. He declared
the need for a greater measure of social justice—a "square deal"—
for the country's many diverse interests; preservation of America's
abundant but limited natural resources; challenged America to
build a Panama Canal for the sake of world commerce and U.S.
national defense; and insisted on mediating both the Russo-
Japanese war of 1904–1905, in the service of East Asian peace for
which TR won the Nobel Peace Prize, and the 1906 Moroccan
crisis, which had threatened to become a European war. For TR,
the White House was a bully pulpit from which he sought to lead
the nation and the world toward a more secure and peaceful future.

After having endured thirty-five years of desultory leadership in
the Oval Office, Americans were thrilled and captivated by Roosevelt's performance. A master of political theater with an instinc-
tive understanding of how to dramatize himself and the policies he
favored, TR was our first modern media president, and a brilliant

huckster. It is true that his rhetoric often outran his actions, especially in behalf of social reform, and he had an undeserved reputation as "a fighting radical" or "strenuous reformer." Wisconsin Progressive Senator Robert La Follette caustically described TR as "the ablest living interpreter of . . . the superficial public sentiment of a given time, and he is spontaneous in his reactions to it." His greatness as a politician, another commentator said, was that he understood the "psychology of the mutt."

While such criticisms were valid, Roosevelt did correctly perceive that the rise of self-serving political bosses and corrupt political machines, concurrent with growing economic inequality and periodic depressions, cast a malaise or psychological pall over the nation. He shrewdly judged that his role as president was in large part to rekindle a sense of national self-worth, by means of essential reforms like limited regulation of the trusts and the railroads and the establishment of a balance of power among competing nations in Europe and East Asia.

But his central purpose, as he saw it, was to launch a "fundamental fight for morality." "My problems are moral problems, and my teaching has been plain morality," he said privately toward the end of his presidential term. Thus, as historian Richard Hofstadter argues, Roosevelt's primary function was to discharge the widespread national fears engendered by the economic and social dislocations of the time. Through "a burst of hectic action" and "by scolding authoritatively the demons that [had] aroused them," Roosevelt served as "the master therapist of the middle classes." Stated in political terms, TR's goal was to remind the country that a successful national future required a restoration of ethics in public affairs—precisely the higher purpose that distinguished America from other nations. Like other great presidents, Roosevelt made a lasting mark on the country by envisioning an American future that hearkened to the past while ultimately transcending it.

Like TR, Woodrow Wilson viewed presidential power as a means toward improving the moral life of the nation. His agenda included reducing disparities of wealth and poverty, protecting the weak from exploitation, broadening democracy by weakening the grip of political machines, and teaching the world's nations "to elect good men" and avoid future wars through an international league practicing collective security. Wilson, the "Presbyterian Priest," as some called him, was a political evangelist intent on preserving democracy at home and expanding it abroad. His fight for the New Freedom in America and the Fourteen Points around the globe made him one of the greatest visionaries in American history.

If much of what Wilson urged between 1910 and 1920 came to seem excessively idealistic in its naive faith that the United States could put its own house in order while permanently altering international relations, his dreams of a better America and a changed world did appeal to the country's best instincts. Consider his attitude toward public office: when asked to run for governor of New Jersey in 1910, he said, without the least sense of posturing, "In view of what I have all my life taught in my classes of the duty of political service on the part of trained men, it would be very awkward to decline if the nomination should come to me unsought and unanimously."

So eloquent an expression of civic duty struck resonant chords with Americans tired of selfish politicians and eager to restore traditional beliefs in government service as a noble enterprise. Imagine what hoots of cynicism would greet such a declaration from most aspirants for office today. When Wilson, however, promised that his governorship would bring "a new and more ideal era in our politics . . . , a renaissance of public spirit, a reawakening of sober public opinion, a revival of the power of the people," voters took him at his word.

Wilson's speeches, which some described as so lyrical they could be danced to, stirred the country as those of few presidential candidates and presidents had in American history. "This great people is not in love with any kind of injustice," he declared on the eve of his first national campaign. "This great people is in love with the realization of what is equitable, pure, just, and of good repute, and it is bound by the clogs and impediments of our political machinery. . . . Our forefathers were not uttering mere words when they spoke of the realization of happiness."

Ever the professor of politics, Wilson viewed himself as an educator who, John Milton Cooper says, aimed "to draw out of people recognition of their own best interests." It was a vision of an

America where the leader reflected the people's needs and wishes, a government once more of, by, and for the people.

Both Wilson's rhetoric and policies during his presidency are notable for their idealism and their genuine belief in the country's capacity to achieve its highest aspirations. In domestic affairs his New Freedom reforms of 1913–1914, lower tariffs, a national banking system, and measures regulating big business were all designed to expand economic opportunity and eliminate a number of the advantages conferred upon the most successful members of the society. In a second burst of reform energy in 1916, when he saw his reelection as partly dependent on more advanced progressive measures, Wilson won passage of aid to farmers; prohibitions on child labor; worker's compensation; an eight-hour day for interstate railroad workers; and higher taxes on the wealthy. It was an agenda that sought to realize greater equity in, and humanization of, the country's industrial system. "The whole nature of our political questions have been altered," Wilson declared during his campaign. "They have ceased to be legal questions; they have more and more become social questions, questions with regard to the relations of human beings to one another." In the future, he added, government would be dealing "with the substance of life itself."

To Wilson's own surprise, his best-known pronouncements on public policy came in the area of foreign affairs. ("It would be an irony of fate if my administration had to deal with foreign problems, for all my preparation has been in domestic matters," he had told a friend shortly before entering the White House.) In Latin America, where he assumed responsibility for promoting democracy and the rule of law, he found himself forced into military actions of which he did not wholeheartedly approve. Yet, as had been the case with TR, he and much of the public viewed his interventions as aimed more at benefiting the Mexican, Central American, and Caribbean peoples than at serving the selfish interests of the United States.

Wilson's most fully developed expression of evangelism abroad came in response to World War I. His defense of neutral rights, his attack on the barbarism of submarine warfare, and his declaration that America was "too proud to fight" were reminders to the country of the differences that set it apart from the Old World. Involvement in the war was presented as purely an act of selflessness, and one that could give the United States no material or strategic advantage. For Wilson and America, this was a "war to end all wars," one that would ultimately make the world "safe for democracy." In its aftermath, the vehicle for achieving such lofty goals was to be a world league, which would replace balance-of-power, sphere-of-influence diplomacy with collective security. No vision in twentieth-century presidential politics has inspired greater hope of human advance or has done more to secure a president's reputation as a great leader than Wilson's peace program of 1918–1919.

Wilson's Democratic successor, Franklin Roosevelt, was nearly his equal in enunciating grand schemes for bettering the life of the nation and the world. Though few could discern a clear program in his 1932 presidential campaign, FDR considered presidential vision as a vital element in the struggle to restore the country's economic health, eliminate the worst abuses of American industrialism, and rally the nation against the Nazi-fascist threat to democracies everywhere.

In his First Inaugural Address, at the low point of the Depression, he helped restore faith in the future by declaring that fear itself was the only thing the American people had to fear, and that he intended to give the country "action, and action now." With eminent political mastery he also quoted the biblical injunction about the need for vision, if America itself were not to perish.

A series of measures intended to advance the national well-being characterized Roosevelt's presidency. The notion of a "Hundred Days" to meet the country's urgent needs; banking reform to rescue a dying monetary system; unemployment relief in the form of a Civilian Conservation Corps, a Federal Emergency Relief Administration, and a Public Works Administration; federal regulation of the securities markets; aid to homeowners and farmers threatened with foreclosure on mortgages; a Tennessee Valley Authority to provide flood control, conservation, and cheap power; an Agricultural Adjustment Administration; and a National Industrial

Recovery Act to restore the country's economic health all made up the program of action launching Roosevelt's New Deal.

When recovery proved elusive, the president established a Commodity Credit Corporation to boost farm prices and a Civil Works Administration to employ four million people to perform blue-collar and white-collar jobs for states and localities. Uncommon congressional gains in the 1934 off-year elections for the incumbent Democrats emboldened FDR in his vision of the role the government should play in the economic and social life of the nation. In 1935 Social Security, which guaranteed old-age pensions; a National Labor Relations law, which authorized collective bargaining; a Public Utilities Holding Company Act and the creation of a Rural Electrification Administration, to advance the cause of cheap public power; and a wealth-tax act, which gave more symbolic than substantive expression to redistribution of wealth, all went far to fulfill FDR's vision of a welfare state imposed on a capitalist foundation. "Without critically challenging the system of private profit," William E. Leuchtenburg has written, "the New Deal reformers were employing the power of government not only to discipline business but to bolster unionization, pension the elderly, succor the crippled, give relief to the needy, and extend a hand to the forgotten men."

Roosevelt gave voice to his conception of the government's new role in American life when he said in 1936: "Governments can err, Presidents do make mistakes, but the immortal Dante tells us that divine justice weighs the sins of the cold-blooded and the sins of the warm-hearted in different scales. Better the occasional faults of a Government that lives in a spirit of charity than the constant omission of a Government frozen in the ice of its own indifference."

FDR's call to action in world affairs was no less passionate and compelling than his domestic activism. Though he followed public sentiment in the thirties by signing neutrality laws intended to assure American isolation from future European and Asian wars, he left no doubt that he wished the United States to stand as the model of a successful democracy in a world of competing ideologies. Nor did he hesitate in 1939 to align the United States with Great Britain and France in the conflict with the Nazis, fascists, and Japanese militarists. After the Atlantic Conference in August

1941, at which Roosevelt and Churchill announced a charter of principles distinguishing Britain and the United States from totalitarian regimes, Supreme Court Justice Felix Frankfurter wrote the president: "We live by symbols and we can't too often recall them. And you two in that ocean . . . in the setting of that Sunday service, gave meaning to the conflict between civilization and arrogant, brute challenge; and gave promise . . . that civilization has brains and resources that tyranny will not be able to overcome."

The United States' entry into the conflict after Pearl Harbor presented an opportunity for Roosevelt to renew Wilson's appeal for international reforms. Describing the war as a contest between proponents of liberty, independence, human rights, justice, and religious freedom "against savage and brutal forces seeking to subjugate the world," Roosevelt turned the war into a moral struggle with which the country could comfortably identify. When he announced the doctrine of unconditional surrender in January 1943, he solidified public support for the war as a crusade against evil.

A speech Roosevelt delivered before a joint session of Congress after the Yalta conference in February 1945 projected an even more irresistible vision of international relations to the American people. His discussions with Churchill and Stalin, he said, promised "the end of the system of unilateral action, the exclusive alliances, the spheres of influence, the balances of power, and all the other expedients that had been tried for centuries—and have always failed." Roosevelt described the alternative as a universal organization of all peace-loving nations practicing collective security as a permanent foundation for peace. Whatever FDR's private doubts—and they were substantial—that such a system of international governance was attainable, he understood that a universalist vision of world affairs was an essential prerequisite to replacing American isolationism with enduring commitments to participation in overseas affairs.

None of our more recent presidents has better understood the need for a grand design, or acted upon it more forcefully, than Lyndon Johnson. After Kennedy's death, he recognized that his first goal was to reassure the American people that he would be faithful to the policies of the previous administration. The death of a president was trauma enough, but the fact that Kennedy was assassinated led to a national crisis in self-confidence, a period of doubt about the durability of the country's democratic system and its tradition of nonviolent political change. "A nation stunned, shaken to its very heart, had to be reassured that the government was not in a state of paralysis . . ." Johnson later recalled. "The times cried out for leadership."

Johnson remembered himself in the first days of his presidency as "a man in trouble." He feared that "the enormity of the tragedy" and "the tide of grief" following Kennedy's death might "overwhelm" him, and that he might "become immobilized . . . with emotion." Not only did the responsibilities of the office frighten him, as they would have any sensible person, but the self-doubt that had throughout his career been the engine of his ambition now began to agitate him. Could he possibly measure up? Was he smart enough? Knowledgeable enough? He was a Texan, a southerner, a man on the fringe with no hold on the imagination of the country and limited experience in world affairs.

Despite his private fears Johnson rose to the challenge and became an inspiration to the nation. To be sure, the country's long-established traditions of political stability and its shared assumptions about the need for cooperative effort to advance the national well-being helped ease Johnson's burden. But his almost uncanny feel for the appropriate word and gesture, honed by thirty-two years in the political arena, was undeniably a crucial factor in making him equal to the task.

In the difficult days after Kennedy's death, words were Johnson's weapons in a war on uncertainty and gloom. His public appearances, his skillful use of language, and his management of the press promoted feelings of continuity and unity. The new president soothed the nation with speeches that conveyed sincerity and wisdom. Proclaiming a national day of mourning on November 23, Johnson invoked the martyred Kennedy as a source of strength: "As he did not shrink from his responsibilities, but welcomed them, so he would not have us shrink from carrying on his work beyond this hour of national tragedy."

Perhaps Johnson's most effective speech in establishing his successful transition to the presidency was a national address he delivered on the evening of November 27. Speaking to a joint session of Congress from the rostrum of the House, a setting that would remind Americans that their new president was a seasoned and highly successful political leader, Johnson's demeanor and rhetoric struck exactly the right tone. Dressed in a dark suit and tie reflecting the country's somber mood, he humbly asked the help of all Americans in shouldering "the awesome burden of the Presidency," which, he admitted, "I cannot bear . . . alone." Invoking memories of FDR, who in another time of crisis began his administration with a call for action, Johnson urged the country "to do away with uncertainty and doubt" and show "that from the brutal loss of our leader we will derive not weakness, but strength; that we can and will act and act now." Johnson recalled Kennedy's dreams of a better America and a more peaceful world and reminded the country of his predecessor's exhortation, " 'Let us begin.' Today, in this moment of new resolve, I would say to all my fellow Americans, let us continue."

During his first months in the White House Johnson began searching for a "big theme" to characterize his presidency. He badgered Richard Goodwin, a speechwriter, to find a popular slogan that would resonate with voters in the 1964 campaign and give his administration its historical identity. During a discussion in the White House swimming pool in February 1965, Johnson "began to talk as if he were addressing some larger, imagined audience of the mind," Goodwin recalled. The president declared his intention to go beyond Kennedy and create a "Johnson program, different in tone, fighting and aggressive." Goodwin "felt Johnson's immense vitality," as he described a plan that could move the nation "toward some distant vision—vaguely defined, inchoate, but rooted in an ideal as old as the country." Eventually settling on the name "Great Society" for his program, Johnson saw it as "a statement of national purpose, almost prophetic in dimension, that would bind citizens in a 'great experiment.' "

An essential element of the Great Society, Johnson believed, would be the fulfillment of constitutional guarantees of equal rights through the legal destruction of segregation. Though he was not unaware of the political benefits to be gained by destroying southern apartheid in 1964, his commitment to this sea change in American life was heartfelt and honest. Johnson, the great political operator and student of power, was at the same time Johnson the underdog, the poor boy from Texas struggling to emerge from the shadows and win universal approval. He despised the sense of entitlement that came naturally to men of inherited wealth and standing. Blacks were the abused minority with talents that went unrecognized and dreams that class and social bias would leave unrealized. Johnson empathized with and viscerally experienced their suffering.

After Johnson, congressional liberals, and Republican Minority Leader Everett Dirksen worked the legislative magic that resulted in the passage of the 1964 Civil Rights bill, Johnson organized a simple, dignified ceremony in the East Room of the White House, to which he invited government officials, foreign diplomats, and civil rights advocates. The moment is captured in a panoramic photograph of Johnson seated at a small table signing the bill before more than one hundred dignitaries. "We believe all men are entitled to the blessings of liberty," Johnson said at the occasion. "Yet millions are being deprived of those blessings—not because of their own failures, but because of the color of their skin. The reasons are deeply embedded in history and tradition and the nature of man. We can understand—without rancor or hatred—how this happened, but it cannot continue. . . . Our Constitution, the foundation of our Republic, forbids it. The principles of our freedom forbid it. Morality forbids it. And the law I will sign tonight forbids it." Such eloquence memorably captured the triumph of America's vision of itself as a moral nation committed to equal opportunity and the rule of law.

The most recent great visionary in American presidential history was Ronald Reagan. Though he had a well-deserved reputation as a president with a limited attention span and little patience for detail, he was at the same time a master of the big picture. He left no one in the country with any doubts about his commitment to liberating the economy and social institutions from federal control through sharply lower taxes, reduced spending on domestic programs, and less regulation, and he was equally resolute in his intention to defeat Soviet Communism through an arms race that could break its fragile economy. Vividly describing his domestic program of supply-side economics as producing a "Reagan Revolution" and declaring Moscow the center of an "evil empire," Reagan impressed Americans as a visionary leader comparable to the greatest of his predecessors in the Oval Office.

When he left office in 1989, Reagan's approval ratings were over 60 percent—as high as any president's in this century with the exception of FDR (whose death occurred at the moment of Allied triumph in World War II). Nevertheless, history has yet to judge the wisdom of Reagan's tax cuts and vast arms buildup. In the generation since he left office, Reagan's personal charm, which played so vital a role in his widespread appeal, has largely been lost from view, and as the legacy of the threefold increase in national public debt of his administration begins to register more clearly on the country, it may well be that Reagan's reputation for effective leadership will be reexamined.

Still, his deftness in making his presidency a statement of a grand conservative design—a design that he was often able to put into effect—will resonate through history. Entering the White House after nearly two decades of mixed presidential records marked equally by sporadic success and ineffectual stumbling, if not outright failure, Reagan restored hope that, in the right hands, the presidency can work and the country can find effective means to deal with its problems. Where Johnson's missteps in Vietnam and Nixon's misdeeds in Watergate destroyed their capacity to fulfill their commitments to a Great Society and détente, respectively, and where Ford and Carter lacked the vision or understanding of politics that could translate into great presidential leadership, Reagan held consistently to an idea of America that captured the public's imagination and encouraged people to believe that the country was getting back on the right track.

Though Reagan's hold on the public had fallen to a 48 percent approval rating by 1992, he can take some comfort from the possibility of the sort of historical reassessment that has raised the estimation of Harry Truman. Current understanding views this once undervalued president as a forceful leader with the courage to act upon his convictions in meeting the challenges of his times, regardless of public opinion.

Truman's Doctrine in March 1947, as well as the Marshall Plan in June of that year, both declaring the need for fresh commitments to meet a threat to democracy and freedom from an aggressive and ideologically driven Soviet Union; Truman's commitment to equal rights for black Americans; his 1948 presidential campaign against a Republican Congress opposing a Fair Deal for everyone; and his dismissal of the legendary General Douglas MacArthur for insubordination are now all judged to be policies that place him in the front rank of U.S. presidents.

During his term of office Truman's relationship with the public rose and fell frequently in response to his handling of a series of domestic and international problems. His 75 percent approval ratings in the closing months of the war plummeted into the forties when inflation, strikes, and Soviet-American tensions gave the lie to dreams of postwar harmony. A spirited response to the Communist threat in the Middle East and Europe, coupled with a brilliant 1948 campaign that invoked memories of FDR and the New Deal, put Truman back in the White House with 49 percent of the popular vote. But with the onset of the Korean War in the summer of 1950, his public standing again went into decline. By the close of his term in January 1953 he held favor with only 31 percent of the country.

Truman's return to popularity in the years since is in large measure a testament to the power of presidential vision. Today he is remembered as a strong-minded leader who was more intent on following what he believed was the proper course of action than on courting public opinion, and he holds a place of honor in the national memory as a chief executive wise enough and courageous enough to lead the country where it needed to go.

Unlike Truman, John Kennedy was during his term a popular president: public support of his administration stood at a respectable 58 percent when he died in November 1963. Since then, however, that figure has reached as high as 84 percent—nine points above FDR, fourteen more than Ike, and sixteen better than Truman. But such polls tell only part of the story, for on the thirtieth anniversary of his assassination, a majority of Americans said JFK was the country's greatest president. When asked who they considered the greatest world leaders of the last one thousand years, a plurality of Americans put Lincoln and Kennedy at the top of the list. While Kennedy's phenomenal appeal has much to do with his martyrdom, with the image of a handsome, boyish, and articulate leader cut off in the prime of life, it also rests on the impression he left as a president with strong convictions about foreign and domestic affairs. His resolution of the Cuban missile crisis in October 1962 and subsequent nuclear test ban treaty with Moscow were dramatic realizations of his declaration that "Mankind must put an end to war—or war will put an end to mankind." Kennedy's combination of toughness and restraint in dealing with the Soviets has come to be regarded as a key part of the strategy that would ultimately lead to America's success in the Cold War.

Likewise, his commitment in June 1963 to civil rights legislation ending racial discrimination in public facilities was a clarion call to overcome the legacy of American apartheid. "One hundred years of delay have passed since President Lincoln freed the slaves," he stated in his greatest presidential address, "yet their heirs, their grandsons, are not fully free. They are not yet freed from the bonds of injustice; they are not yet freed from social and economic oppression. And this nation, for all its hopes and all its boasts, will not be fully free until all its citizens are free." He asked that the law be passed "not merely for reasons of economic efficiency, world diplomacy and domestic tranquillity—but above all, because it is right."

III

Yet unwavering commitment to policies he believes essential to America's advance, has been no guarantee of a president's success or high historical standing. A chief executive with unrealistic or unrealizable hopes is a leader marked out for failure and defeat, with Wilson, Hoover, and LBJ as notable cases in point. Wilson and Johnson deserve recognition as great visionaries, but surely presidential greatness rests on more than the articulation of utopian goals at home and abroad.

Woodrow Wilson's dream of a new world order following the carnage of World War I was a vision much ahead of its time. His assumption that the mass slaughter committed by advanced industrial nations in the war would be sufficient to revolutionize the conduct of international affairs was misplaced. While a program of open covenants, openly arrived at; arms reductions; freedom of the seas; free trade; adjustment of colonial claims; self-determination for all peoples; and the replacement of alliance systems and spheres of influence by a league of nations guaranteeing political independence and territorial integrity to all nations through collective security seemed a reasonable foundation for an enlightened peace plan, in reality the victorious powers could not conceive of abandoning the fruits of their sacrifices for untried arrangements at odds with all historical experience.

Similarly, while the president's proposals appealed to most Americans in principle, they also had a healthy skepticism about giving up traditions of diplomatic autonomy and isolationism for a peace program that might lead not to a brave new world but instead to the United States' involvement in traditional power politics and other nations' wars. Recognizing that America's allies would resist his Fourteen Points and that Americans also had doubts about their viability, Wilson made the 1918 congressional elections a referendum on his peace plan. In October he told voters, "If you have approved of my leadership and wish me to continue to be your unembarrassed spokesman in affairs at home and abroad, I earnestly beg that you will express yourself unmistakably . . . by returning a Democratic majority to both the Senate and the House of Representatives."

Partly because they were uncertain about the president's conception of a postwar world and eager to assure a dialogue about the future of U.S. diplomacy, voters installed Republican majorities in both houses of Congress. The Democratic defeat was a powerful blow to Wilson's prestige and ability to achieve his peace aims in the Versailles negotiations in 1918–1919. Despite his presence at the head of the American delegation, Wilson could not bend other government chiefs to his will. The treaty provisions made a mockery of a peace among equals, self-determination, arms control, adjustment of colonial claims, free trade, and an end to spheres of influence. Only the League of Nations survived as the hope of fulfilling Wilson's dream of a just world enjoying perpetual peace.

Politically weakened by his defeats in the elections and at the peace table, Wilson faced a Republican-controlled Senate with Henry Cabot Lodge of Massachusetts, a strong critic and foe, at the head of the powerful foreign relations committee. In the fall of 1919 Wilson took his case to the country for the Treaty and the League. "The real issue," he declared in one speech, "is whether the United States could refuse to accept the moral leadership of the world. The stage is set, the destiny disclosed. We cannot turn back. We can only go forward, with lifted eyes and freshened spirit." If America failed to implement the current peace program, he warned prophetically, "there will come some time, in the vengeful Providence of God, another war in which not a few hundred thousand men from America will have to die, but as many millions as are necessary to accomplish the final freedom of the peoples of the world." Though a convinced *New York Times* reported that "the President has steadily advanced his cause since he started out on his nationwide tour," a physical collapse in September ended his trip and any possibility of defeating Senate opponents.

Ironically, Wilson's reputation soared during World War II, when the country came to view the failure of his international vision as a cause of the current conflict and adopted the principle of a league of nations as essential to postwar peace. *Time* described a 1944 film biography of Wilson as a "worshipful sermon on internationalism" likely "to bring millions of Americans a few steps forward on the sawdust trail." While Wilson continues to hold a place among the handful of great presidents, his adherence to an overly idealistic vision of a new world order, which the postwar history of the United Nations has demonstrated is still well beyond reach, has been a blemish on his reputation and given "the vision thing" something of a bad name.

Like Wilson, Herbert Hoover had very specific notions of where he wished to lead the country and held to them in the face of changed conditions and public sentiments that made them unworkable. In the words of presidential scholar Richard Neustadt, there is "no guarantee that any man brings with him to the White House the degree and kind of feeling for direction that can help him once he gets there. Former Commerce Secretary Hoover had a sense of purpose so precise as to be stultifying."

Hoover's vision or "sense of purpose" had stood him in good stead prior to his presidency. In his 1919 book, *The Economic Con-*

sequences of the Peace, John Maynard Keynes describes Hoover at the Versailles conference as a man with a steady gaze at "the true and essential facts of the European situation," which made him the only realistic, knowledgeable, magnanimous, and disinterested statesman in Paris who understood how to achieve a "Good Peace." Likewise, in the twenties, as secretary of commerce, Hoover had successfully embodied America's faith in free enterprise, individualism, and a New Era partnership of government and trade associations to eliminate wasteful competition and make American capitalism more productive. He saw this national political economy as a "third alternative" to laissez-faire capitalism and state socialism—a voluntary, cooperative system based on the scientific principles of coordination and efficiency.

Hoover's faith in the economic principles he favored was unshakable. The stock market crash in 1929 and the onset of the Great Depression did little to shatter his belief that American economic arrangements could "banish poverty from this nation" and, in the conventional Republican wisdom of the twenties, put a chicken in every pot and a car in every garage. Though he responded to the Depression with the first systematic effort by a president to restore national prosperity, his rigid views concerning limited government and private initiative prevented him from taking the sort of bold, innovative steps needed to face an unprecedented American crisis. Hoover clung to a vision of the country's future that was largely consonant with its recent past. But it was the wrong vision for a nation mired in an economic disaster unresponsive to conventional solutions. In the late nineteenth century and first thirty years of the twentieth, Richard Hofstadter said, these ideas "had had an almost irresistible lure for the majority of Americans." But in the crisis of the thirties, they had become "stale and oppressive," even "outlandish and unintelligible." In that context Hoover, the engineer and economic rationalist, Hofstadter concluded, "had become a wild-eyed Utopian capitalist."

Like Woodrow Wilson, Lyndon Johnson, who enjoyed his share of domestic triumphs, fell victim to events overseas that would not conform to his convictions about U.S. national security and world peace. Johnson inherited a conflict in Vietnam that his two immediate predecessors had described as vital to the U.S. national interest. If South Vietnam fell to Communist Viet Cong guerillas supported by Communist regimes in Hanoi, Peking, and Moscow, Eisenhower and Kennedy asserted, it would be the first in a series of Southeast Asian dominoes to come under Communist control. This would mean not only the loss of a resource-rich region to Communist power but would also signal America's allies and other Third World countries that the United States would not actively resist Communist aggression in all parts of the globe. Abandoning Vietnam would be a dangerous departure from the containment doctrine that had led the United States to halt Communist expansion in Europe, the Near East, Latin America, and north Asia. Indeed, remembering the "lessons" of Munich and World War II, presidents from Truman to LBJ preached the need to stop attacks on small countries by more powerful aggressors as essential to preventing miscalculations leading to a third world war.

Astute critics at home and abroad argued that the Vietnam conflict was in fact a civil war and warned that any substantial involvement by America in the fighting would lead to a struggle it could not hope to win, short of an all-out escalation against Hanoi and possible nuclear exchanges with China and Russia. Johnson, however, dismissed such advice as the recommendations of "nervous nellies" who lacked the wisdom and strength to hold fast in Vietnam. Likewise, he did not heed the counsel of some of his close advisers and old congressional colleagues that the American public would not sustain support for a limited conflict costing thousands of American lives and billions of dollars. Rather, the majority of Americans felt that, if the war was worth fighting, it should be fought without the kinds of constraints the president was putting on America's power to quickly defeat North Vietnam.

Because Johnson feared that a more substantial commitment than the considerable bombing of the North and the 535,000 troops sent to the South would turn into the wider war with China and Russia he was trying to prevent, he refused to carry escalation too far. But the middle ground he had chosen between withdrawal and an all-out effort became a trap from which he could not escape. Having made the rescue of South Vietnam from Communism and its independence a sine qua non of his presidency and having convinced himself that his policy was the only means to secure America's vital interest in Southeast Asia, he stubbornly clung to a failing strategy. The result was a stalemate in South Vietnam and civil strife at home that destroyed his hopes for a Great Society and another presidential term.

Instead of withdrawing from Vietnam, as Kennedy might have after the 1964 elections, or more likely after the war had become a stalemate in 1966–1967, and as Nixon finally did in 1973 by masking U.S. defeat behind the façade of Vietnamization, Johnson accepted withdrawal from the 1968 campaign as the price of having continued the war. Whatever may be said for the courage of LBJ's convictions, his wisdom in pursuing an outdated vision of America's foreign policy interests is certainly questionable. The Sino-Soviet split and historic antagonisms between China and Vietnam made a Communist victory in Vietnam much less of a threat to America's national security than LBJ and the war's supporters believed. Ho Chi Minh and the Hanoi government were first and foremost Vietnamese nationalists and only secondarily international Communists. As with Wilson's peacemaking in World War I and Hoover's response to the Depression, Johnson didn't lack for a grand vision of America's role in Southeast Asia. All three men, however, lacked the flexibility to modify and renew their visions in response to the changing conditions that are the inevitable course of history.

IV

The only thing worse than having allies, Winston Churchill said, is not having them. For a president, the only thing worse than holding to a failed vision is having no vision at all. Our least successful chief executives have been those who had no clear idea of where they wished to steer the ship of state, especially in domestic affairs. Taft, Harding, Carter, Bush, and now Clinton have all come to political grief over their inability to define and convey their goals. True, all of their administrations had coherent foreign policies (though the jury is still out on Clinton's): Taft's dollar diplomacy, Harding's (or really Secretary of State Charles Evans Hughes's) nonaggression and arms control agreements at the Washington Conference of 1921–1922, Carter's emphasis on human rights and Camp David accords advancing Middle East peace, Bush's advocacy of a New World Order and success in implementing it in the Persian Gulf war, and Clinton's peacemaking in Haiti, the Middle East and Bosnia are notable achievements. But no one reviewing the history of these presidents' administrations—or making initial judgments on Clinton's—can point to any organizing theme in domestic affairs that gives them a distinctive identity. In a mass democratic society like ours, in which the government derives its power from a citizenry demanding accountability for the direction of the country, vagueness or ambivalence is an insurmountable flaw.

William Howard Taft was Theodore Roosevelt's handpicked successor in 1908. An amiable, highly intelligent man from a prominent Ohio family, Taft was a jurist with a Yale law degree who had served on his state's Superior Court, as solicitor general of the United States, and a judge of the federal circuit court. He also had a distinguished record as governor general of the Philippines and as TR's secretary of war. But except for one election campaign for a seat on the Ohio Superior Court, Taft had no track record as a political candidate. Moreover, had it not been for the urging of his wife, who stoked his ambitions, he would have accepted appointment to the U.S. Supreme Court and never have run for president. A large man who weighed three hundred pounds, and who enjoyed eating, talking, golfing, and sleeping, Taft disliked politics and had no compelling passion to accomplish anything particular during his term in office. While he vouched his loyalty to TR's progressive policies and promised to fulfill his predecessor's plans, he regarded the election contest of 1908 as having little significance for the future: Had the Democrats won, he believed, they would be behaving much the same as he was. Taft's campaign, one Republican newspaper commented, was "loaded down with calm." Where a TR run for office had resembled a cross between "a bullfight and a national camp meeting," Taft's idea of a campaign was to read dull speeches that made Roosevelt's programs sound like "a statistical report."

A month after he became president Taft told a friend that he would have been more comfortable as chief justice; he described himself in the presidency as "just a bit like a fish out of water." He depended on his wife, who was the real politician, to guide him in responding to all the issues he would confront as president. When Helen Taft took ill at the start of his term, however, the president had to rely on other advisers with whom he was less comfortable.

However much he struggled to make sense of his job, Taft did not lack convictions. He was a warm advocate of traditional laissez-faire policies, filing a number of antitrust suits to promote freer enterprise. In spite of such measures, however, he tended to favor distinct limits to government intervention in the country's economic and social affairs. His commitment to continue the program of government activism favored by Roosevelt had more to do with personal loyalty to the man who made him president than with any genuine conviction about the need for and value of implementing a progressive agenda. In issue after issue during his presidency—such as the progressive attempt to wrest power from the dictatorial and rigidly conservative House Speaker "Uncle Joe" Cannon, and progressive-conservative fights over conservation policies and lower tariffs—Taft revealed himself to be an uninspiring leader who shifted positions so often that no one believed he had firm views on any subject.

After six months in office Taft laid plans to overcome the damage he had been done in these initial political fights by undertaking a transcontinental speaking tour. But, as he confided to friends, he didn't know "exactly what to say or how to say it." Though he would make clear in the course of his trip that he was wedded to the conservatives in his party and had little regard for the progressives, his speeches were notable for their "barrenness of ideas." By the close of his tour, Taft was on a downward path that would lead to political defeats in the 1910 congressional elections and the three-way 1912 contest against TR and Wilson. Dismissed as the head of "a lawyer's administration" and as "totally unfit" to lead the country, Taft won only 8 electoral votes and 3.5 million popular votes out of 13.9 million cast for president in 1912.

Warren G. Harding, Wilson's successor in 1921, exhibited traits similar to Taft's. Most of his contemporaries viewed him as a political cipher whose passivity perfectly matched the country's post-progressive and postwar mood. After service as Ohio lieutenant governor and a failed bid in 1910 for the governorship, Harding won election to the Senate in 1914, where he became known as a reliable but undistinguished conservative. The prominent Kansas editor William Allen White described him as "a mere bass drum, beating the time of the hour, carrying no tune, making no music, promoting no deep harmony; just a strident rhythmic noise."

Harding, who enjoyed being a senator, had no strong ambition to rise higher. But his wife, Florence, whom he called the Duchess, and Harry M. Daugherty, a leading Ohio corporation counsel and lobbyist, pressed him to run for president. "I found him," Daugherty later said, "sunning himself like a turtle on a log and I pushed him into the water." A thoroughly conventional man who could have been a character in Sinclair Lewis's novel *Babbitt*, Harding was at heart a small-town joiner. During his early years in Marion, Ohio, he had belonged to all the town's fraternal organizations— the Elks, the Odd Fellows, the Hoo Hoos, the Moose, and the Red Men.

Many historians consider Harding the worst president in the country's history, a man thoroughly out of his depth in office. On being told of his election, he exclaimed: "God help me, for I need it." When Columbia University president Nicholas Murray Butler visited him at the White House, Harding told him: "I knew this job would be too much for me. I am not fit for this office and should never have been here." Confronted by a tax question on which various advisers gave him conflicting advice, he told a secretary, "John, I can't make a damn thing out of this tax problem. I listen to one side and they seem right, and then—God!—I talk to the other side and they seem just as right, and here I am where I started. I know somewhere there's a book that will give me the truth, but, hell, I couldn't read the book. I know somewhere there is an economist who knows the truth, but I don't know where to find him and haven't the sense to know him and trust him when I find him. God! What a job!"

And to borrow Theodore Roosevelt's description of President William McKinley, Harding had "the backbone of a chocolate eclair." Possibly his most memorable contribution to American politics was the oft told story about his father's pronouncement on Warren's good fortune at not having been born a girl: "Otherwise you'd always be in the family way. You can't say no!"

In and of itself, Harding's difficulty in making a decision on a complicated question is no indictment of the man or his presidency. Every president has confronted painful choices on how to meet the challenges of his day. Harry Truman complained about financial advisers who refused to come down decisively on one side or the other of an issue, saying, "Just once in my life I'd like to meet a one-armed economist." Moreover, having a conventional mind and being less than a deep thinker do not necessarily prevent a man from being an effective leader, as Ronald Reagan demonstrated. The key to Reagan's success was in knowing where he wished to lead the nation and understanding how to convince the country to follow him. By contrast, Harding had neither a policy nor a moral compass for setting a national course that Americans could follow. Harding urged a "return to normalcy," but he had no clear idea of what this meant. When his administration was beset by scandals, he complained that it was his friends, "his Goddamn friends," who kept him walking the floors at night. But it would have been more accurate to say that it was Harding's own lack of standards and vision that left his administration vulnerable to corruption and marked out his presidency as a national embarrassment devoid of lasting or even significant accomplishments.

High moral standards, intensity of purpose, and devotion to duty were among the notable qualities that distinguished Jimmy Carter from Taft and Harding. But with his two predecessors Carter shared a reluctance to set a national domestic agenda that could inspire hope in the future. "Government cannot solve our problems," he declared after a year in office. "It can't set our goals. It cannot define our vision. Government cannot eliminate poverty, or provide a bountiful economy, or reduce inflation or save our cities." While Carter was undoubtedly correct in arguing that government has a limited capacity to solve problems, it *does* have the power to exercise a substantial influence on all the difficulties he mentioned in his 1978 State of the Union speech. Moreover, it is the responsibility of the government, or the president, more precisely, to define the national vision. If he fails to do so, he ends up dissipating much of the good will he holds by virtue of entering office.

Carter's economic policies are the best illustration of his short-comings in this area. In much of his economic policymaking, as James MacGregor Burns has shown, Carter seemed to lack a blue-print for action: "The White House sent out mixed signals as to what it wanted. Advance preparation was inadequate, follow-through sporadic, lines of communication and delegation scrambled. The normal friction between the executive and legislative branches was exacerbated by exceptionally poor staff work in the White House's congressional liaison office. Above all a clear sense of priorities was lacking."

Carter's plan, in general, was for less government intrusion in the country's economic affairs. To reduce its 8 percent unemployment rate and keep inflation, which had been running at over 10 percent, under 5 percent, he focused on cutting taxes and increasing national productivity by limiting government controls over industries and banks. The one area in which he did favor strong government involvement was energy, and he supported a policy that would conserve fuel and hold down oil and natural gas prices.

But it was this very policy that gave clearest definition to the problems of his administration. During 1977–1978, his energy plans fell victim to his inability to persuade oil and gas companies to accept changes that might serve the larger national interest. When he tried to rally the nation behind an energy program in 1979, he instead created a sense of crisis that further undercut his authority. Before delivering a major speech on the subject in July, he consulted over 130 people on what he should say. Many urged him simply to lead: "Talk to us about blood and sweat and tears," one of them advised. Another counseled, "If you lead, Mr. President, we will follow."

This, in fact, was precisely what Carter had been unable to do. He acknowledged in his speech that Americans were losing faith in the future of the country and had come to regard the government as divided and unable to act. The country faced a "crisis of confidence"—a national "malaise" that threatened to immobilize it and endanger its national security. An unemployment rate barely below what it had been in 1976, prime interest rates reaching a record 21.5 percent, and an annual 13 percent inflation were sufficient proof of the truth of Carter's remarks. But the real problem, as people saw it, was Carter's inability to formulate an articulate policy to meet these very difficulties. Carter's presidency reminded one Washington insider of "the king who told his minister that he had been looking out of the window and perceived that his country was in trouble. 'But sire,' replied the minister, 'that's not a window—it's a mirror.' " Inevitably, millions of Americans came to believe that Carter had no clear idea of what to do as president, and so did not deserve a second term.

George Bush, Reagan's vice president for eight years and his successor in 1989, suffered a similar fate. Bush had impressive family, educational, business, and political credentials. The son of Prescott Bush, a U.S. senator from Connecticut, Bush attended Phillips Andover Academy and Yale, served with distinction as a Navy pilot in World War II, and ran successful oil exploration and equipment companies in Texas. Aside from a term in Congress and his vice presidency, Bush had spent his career in appointed administrative and diplomatic posts—as ambassador to the United Nations, chairman of the Republican National Committee, U.S. representative to the People's Republic of China, and director of the Central Intelligence Agency. He defined himself as a moderate conservative on social and economic questions, and while as a congressman in the sixties, he opposed most Great Society legislation, he did vote for civil rights, and in the 1980 nomination fight against Reagan, decried the Californian's connections to right-wing groups and complained that Reagan's supply-side ideas were "voodoo economics."

As Reagan's vice president, however, he bent to the president's wishes, supporting him on all domestic and foreign policies. Although this turnabout indicated little more than that Bush was playing the role traditionally expected of a vice president, when he himself ran for the White House in 1988, numerous commentators complained that he was an undefined figure who had made no distinctive marks during his twenty-five years in public life.

While his experience at the U.N., as representative to China, and as CIA director prepared him well to deal with foreign affairs, Bush seemed less ready to address the more pressing domestic issues troubling the country at the end of the eighties—crime, drugs, massive government debt and deficits, bank failures, a faltering educational system, homelessness, increased poverty, and racial divisions. With conventional campaign bravado, Bush promised to grow the country out of its deficits with the memorable phrase, "Read my lips: No new taxes," a pledge he would come to regret, said he would be the "education President," and urged voluntarism ("A thousand points of light") as a substitute for government help to the needy and a means of creating a "kinder, gentler America."

No less a political veteran than Richard Nixon called the 1988 campaign "trivial, superficial, and inane," a characterization that turned out to be an equally apt assessment of Bush's response as president to domestic problems. He broke his vow on taxes to stem the rising tide of red ink, and set forth no clear course of action to address any other of the country's ills. His ineffectualness was most forcefully revealed to voters in his inability to deal with a recession in July 1990, which brought an end to the economic boom of the eighties. Unemployment above 7 percent, yearly deficits approaching $300 billion, and a debt above $3 trillion put Bush's reelection in doubt. In 1992 Governor Bill Clinton of Arkansas, styling himself a new (more conservative) Democrat, captured public attention by making the economy the focus of his campaign. Bush, in contrast, showed himself to be so out of touch with problems of ordinary Americans that he failed, in a national forum, to answer effectively a question about shopping in a supermarket. With the help of Ross Perot's third-party candidacy, Clinton went on to win the presidency.

After three years in office, the well-educated and highly intelligent Bill Clinton, who holds degrees from Georgetown and Yale Law School, and was a Rhodes Scholar at Oxford, had run an erratic course. The strongest and most often made complaint against him was that he never stayed fixed on an issue. He was a new Democrat but spent much of his administration catering to traditional party constituents among the country's minorities. He advocated allowing gays in the military but under conditions that managed to antagonize both gays and opponents of the policy. He favored affirmative action but wavered in his backing after Newt Gingrich and conservative Republicans took control of Congress in 1994 and stated their intentions to dismantle the increasingly unpopular policies. Then, when advisers counseled the importance of obtaining the support of liberal Democrats both for his 1996 reelection bid and as a way to head off a Jesse Jackson challenge from the left, he restated his faith in affirmative action. In foreign affairs, he waffled in trade dealings with Japan and China and, for a time, on a policy to deter Serbian aggression in Bosnia. As a president who seemed intent on being all things to all people, he alienated most everyone by seeming to have no firm opinions on anything.

"For Bill Clinton's natural supporters," *New York Times* columnist Anthony Lewis wrote in July 1995, "the most painful realization of his presidency is that he is a man without a bottom line. He may abandon any seeming belief, any principle. You cannot rely on him." In the same month Maureen Dowd, another *Times* columnist, predicted that in 1996, Bill Clinton would be "running against himself. The President is playing to his strength. You cannot run against yourself if you have only a self. You need selves. Mr. Clinton is the perfect candidate of change, since he is forever changing." She called him "President Proteus," although he was more often known by the nickname that had attached to him in Arkansas, "Slick Willie." Dowd also imagined a Clinton campaign highlighted by the president's repudiating himself. " 'Tired of me?' " she saw him asking. " 'I have vowed not to run for public office again after one more term. So stick with me and you'll be rid of Bill Clinton forever. The record speaks for itself. Dump me. I have. And then vote for me. Remember, a vote for Bill Clinton is a vote against Bill Clinton.' "

Until the fall and winter of 1995–1996, the want of clear vision in Clinton's leadership had led to the predictable consequences of diminished influence and loss of political control. In the summer of 1995, after months in which Gingrich; Bob Dole, the Senate Republican Majority Leader; and the Congress generally had taken the headlines away from Clinton by fighting for a comprehensible program of change called a Contract with America, Clinton tried to recapture the public's attention. Acknowledging that the president was seen as too much of "a conciliator, an appeaser, a waffler," White House advisers mapped out for him a strategy of taking firm stands on tough issues like welfare and federal curbs on smoking as a way to reduce voter concern that Clinton lacked leadership.

Yet try as they might, aides could not rein in Clinton's proclivity for changing his public positions, which raised doubts about his commitment. In October 1995, after Clinton angered Democratic congressmen and senators by expressing regret at having raised taxes too aggressively in 1993, Senator Bob Kerrey of Nebraska released an undelivered speech to the *New York Times* in which he complained that "after three years as President, he [Clinton] doesn't appear to know where he wants to lead America. He is developing some interesting theories about where we have been and where we are, but he doesn't talk consistently about where we should be going. He has a handful of programs for which he is prepared to fight, like national service and Head Start, but even they don't seem to be connected to a clear vision of where he believes America could and should be going. He is very clear about where he wants to go—back to the White House for four more years. But as to the country? Well, that is much less clear."

By November, however, Clinton had begun to take more focused stands in both domestic and foreign affairs. Vetoing Republican budget proposals for welfare, medicare, medicaid, education, and environmental reforms, and committing twenty thousand U.S. troops to a peacekeeping role in Bosnia, he gained higher marks from a public responsive to a president opposed to excessive changes in social programs and for a direct American presence in restoring peace in Bosnia.

Why was Clinton initially so reluctant to align himself to well-defined policies? He clearly understands the value of inspirational leadership to the most successful administrations in history, and has stated, for example, how much he admired and learned from the presidencies of FDR and JFK. But until late in 1995 he had been unable to imitate them, or, more to the point, to find his own unique voice or identity as president. Some believe it is because he lacks core beliefs and above all aims to be universally liked if not loved. Yet his track record suggests otherwise, for however ardent his desire for public affection, he is nevertheless clearly disposed toward overcoming the country's legacy of discrimination

against minorities and women and was eager to put
national health care system assuring access to everyo

What, then, deterred him from announcing a grand
domestic change, led by health care reform? Clinton's problem
may be the classic dilemma of a searching, subtle mind that finds
it almost impossible to accommodate itself to simple solutions, or
at least publicly appealing ones, to large problems. His aides assert
that his ability to grasp the details of both sides of an issue in rich
detail is immobilizing. The health care plan that he promised at
the start of his term turned into a 1,300-page bill, which most
Americans feared would give birth to a bureaucratic nightmare.

Clinton's affinity for the center or for balancing competing ideas
and interests also handicaps him, for it is difficult to be a moderate
evangelist. As TR, Wilson, FDR, and Reagan vividly demonstrated,
vision and the ability to mobilize public sentiment in its behalf
require passion or faith or moral certainty. Preaching presidents
must have the conviction of warriors at Armageddon battling for
the Lord. As the country moved into the 1996 campaign season
and Clinton began to hit his stride as a president with sharply
etched domestic and foreign policies, his leadership ability remained in question, but there were promising signs that he was
learning on the job and that he could yet emerge as an effective
visionary.

A discussion of presidential vision cannot end without some consideration of Richard Nixon. If he is the final subject of this survey
it is not because he lacked vision or carried it to excess, or failed
in his assessment of the future. Rather, it is because he is a case
unto himself.

Nixon was primarily a foreign policy leader, as he was the first
to assert. His commitment (in collaboration with Henry Kissinger,
his national security adviser and then secretary of state) to détente
with Russia and China and his determination to play one off against
the other in order to build a stable peace has given him a reputation as one of the great foreign policy realists of the twentieth
century.

Yet, as Tom Wicker effectively argued in his book *One of Us,*

Nixon was also a forceful and successful domestic leader. His record on revenue sharing, environmental protection, desegregation of schools, antihunger and antidrug policies, pension reform, aid to the arts and humanities, replacement of the draft with a volunteer army, Keynesian deficits in the service of more jobs and an expanding economy, and proposals to assure health insurance to greater numbers of Americans and to supplant welfare handouts with a family assistance plan or guaranteed annual income, added up to the most progressive Republican administration of the postwar era, one that was in many respects a worthy heir to Franklin Roosevelt's New Deal.

Nixon, Wicker asserts, "actually had a certain definable domestic vision, a commodity not every president has brought to the White House: he wanted, and to some extent achieved, a government doing what needed to be done for the welfare of the nation. . . . This strange and reclusive figure, cynical as he certainly was . . . was not personally an activist or a progressive *man;* but—vastly more significant—in his first term he was both an activist and a progressive *president,* mostly because he had to be. The element of political compulsion is not to be despised; the American people may want more from the White House than Nixon the man ever promised, but they usually get considerably less than Nixon the president delivered."

Compared with most presidents, then, it seems reasonable to conclude that, in both foreign and domestic affairs, Nixon stands relatively high in the ranks of U.S. chiefs. But a major proviso will always have to be made in any evaluation of Nixon's presidency, cautioning historians to take into account the great qualifier of Watergate before rendering final judgment. For alongside Nixon's achievements at home and abroad is the disturbing fact that Nixon the man and president had little regard for accepted national tenets that the country believed should define its future as decidedly as they had shaped its past.

Watergate and the coverup that followed were exercises in constitutional subversion. Dick Nixon may have read the Constitution, Harry Truman said, but if he did, he sure as hell didn't understand it. There was a barrenness of vision on Nixon's part with regard to the rule of law that stood at the center of the Watergate crisis, the articles of impeachment drawn up against him by the House, and his decision to resign that make him the only president in the century to be fairly described as a great visionary leader who was at the same time a scoundrel devoid of vision.

CHAPTER 2

CHAMELEONS ON PLAID

While every great president has been a visionary, he has also served the office as a sensible realist or instrumentalist, a leader who understood that political accomplishments often required flexibility of means to reach desirable ends. In a nation composed of a vast array of competing interests, presidential success has always depended at least partially on compromise with determined opponents. The corollary to the proposition that presidents without vision will perish is that, without the right balance of political give and take, little, if anything, can be achieved by a chief executive. Abraham Lincoln "was a sad man because he couldn't get it all at once," said FDR, the greatest political practitioner in American history. "And nobody can. . . . You cannot, just by shouting from the housetops, get what you want all the time."

The minefield of national politics is strewn with presidents who were either too ideological to bend and make concessions, like a Herbert Hoover, or so lacking in political direction that their administrations faltered under the burden of their drift and opportunism, like Taft's, Ford's, Carter's, and Bush's. The men who have survived and prospered in the White House have been those with the keenest political sense: presidents who combined a clear sense of purpose with both a carefully judged assessment of what degree of change the country was ready to accept and a strategic

sense of when to accommodate themselves to opponen
ready to yield on at least some points. Winston Chu
stood that "the duty of governments is to be first of all pra⸍⸍.
I am for makeshifts and expediency. I would like to make the people who live on this world at the same time as I do better fed and
happier generally. If incidentally I benefit posterity—so much the
better—but I would not sacrifice my own generation to a principle—however high or a truth however great."

Yet political intelligence is not an imperishable commodity or
fixed attribute. Even our greatest presidential operators have made
their share of political mistakes or been wedded to a program that
ultimately wouldn't work and caused them considerable political
grief. If politics is indeed an impossible profession, it must nonetheless be practiced as an art, with a palette of just the right shades
of principle, bravado, and compromise. No one, for example, can
be an effective pragmatist without holding to a foundation of some
larger design. Pragmatists without vision are seen as opportunists;
pragmatists with vision are seen as statesmen, or at the very least,
good politicians. American politics, then, requires a masterly sense
of proportion and balance, and will almost certainly defeat those,
who, in LBJ's famous description of Gerald Ford, couldn't walk a
straight line and chew gum at the same time.

Johnson had an even more colorful way of explaining what a
politician must do to survive and succeed. After Vice President
Richard Nixon was stoned and spat upon in Latin America in 1958,
he received a hero's welcome at Andrews Air Force Base in Maryland, where LBJ, who was then the Senate majority leader, em-
braced him. The following day a reporter caught up with Johnson
on Capitol Hill. "I saw you greeting Nixon yesterday," the journalist said. "I thought you told me a few weeks ago that Nixon
was 'nothing but chicken shit.' " "Son," Johnson replied, "you
have to understand that in politics, overnight chicken shit can turn
to chicken salad."

Johnson and other successful political leaders have always realized that they could not get very far without accommodating to
change—change in circumstance, change in mood, change in ideas;
change that offered opportunities to advance America's grand
experiment in democracy and freedom. "The mission of democratic statecraft," Arthur Schlesinger, Jr., explains, "is to keep in-

stitutions and values sufficiently abreast of the accelerating velocity of history to give society a chance of controlling the energies let loose by science and technology. Democratic leadership is the art of fostering and managing innovation in the service of a free community." "I simply experiment," the great American essayist Ralph Waldo Emerson said. "An endless seeker, with no Past at my back."

I

When he became president in 1789, George Washington considered himself to be "entering upon an unexplored field, enveloped on every side with clouds and darkness." He saw that "liberty and the destiny of the republican model of government," as well as his personal reputation, were staked on the "experiment" fostered by the Constitution of 1787 and the new government that was to give it meaning. Since the Constitution was so general in its provisions for so many topics, but particularly on the role of the president, which was described in five paragraphs measuring half a printed page, Washington knew that the success of the presidency, and the government as a whole, would depend in large measure on what he and his colleagues in the executive, legislative, and judicial branches actually did in office. As the historian Marcus Cunliffe explains, Washington, who was "not an expert on finance, or a nimble political tactician, or a constitutional theorist, or a diplomatist acquainted at firsthand with foreign affairs," feared he would fail as the first president. In every respect, his presidency was to be a learning exercise for himself and the country.

On all matters of both protocol and substance Washington had to choose among competing influences that might strengthen or undermine the new government. How, for example, was he to deal with the incessant demands on his time for public audiences and access to his residence (or the "people's" house), where they felt entitled to drink and dine at public expense?

Though such questions seem relatively minor in retrospect, their resolution would have a significant impact on public confidence in the new government's ability to build traditions of sensible republican rule. Washington searched for a middle ground between "too free an intercourse and too much familiarity," on the one hand, and a monarchical detachment unseemly for the president of a republic, on the other. Settling on once-weekly dinners for government officials and their families and twice-weekly open houses of limited duration for anyone properly attired, Washington established the dignity of his office without divorcing himself from the citizenry he was asked to serve. Similarly, he was content to be addressed as "Mr. President" rather than as "His Highness, the President of the United States of America, and Protector of Their Liberties," as Vice President John Adams proposed. "Mr. President" bespoke an unpretentious republican regard, which Washington believed struck just the right note between old-world ideas of inherited wealth and power and excessive leveling at the expense of a president's dignity.

On more weighty matters of government organization and administration he was equally as perspicacious. A typical problem he faced was how to interpret the Constitution's requirement that he seek the advice and consent of the Senate in making treaties, with which two-thirds of senators present would have to concur.

Initially, Washington was convinced that obtaining "advice and consent" would have to precede the taking on of any external commitments if the country was to be consistent, act honorably, and not embarrass itself in world affairs. Early in his term, therefore, as his representatives negotiated with various Indian tribes, he asked the Senate to support instructions he intended to give his envoys. Arriving unannounced at the Senate on a Saturday morning, he asked John Adams, who was presiding over the meeting, to read a seven-point document on which he wished "advice and consent," though in fact consent was all he required. But jealous of their prerogatives as a separate government branch and eager not to set a precedent that would allow presidents to intimidate them by coming to their chamber, the senators refused to act, postponing decisions on the questions before them. Their response angered Washington, who regarded it as defeating "every purpose of my coming here." But soon recognizing the legitimacy of the Senate's concern and the value of presidential freedom to maneuver abroad with as few domestic constraints as possible, he reached tacit agreement with senators that advice and consent would follow rather than precede negotiations, leaving Washington and all future presidents with the authority to make treaties first and consult later.

The first great test of presidential autonomy in treaty-making came with the negotiation and approval of Jay's Treaty, an agreement to resolve post-Revolutionary differences with Great Britain over trade, neutral rights, and forts in America's northwest territories. Because the stakes were so high, some in the Senate asked Washington to consult through periodic written messages on developments in the talks. After reflecting on the possible consequences of such action, Washington refused to give senators access to tentative and secret proposals and counterproposals, believing that premature public debate would adversely affect the possibility of reaching an agreement. A majority of senators voted to accept the president's policy, but when the signed treaty reached the Senate for confirmation, it provoked a firestorm of controversy. Few in America, including Washington, could accept the concessions Jay had made. But fearing the alternative was a war that would threaten the stability of the new republic, Washington and twenty out of thirty senators opted for an imperfect treaty.

The greatest test of Washington's political judgment and skills came in response to policies aimed at stabilizing and expanding the nation's economic well-being. James Madison had worried that any efforts to set a national economic course would only stimulate the country's natural impulses toward partisanship and formation of parties, and in turn Washington himself was anxious lest such national divisions threaten the cohesion of the Union, make it more vulnerable to external dangers, and thwart his efforts to be a successful chief. He feared that the solidification of Federalist and anti-Federalist factions denouncing each other as "monocrats" and "mobocrats" might be a death knell for a unified republican nation.

Yet Washington concluded that such risks were outweighed by commitments to economic and fiscal policies essential to the country's future. Following the lead of Secretary of Treasury Alexander Hamilton, Washington endorsed federal assumption of the national debt, promising to repay fully bonds issued during the Revolutionary War by the Continental Congress and the states. Agrarian spokesmen, led by Secretary of State Thomas Jefferson, declared the Hamilton program, which included creation of a national bank and passage of a whiskey tax to supplement import duties, at odds with the substance and spirit of the Constitution, since repayment would chiefly benefit northeastern commercial interests and hurt debtor farmers.

But Washington, convinced that economic stability would be a critical anchor for the new nation, agreed to Hamilton's entire program. And having so decided, the president did not hesitate to enforce his policy. In 1794, after three years in which western Pennsylvania farmers, whose livelihood largely depended on whiskey sales, openly defied federal demands for tax payments, Washington declared a state of insurrection in the region and called upon four state governors to provide militia forces to suppress it. Despite considerable anguish at having to take up arms against fellow citizens, Washington felt he had no choice but to establish the precedent of enforcing federal authority against Americans defying national laws.

The spirit of practical politics in the service of national advance found its final and most eloquent expression in his Farewell Address of September 1796, which took the form of a state paper printed in newspapers across the country. Devoting two-thirds of his valedictory to domestic affairs, Washington counseled his countrymen against state, sectional, and party affiliations that overrode American or national interests. Only through avoidance of factionalism, which divided Americans against one another and made them tools of foreign powers, could they achieve the personal happiness and national greatness that was already within their reach.

"Nothing is more essential," Washington warned, "than that permanent, inveterate antipathies against particular nations and passionate attachments for others should be excluded, and that in place of them just and amicable feelings toward all should be cultivated. The nation which indulges toward another an habitual hatred or an habitual fondness is in some degree a slave."

The message was simple enough: a successful nation was one that operated by calculation of national interest, not by individual ideology or passion. Permanent alliances at home or abroad were a poor idea, but "temporary alliances for extraordinary emergencies" were essential in a world of shifting conditions and unpredictable events. The path to private contentment was through flexible public actions serving national designs. It was a fitting prescription not only for a national agenda but for presidential effectiveness in years to come.

Thomas Jefferson, an architect of the anti-Federalist or Democratic-Republican party, which was at odds with the expansive view of the Constitution and government adopted by Washington, was as flexible a politician as his great predecessor in the presidency. Sharing Washington's concern to minimize conflicts that could destroy the democratic experiment of the United States, Jefferson declared at the start of his presidential term in 1801, "We are all republicans—we are all federalists."

Anyone acquainted with Jefferson's prepresidential career might have predicted the temperate tenor of his term of office. Jefferson was a centrist with a strong practical bent that led him to be more interested in the mechanical arts than in political theory. He was a man of striking contradictions—an associate of the wealthiest and most learned men of his age as well as a confidant of the most radical thinkers in France and the United States; the head of a party devoted to the interests of yeoman farmers, yet a friend of the country's great planters and commercial innovators—but above all he was a rationalist who sought progress in considered compromise.

However much he shrank from controversy, Jefferson was also a man with strong views on politics and national affairs. He was intent on dismantling as much of the federal government's hold over the individual as possible. In his first message to Congress in 1801, he declared federal authority responsible for only the external and mutual relations of "these states." The "principal care of our persons, our property, and our reputation, constituting the great field of human concerns," would rest in the hands of the localities. As a guarantee against excesses of federal power, the Jeffersonians eliminated the internal excise taxes imposed by the Federalists. In the words of one historian, "For many citizens the federal presence was now reduced to the delivery of the mails."

But for Jefferson, the government did have a larger function to perform, one central to everything he associated with public power and control—namely, the development of the individual in his pursuit of happiness. And in Jefferson's mind individual contentment was tied closely to landholding and farming. "Those who labor in the earth are the chosen people of God, if ever he had a chosen people," Jefferson declared in his 1781 treatise, *Notes on the State of Virginia*. Seven years later he predicted that the state governments "will remain virtuous for many centuries; as long as they remain chiefly agricultural; and this will be as long as there shall be vacant lands in any part of America." During the period of Federalist rule, he became all the more convinced that "farmers, whose interests are entirely agricultural . . . are the true representatives of the great American interest, and are alone to be relied on for expressing the proper American sentiments."

The Louisiana Purchase of 1803, the greatest act of Jefferson's presidency, was in the service of this very concern—to sustain America as an "empire of liberty" through the availability of abundant Western lands. American dreams of gaining a domain equal in size to its existing territory had been challenged in 1800 by a powerful nation's laying plans for renewed presence in the New World, when France regained the trans-Mississippi West from Spain. A French empire that controlled New Orleans, navigation of the Mississippi River, and access to the Gulf of Mexico had serious implications for Americans generally and western farmers in particular. Consequently, when Napoleon, worried by prospects of the resumption of European warfare, offered to sell the Louisiana Territory to the United States for $15 million, Jefferson found the proposal irresistible. But constitutional scruples stood in the way of his immediately accepting it. An advocate of strict constitutional construction, which had been a hallmark of his opposition to the Federalist, Jefferson now saw that his principles were clearly at odds with the decision to buy Louisiana. Where in the founding document could one locate presidential authority for undertaking such a major step? Jefferson freely acknowledged that he saw none. He privately called the transfer of territory "an act beyond the Constitution" and hoped that Congress and the states would later add a constitutional amendment that would legalize his action. In a letter to a friend he compared himself to the guardian of a ward whose money he invested for his future good, even though the investment did not bind the ward forever and could one day be disavowed as an unwise and illegal act. For the moment, though, Jefferson felt compelled to put himself at "risk" for the good of the country and to let history weigh the wisdom of his bold and probably unconstitutional step.

The judgment of historians on this matter has, in fact, been almost uniformly positive. Finding sufficient authority to be granted in the treaty-making clause of the Constitution to warrant Jefferson's action, commentators celebrate his decision as a demonstration of practical good sense on behalf of the nation. Although contemporary Federalist opponents attacked Jefferson's hypocrisy, taunting him as a sanctimonious constitutionalist who was "tearing the Constitution to shreds," the elasticity of the document made their complaints—as well as Jefferson's own concerns—less than compelling. More important, the practical advantage to a young nation throwing off European colonial entanglements, assuring itself of control over the West as far as the Rocky Mountains, and opening the way to U.S. dominance or "free security" in the Western Hemisphere were all benefits no wise leader could have rejected.

Despite his popular image as a man so private and principled as to be almost above the fray of politics, Abraham Lincoln was as great a political operator as anyone who ever sat in the White House. Historian David H. Donald argues that despite Lincoln's failure "to win the press, the politicians, and the people [who never gave him anything resembling national majority support] he was nevertheless a successful politician." And by virtue of his political acumen, Donald adds, Lincoln "gained the opportunity of becoming a superb statesman." The techniques he used to achieve his ends involved first and foremost avoiding doctrinaire positions. As he told the Congress in an annual message, "The dogmas of the quiet past are inadequate to the stormy present. The occasion is piled high with difficulty, and we must rise with the occasion. As our case is new, so we must think anew, and act anew. We must disenthrall ourselves, and then we shall save our country."

Above all, he believed it essential to be responsive to changing conditions and to accommodate to them in the service of preserving the Union. Like Emerson he considered consistency the hobgoblin of little minds. When people pressed him to state his policies on a variety of issues, he resisted by saying he was still undecided or by obscuring his uncertainty in a cloud of words that might amuse an audience but left it no closer to knowing what he planned than before he spoke. His refusal to share his plans sprang from his realistic understanding that, until events made clear what he must do, those plans had to remain unformulated.

The evolution of his emancipation policy is an excellent case in point. On principle, Lincoln considered slavery immoral. "If slavery is not wrong," he declared, "nothing is wrong." But he perceptively determined that eliminating it would have to wait until the military and political necessities of saving the Union were addressed. In the summer of 1861, General John C. Frémont, the commander of Union forces in the West, announced a policy of confiscating rebel property, including slaves, who would then be granted their freedom. Lincoln, however, insisted that only slaves used directly to help the rebellion could be seized. Anxious that Kentucky not join the Confederacy, he stipulated a policy that removed a threat to the state's slaveholders, which might otherwise have precipitated Kentucky's secession.

Abolitionists did not see any wisdom in Lincoln's action. "How many times are we to save Kentucky and lose our self-respect?" one asked, while another protested, "Such ethics could only come of one born of 'poor white trash' and educated in a slave state." But as historian Phillip Paludan asserts, Lincoln had larger concerns in mind. "Although equal justice under law was the moral high ground and the purpose behind much Union warmaking, the President had to think about both ends and means, ideal and immediate necessity. The strategic position of, and the delicate balance in, Kentucky restrained antislavery action this time. But Lincoln was a master of longer-ranged visions, of a time when means and ends entwined." Since Kentucky's secession might also have brought Missouri and Maryland to the Confederate side, Lincoln could not risk losing three additional states by advancing the date of what he thought was inevitable in any case.

Believing it crucial to end slavery first in the border states, Lincoln asked Congress in 1862 to provide financial compensation to any state agreeing to "gradual abolishment of slavery." Since this policy would grant a kind of legitimacy to slavery by paying slaveholders to give up "their property" and since it made no provisions for civil and political rights for the freedmen, abolitionists remained opposed, although Wendell Phillips acknowledged that Lincoln's proposal was at least a conscientious beginning: "The President has not yet entered Canaan, but he has turned his face Zionward."

But the failure of the border states to act on Lincoln's proposal forced the president to recast his strategy. With the help of Congress his subsequent agreement to abolish slavery in the District of Columbia, refusal to return escaped slaves from the North to the South, and abolition of slavery in the territories, signaled that slavery was doomed. In the summer of 1862, with the border states still unmoved by his appeal, Lincoln fashioned his Emancipation Proclamation, which granted freedom to all slaves in states still in rebellion on January 1, 1863. By now a number of forces had come into play that persuaded Lincoln that the time had come for decisive action. Emancipation would weaken the Confederacy by bringing blacks to Union lines, would discourage European states from recognizing the Confederacy, would enlist renewed enthusiasm for the war effort among many in the North, and would ease the way to mustering and mobilizing black troops against the South. In the form it was actually issued in September of 1862 the Proclamation did not give the abolitionists all they wanted, but it freed 74 percent of all slaves in the United States and 82 percent of those in the Confederacy.

Lincoln's decision finally to abolish slavery was the product of pragmatic considerations. As he himself acknowledged, the Proclamation had "no constitutional or legal justification, except as a military measure." In 1864 he wrote privately in regard to the Emancipation declaration, "I claim not to have controlled events, but confess plainly that events have controlled me." But with this act Lincoln had put practical politics in the service not only of the war effort but of the country's highest ideals. Emerson declared that through emancipation the "government has assured itself of the best constituency in the world: every spark of intellect, every virtuous feeling, every religious heart, every man of honor, every poet, every philosopher, the generosity of the cities, the health of the country, the strong arms of the mechanic, the endurance of the farmers, the passionate conscience of women, the sympathy of distant nations—all rally to its support."

Lincoln, the great pragmatist, had wanted to do the right thing at the right time. Though some contemporaries carped at his expediency in dealing with the "crime" of slavery, most unionists judged his policy to be a commonsense step necessary to the United States' future. His Proclamation eased the moral burden on a nation of "free men" at the precise moment that it could offer the most benefit toward defeating the South and preserving the Union.

II

The greatest presidential pragmatists of the twentieth century have been no less cognizant that changing historical conditions called for adaptability and fresh, sometimes even unprecedented, action. Theodore Roosevelt, Wilson, FDR, Truman, Eisenhower, JFK, LBJ, Nixon, and Reagan were, like their most successful predecessors, realists who occasionally erred when their hopes and beliefs failed to take into account unpalatable truths, to which they were subsequently slow to accommodate. But these were exceptional circumstances in political careers marked by a faith in long-term goals that made short-term adjustments and sacrifices acceptable elements in a larger design.

TR and Wilson were of one mind in being essentially conservatives eager to reinforce traditional economic, political, and social habits. But recognizing that industrialization had changed America forever and that hallowed values would need to be restored under a new flag, both men bent themselves to progressive assumptions about making the federal government the country's principal arbiter in addressing the problems of their time. TR, who feared big business and organized labor as the advance guard of class warfare that, if unchecked, would destroy the American middle class, pressed for federal regulation of the interests threatening economic and political democracy, the forces guaranteeing realization of every individual's American dream. Wilson, the advocate of a New Freedom (or more accurately the champion of the reinstatement of old freedoms) through the break-up of early twentieth-century trusts and political machines, concluded that he would have to remedy current ills by relying on TR's New Nationalism—a federal government that had assumed responsibility for economic and social issues previously off-limits under the sacred doctrine of laissez-faire.

In foreign affairs as well, the warrior and the priest, as John Milton Cooper has called Wilson and TR, were also ruled by similarly pragmatic impulses. Roosevelt, who preached overseas activism in the name of world good, made American self-interest the cornerstone of all his policies. Acquisition of the Panama Canal, mediation of the Russo-Japanese war, and the Corollary to Monroe's Doctrine, which declared America the policeman of the Western Hemisphere, all rested on compelling moral justifications about serving international prosperity, law, and peace. But they were actions that, first and foremost, served the vital interest of the United States as defined by shifting balances of power and new technological developments on the world scene.

Though he preferred to believe otherwise, Wilson's military interventions: Mexico, 1914; Haiti, 1915; Mexico, 1916; Santo Domingo, 1916; Cuba, 1917; Europe, 1917; Russia, 1918, were little different from those of TR, and were rationalized with the same high-minded rhetoric that could not disguise America's laying claim to a superior position in an altered world. Nor, for all his protests about being "too proud to fight" and his holding forth of the United States as the last bastion of sanity in a world gone mad with war, could Wilson resist the arguments to enter the Great War as an essential step toward preserving American democracy. Wilson's subsequent peace program enjoyed a reputation as "universalist" or based on enlightened ideals for the benefit of all mankind, but once again, its actual provisions spoke volumes about Wilson's understanding of both America's status among nations and of how his plan's realization would have meant the onset in 1920 of "The American Century" that publisher Henry Luce saw coming to life years later, during the Second World War.

Franklin Roosevelt, the greatest of our modern pragmatic presidents, made "the rest of the fellas around here look like kids," LBJ once said. FDR had all the attributes of an effective political leader, especially the capacity to enunciate a grand design for which he developed substantive programs gradually and only when they became feasible. As had been true of Lincoln, no one could tell where Roosevelt stood on a particular policy until he calculated just how far current opinion would allow him to go. "You are one of the most difficult men to work with that I have ever known," Secretary of the Interior Harold Ickes once told him. "Because I get too hard at times?" the president asked. "No," Ickes answered, because ". . . you won't talk frankly even with people who are loyal to you. . . . You keep your cards close up against your belly. You never put them on the table."

Roosevelt was a master change artist. During the 1932 campaign he vacillated on so many matters that Herbert Hoover dubbed him a "chameleon on plaid." His evasiveness during the election fight was a foreshadowing of his constant maneuvering during his twelve years in office. The New Deal programs he introduced to provide relief and recovery from the Depression and the reforms he initiated that could prevent another such mishap from occurring emerged from Roosevelt's canny reading of the changing economic and political realities he saw.

His openness to domestic change was not curtailed by the pressure of U.S. involvement in the war. At the end of 1943, the president had tried to convince the country that much remained to be done in the fighting by announcing that Dr. Win-the-War had replaced Dr. New Deal as the principal concern of his administration. "The overwhelming first emphasis should be on winning the war," Roosevelt told the press. But after eleven years in office, he was still contemplating dramatic innovations to promote national economic reform. Only two weeks later, in his State of the Union address, the most radical speech of his presidency, he indicated that he was more prepared than ever to challenge the country to adopt bold measures that could transform American life.

Though still urging that the country extend its efforts to win the war, he now pressed the case for an economic bill of rights which he planned to make his principal order of business in the postwar part of his fourth term. The columnist Walter Lippmann commented that it was "good politics in the year 1944 to propose the very things which no other politician has ever regarded as anything but straight political suicide." Moreover, the sudden shift in tone and content from two weeks earlier was the sort of tactic that gave Roosevelt a reputation as a "politician" with a predilection for cutting corners. All the leaders of the forties had their symbols, Clare Boothe Luce once said. Hitler's and Mussolini's were the upraised arms; Churchill's the V sign. Roosevelt? Luce wet her finger and held it up to test the wind.

However much Roosevelt's economic-bill-of-rights speech can be viewed as the opening salvo in his 1944 presidential campaign, it was nevertheless the statement of a bold idea whose time had come in an administration notable for small domestic gains since the onset of the world crisis in 1939. Roosevelt, with his feel for shifting political currents and a determination to make his fourth and last term the occasion of a program assuring economic security against hunger, homelessness, and joblessness, seized the moment to outline a program for the future—a program that victory in the war and the personal influence of the longest serving and most successful president ever might convert into as lofty a political achievement as anything in the country's history.

Harry Truman's largely successful presidency was a small miracle made possible by both the course of international events and by his own effectiveness as a politician. Vice-presidential successions have traditionally profited from the good will generated by the death of a president in office. TR after McKinley, Coolidge following Harding, and LBJ replacing Kennedy were all beneficiaries of national unity, for few Americans wished to add to the burdens of an unelected chief executive confronting challenges he never expected to face. Truman's case, however, was unique: he was "the second Missouri compromise," "the little man from Missouri" almost no one thought could measure up to the legendary Franklin Roosevelt. The inevitable comparisons put Truman at a huge disadvantage and marked him out for failure after less than one term.

But Truman was an individual with extraordinary inner resources and political instincts as finely honed as those of his most illustrious White House predecessors. He had faith in his own judgment about men and events—"the buck stops here," he said in a famous comment about where responsibility lay in his administration. The clarity of purpose he brought to ending World War II, reaching for Fair Deal reforms, and meeting the Soviet Communist challenge reduced the anguish of the many difficult decisions he had to make later during his term.

In 1948 few pundits expected Truman to win election to office in his own right. The inevitable economic dislocations of the post-war conversion period, highlighted by strikes and inflation, and the collapse of hopes for world harmony through U.S.-Soviet coop-eration and an effective United Nations, had led in 1946 to the first Republican-controlled Congress since 1930. After the Dem-ocratic defeats Senator J. William Fulbright of Arkansas suggested that Truman resign and turn the presidency over to a Republican. Truman replied that henceforth Fulbright should be known as "Senator Halfbright." While this sort of feistiness made Truman a folk hero with millions of Americans, as the election year arrived the Republican campaign confidently predicted that the country was ready for a political sea change.

But brilliant political maneuvering carried Truman to the biggest upset victory in American political history. Despite defections by the left and right wings of his party, which seemed to portend the loss of traditional southern states and northern big cities, Truman accurately concluded that a hard-hitting attack on the Republican Eightieth Congress, combined with appeals to New Deal voters to help him fill out FDR's fourth term, would keep him in the White House. Sensing that a majority of Americans remained indebted to Democratic reforms, were suspicious of "progressive" Democrats celebrating outdated notions about Soviet-American cooperation, and were offended by Dixiecrat opposition to equal rights, Truman struck all the right notes against Henry Wallace, Strom Thurmond, and Republican candidate Tom Dewey, who had all the appeal of "a certified Public Accountant in pursuit of the Holy Grail." Alongside the animated and down-to-earth Truman, the lackluster Dewey impressed voters as arrogant: "He is the only man I ever met," one critic said, "who could strut sitting down."

Truman's political astuteness in the campaign served him equally well as a successful leader in foreign affairs. When he came to the presidency, Truman had no claim to expertise in world politics, and faced both a rapid deterioration in Soviet-American relations and the outbreak of civil war in China, where he had sent General

George C. Marshall to mediate a settlement. Convinced by early 1946 that the United States would have to confront Soviet expansionism in a contest between totalitarian Communism and Western democracy, Truman formulated a policy of containment through a series of international actions that rallied Americans at home and allies abroad. The Truman Doctrine in March 1947, promising help to Greece and Turkey; the Marshall Plan that June for the rehabilitation of Western Europe; the NATO alliance in 1949, a mutual security pact among the U.S. and eleven Western nations; and the decision to defend South Korea in June 1950 from a North Korean attack decisively ended American isolationism by creating a national consensus for long-term U.S. involvement abroad. Truman's timing, rhetoric, and flexibility in responding to the post-1945 world crisis was an object lesson in how pragmatic politics tied to long-term goals are essential to effective presidential action.

Contemporary critics of Dwight Eisenhower described him as something of a White House dolt, an apolitical general who preferred golf and bridge to policymaking and assuming the leadership of his own administration. His platitudinous speeches, notorious for their tortured syntax, made the president an object of derision by intellectuals, who compared his ineptness on the hustings and before the press to that of Warren G. Harding. After one of his illnesses, liberals joked, Ike's doctors told him to stop reading so many presidential documents, because it was tiring out his lips.

But criticisms like these could not account for how so limited a man could have exercised such effective leadership during World War II; won two decisive election victories against Adlai Stevenson, one of the most intelligent and attractive candidates to grace the twentieth-century American political scene; and maintained the confidence of people at home and allies abroad during eight tumultuous years in domestic and foreign affairs. When in the late 1970s, historians and political scientists gained access to Eisenhower's diaries and were able to investigate the inner workings of his presidency, they discovered a significantly different man from the one so often ridiculed in the critical literature of the fifties and the sixties.

The Eisenhower that has been revealed in recent historical writings was far more a politician than previously suspected. He not only had a much greater interest in the epochal domestic and foreign policy issues confronting his administration but was also considerably more astute about how to lead the government and country toward what he considered vital national and international goals.

In the fifties, for example, it was accepted wisdom that Secretary of State John Foster Dulles was responsible for establishing foreign policy. Dulles was viewed as an evangelical anti-Communist ready to take America to the brink of war and, if need be, to engage in massive nuclear retaliation against an act of Communist aggression. Eisenhower himself, it was thought, had more temperate views on nuclear weapons and dealings with Moscow and Peking, but he had fallen under Dulles's spell. The record of Ike's presidency, however, indicates that he met regularly with Dulles and that, as Eisenhower put it, Dulles "never made a serious pronouncement, agreement, or proposal without complete and exhaustive consultation with me in advance and, of course, my approval." Eisenhower had nothing but admiration for Dulles's "wisdom" and "knowledge in the delicate and intricate field of foreign relations," but it is clear that the secretary's actions were consistently the product of their shared ideas and were ultimately the president's decisions.

The fact that Eisenhower's actual foreign policy was much more restrained than Dulles's rhetoric is telling evidence of Ike's control in this area. In 1956, for instance, after much discussion in the administration of the "rollback" of Communism and the liberation of subject peoples from Soviet dominance, Eisenhower refused to intervene when Russian tanks and troops ousted a Hungarian government for threatening to withdraw from the Warsaw Pact. Mindful that any follow-through on threats to reduce Soviet power might lead to a nuclear war, Eisenhower took a more measured position repeatedly during his eight years in office to make a less bellicose containment policy the principal means of assuring Western security. While he may have wavered in his strategy on how to overcome the Soviet threat, no one ever accused him of backing away from a tough anti-Communist policy, and no one doubted that this remained his primary goal.

Ironically, it was Eisenhower himself who encouraged the notion that Dulles guided his administration's dealings with the out-side world. This ploy was partly Eisenhower's way of making a subordinate a lightning rod who would be the focus of the press and the public in the event of any missteps. Moreover, Eisenhower believed it shrewd politics to obscure his own role in policymaking at home and abroad as a way of sustaining his political influence with the Congress and the mass of Americans.

Similarly, he obscured his intentions on a variety of issues by intentionally making vague and sometimes muddled statements at press conferences and in public addresses. He operated, in effect, by the same principle relied on by Lincoln and FDR: keep your options open until you know what current conditions and mood will allow in pursuit of some larger goal. In 1955, when Com-munist China threatened to seize the offshore islands of Quemoy and Matsu as a prelude to invading Taiwan, Eisenhower suggested that the United States might consider using nuclear weapons as a response to any such attack. "I see no reason why they shouldn't be used just exactly as you would use a bullet or anything else," he told the press. Whether he was bluffing or not, he would never admit. But his statement had the desired effect of discouraging the Chinese from a course of action inimical to U.S. interests and risk-ing a nuclear war.

The surprising aspect of Eisenhower's manipulativeness is not the depth of his practical political skills, but that contemporaries and historians misinterpreted it until almost twenty years after his term. Popular presidents are rarely the fools intellectuals would sometimes have them be. It should be a truism for all president-watchers that effective, well-liked chiefs are, in one way or another, political realists or sensible pragmatists using their skills in the ser-vice of some public design. Indeed, as the history of the country makes abundantly clear, Americans as a rule hate politics and often mistrust politicians as opportunists who are intent only on gaining access to public funds. It should come as no surprise that aspirants to elective office increasingly present themselves as amateurs or cit-izen politicians eager to save the country from the professional, self-serving pols. This may be good campaign strategy and even useful while in office, but it should never fool students of politics and the presidency.

*   *   *

If Lincoln, FDR, and Eisenhower achieved their goals through patience and the artfulness of statecraft, Lyndon Johnson announced them with a passion and clarity that made him seem more like a tub-thumping preacher than the most effective backroom wheeler-dealer ever to serve in the Senate and possibly the White House. Whatever LBJ's failures as president—which were ruinous to his hold on the office and ultimately his historical reputation—he was, along with FDR, the greatest presidential legislator in the country's history.

Circumstance played a part in Johnson's success. Turning Kennedy's death and the hapless candidacy of Barry Goldwater to good effect, Johnson won a landslide victory in 1964, which gave him the most liberal Congress in the country's history. While the least experienced politician would have found it possible to get major bills passed in this legislature, Johnson was no amateur. His twenty-four years in the House and the Senate, including six years as Senate majority leader, had made him a master of the congressional procedure and deal-making. The passage in 1957 of the first civil rights bill in eighty-two years and the creation of the National Aeronautics and Space Administration (NASA) in 1958 were impressive trial runs for what Johnson would achieve as president.

Yet even Johnson's experience on the Hill and the liberal majorities in Congress could not have guaranteed the successful passage of the Great Society laws of 1964–1968 were it not for a national mood receptive to equal rights for blacks; medicare for the elderly; medicaid, food stamps, Headstart, and better housing for the poor; federal aid to elementary, secondary, and higher education for wider and improved learning; truth in lending and packaging for consumers; a Department of Housing and Urban Development, Model Cities, and Urban Mass Transit for the betterment of the cities; public radio and television and national arts and humanities endowments for a more cultured America; clean air and water; and product, highway, traffic, and tire safety for everyone.

It was Johnson's keen sense of national political possibilities, and his skills as an accommodationist or coalition-builder, that helped win enactment of the many landmark Great Society measures. He knew that the key to the success of his program would be in making the Congress feel that it was the center of the political universe. "The most important people you will talk to are senators and congressmen," Johnson told one of his aides. "You treat them as if they were president. Answer their calls immediately. Give them respect. They deserve it." Texas congressman Jake Pickle recalls that Johnson had a rule that aides had to return a congressman's or senator's call in "ten minutes or else!" Johnson himself, Pickle explains, "contrary to almost any president I've ever heard of, was on the phone constantly, talking to members of the House and the Senate. It would be nothing for him to talk to fifteen, twenty, or thirty different congressmen or senators during a day about some matter." And he was "awfully persuasive. He's about the best close-in, eyeball salesman that you'll run across."

White House aides not only listened to what legislators had to say but also made regular inquiries about how the White House could help them, as attested to by a "what can we do for you this week" file in the LBJ presidential library. While explicit promises of rewards for votes were rarely given, it was an unspoken assumption of the process that cooperation with the administration would lead to White House favors and attention that would serve the legislator's district or state and strengthen their standing with constituents.

Senate Republican Minority Leader Everett Dirksen was a particularly favored object of Johnson's attention. LBJ assistant Jack Valenti recalls how Johnson and Dirksen would sit in the living quarters of the White House, "their knees almost touching," sipping refreshments. " 'Now, Mr. President,' the organ tones would pour forth like melodic molasses flowing over tiled slopes, 'there is that matter of . . . ' And here Dirksen would mention some regulatory agency or commission, and inevitably the minority leader would have on the tip of his tongue the names of several people who were, in Dirksen's words, 'ably suited.' " Johnson "would pretend mock outrage" at the incessant demands for appointments and long lists of candidates. But by the close of their meeting, "a deal had been sealed. Dirksen would have an appointment of one of his friends, and the president would have a commitment on some piece of legislation."

By contrast, uncooperative legislators paid a price for the independence of their opinions. Democratic Senator Frank Church of Idaho, who went against the president on a major bill, defended his vote by saying that noted columnist Walter Lippmann shared his views. Johnson replied: "I'll tell you what, Frank, next time you want a dam in Idaho, you call Walter Lippmann and let him put it through for you." When Democratic congressmen persisted in defying the president's wishes, House Speaker John McCormack arranged to strip them of committee seniority, a substantial blow to the influence of long-term members.

Yet in spite of all the steps Johnson took to control the Congress, he faced formidable obstacles to every major bill he proposed. His struggle to provide federal aid to elementary and secondary education is an instructive example. Past attempts to create such assistance had repeatedly failed, for to many Americans, federal aid meant unconstitutional support of parochial schools. Instead of proposing general aid to public schools, which would have antagonized Catholics and reignited "a bitter battle" over helping parochial education, the administration suggested a plan of "categorical aid" to poor children in city slums and depressed rural areas. Partly inspired by *Everson* v. *Ewing Township*, a 1947 U.S. Supreme Court ruling that federal aid to parochial students was constitutional if it went directly to children rather than to schools, the proposal would help the needy regardless of whether they attended public or private schools. In addition, Johnson resisted proposals that funds go only to poor school districts, broadly interpreting "categorical aid" as available to children all over the country. Although advertising his bill as aimed at educating the underprivileged, he believed it would have a better chance of passing if it also offered substantial sums to middle-class and well-to-do children.

The Washington *Post* praised Johnson's bill as "political realism at its pragmatic best." It attacked "the most glaring and urgent aspects of the country's educational problem," and "without imperiling vital constitutional principles," it put aside "the religious conflict which has for so long frustrated every effort to extend Federal aid to education." Implicit in the *Post*'s assessment was the conviction that Johnson the great political operator was, more importantly, a far-seeing idealist who was acting to save and improve the country's schools and the principle of universal education by committing federal money and support to the service of an American ideal as old as the country itself.

The end of the Cold War and the compelling need for a new overall plan or direction in foreign policy supplied both Nixon in the seventies and Reagan in the eighties with a context ripe for the combination of larger purposes with flexible means in conducting overseas affairs.

Nixon had come to the White House with a justified reputation as an uncompromising anti-Communist. His role in bringing down Alger Hiss for lying to Congress about passing government secrets to a Communist agent; his readiness to pillory Democratic foreign policy as soft on Communism in the 1952 and 1956 campaigns; his famous "kitchen debate" with Soviet leader Nikita Khrushchev in 1959; his tough talk during the 1960 presidential contest about how to deal with Moscow, Peking, and Castro's Cuba; and his support in 1964 for Barry Goldwater, who spoke of "lobbing one" into the men's room of the Kremlin, all suggested an intransigence that frightened critics into viewing him as capable of provoking a nuclear war with the Soviets and Chinese.

Yet his presidency developed into anything but a single-minded crusade against the Communists. Although he continued the Vietnam war for another four years, helped topple Salvador Allende's constitutionally elected left-wing regime in Chile, and made anti-Sovietism the initial focus of his Middle Eastern policy, he also displayed a degree of realism and flexibility that with the passage of time has come to be seen as effective and forward-looking.

Recognizing that Vietnam had shattered America's Cold War consensus and that Russia and China were as intent on protecting their national security interests against each other as against the United States, Nixon and Henry Kissinger devised a policy of détente that aimed to create a foundation for a long-term "structure of peace" in "an increasingly heterogeneous and complex world." Its principal features were to be reduced arms competition, diminished Chinese-Soviet expansionism and support for Third World revolutions, and expanded trade between the United States and the two Communist superpowers—an ambitious program helped in no small measure by a secret Kissinger mission to China in 1971 and a very public one by Nixon the following year. The president's pronouncement on what he was trying to accomplish in Beijing made clear how far he had come from his early days as a kneejerk anti-Communist. "What brings us together," Nixon told Chairman Mao Zedong, "is a recognition of a new situation in the world and a recognition on our part that what is important is not a nation's internal political philosophy. What is important is its policy toward the rest of the world and toward us." Agreeing to oppose "hegemony" by any one country over another, which was a coded declaration of intention to block Moscow's "geopolitical ambitions," Nixon and Mao signed a communiqué opening a new era in Sino-American relations.

A similar approach to Moscow in the spring of 1972 produced a substantial thaw in the Cold War. As in China, Nixon stressed his regard for each nation's autonomy or right to have whatever domestic political system it preferred, as long as it did not seek to impose its ideology on other states around the globe. "There must be room in this world for two great nations with different systems to live together and work together," Nixon told Soviet leader Leonid Brezhnev. Eager to reduce Soviet-American tensions, inhibit the United States from lining up with Beijing, and ease domestic economic problems, the Soviets agreed to a Strategic Arms Limitation Treaty (SALT I), to restrain its adventurism abroad, and to trade more freely with the United States, including the purchase of badly needed grain supplies.

Like Nixon, Reagan proved to be more of a foreign policy pragmatist and realist in the White House than anyone would have predicted. During his years as a conservative spokesman for General Electric, a warm Goldwater supporter in 1964, and a governor of California from 1967 to 1975, he outdid almost everyone on the national scene as a proponent of defeating the Communist threat. He advocated stronger measures in Vietnam to assure an American victory, and he criticized the Nixon-Kissinger détente policy as a misguided approach to an "evil empire" with which there could be no compromise.

As president, Reagan initially spoke of defeating Communism

and denounced Soviet leaders as willing "to commit any crime, to lie, to cheat" in the service of their cause. America's conflict with Moscow was a "struggle between right and wrong, good and evil." In the course of his term in office, moreover, Reagan devoted himself to a trillion-dollar defense buildup, including a possibly unworkable Strategic Defense Initiative (SDI or "Star Wars," as critics dubbed it) to construct a shield against nuclear attacks, and by so doing eliminate the Soviet threat to the United States. Moreover, until November 1985, almost five years into his presidency, Reagan had refused to meet with Soviet leaders, making him the first chief executive in fifty years not to have a summit conference with his Soviet counterpart.

All this changed in 1985 after Mikhail Gorbachev came to power. Believing that the only way to preserve the Soviet system was through economic reforms that included massive cuts in defense spending, Gorbachev proposed a meeting with Reagan at Geneva in November 1985 to improve relations and promote arms control. Reagan, seeing a chance to reduce Soviet-American tensions and wean Moscow away from Communism, agreed. For all his ideological posturing, Reagan was fundamentally a political realist who valued concrete achievements over rhetorical flourishes. As governor of California, for example, despite his vocal opposition to withholding taxes and abortion, Reagan had signed bills endorsing both policies, which he had come to see as necessary to the state's economic and social well-being.

Between 1985 and 1989, Reagan and Gorbachev met four times and forged a landmark arms reduction agreement that eliminated land-based intermediate-range nuclear missiles from both countries' arsenals. At their final conference in Moscow in June 1988, Reagan described the moment as "one of the most exciting, hopeful times in Soviet history," "when the first breath of freedom stirs the air." Accurately discerning that Soviet Communism was giving way to something resembling Western-style free enterprise and that Soviet domination of Eastern Europe was nearing its end, Reagan could justifiably be confident that his receptivity to dealing with and supporting Gorbachev had contributed to the transformation of the Soviet Union and the end of the Cold War.

III

One of the many puzzles in presidential history is why so many of the country's most successful twentieth-century pragmatists, from Wilson to Reagan, made at least one major blunder during their administrations, each of which was the product of a want of good political sense. Why did executives who in almost every other instance seem to be tough-minded realists aggressively pursue plans that would come to embarrass them and weaken their hold on power? While one might attribute such behavior to the simple fallibility of human judgment, a closer look at how things occasionally went wrong for each of these leaders reveals a more complex underlying cause.

Woodrow Wilson, who had been so astute in leading his legislative program through the Congress in 1913–1914 and again in 1916, in converting his 1912 plurality into a successful reelection campaign, and in building a national consensus for support of World War I after U.S. entry, failed badly in gaining support for his peace program. It is understandable that he tried, however slim his chances of success, to convince voters to give him a Democratic Congress in 1918. Would he have been significantly less repudiated by a Republican victory without such a plea? It is doubtful. Moreover, he cannot be faulted for having conceded several of his Fourteen Points in the Paris peace talks. International realities required that he accommodate himself to his allies, who recognized the political impossibility of selling their publics on a peace without victors. To his credit, Wilson understood that the conclusion of the fighting had stripped him of his power to exert much influence on the European governments. Moreover, he realized that international events, particularly the revolution in Russia, were moving too quickly for him to shape the world along the lines of the postwar peace arrangements he had enunciated in January 1918.

More bewildering is why he failed to compromise with the Republican-controlled Senate in 1919 as a way to win approval for a modified peace treaty and the League of Nations. Having conceded so much already, it is understandable that he wished as a minimum the ratification of the Treaty and the League. But in refusing to accept amendments that could have given him the two-thirds votes needed for Senate approval, he turned a political fight into a moral contest, which was bound to end in political defeat. Wilson, the practical politician, abandoned political realism at the very moment he was battling for what he considered the most important legislation concerning international relations in modern history. Although limited U.S. involvement in the League in 1919 would most likely have given a physically impaired, lame-duck president too little means and time to make the world organization into the universalist instrument he had initially envisioned, arranging America's membership in a world peace body would have been a landmark step that could have opened the way for like-minded successors to move the League toward what Wilson hoped it might be.

Biographers have tried for seventy-five years to explain Wilson's refusal to compromise in 1919–1920. Some have ascribed it to just plain stubbornness, and some to psychological forces urging Wilson toward self-defeat. Yet none of these interpretations takes into account the balance of Wilson's record, which was a considerable success. The more likely reason for Wilson's failure lies in his physical collapse, which was brought on by a major stroke in September 1919. His illness intensified a propensity for self-righteousness and made him uncharacteristically rigid in dealing with a political issue that cried out for flexibility and accommodation. As Edwin A. Weinstein has argued in his medical and psychological biography of Wilson, "The cerebral dysfunction which resulted from Wilson's devastating strokes prevented the ratification of the Treaty. It is almost certain that had Wilson not been so afflicted, his political skills and facility with language would have bridged the gap between . . . [opposing Senate] resolutions, much as he had reconciled opposing views of the Federal Reserve bill . . . or had accepted the modifications of the Treaty suggested in February 1919."

In 1937, when Franklin Roosevelt undermined the political influence he had enjoyed after his 1936 landslide reelection, he was anything but ill. To the contrary, he had reached his peak as a national leader, enjoying as much public backing as any president has had in the country's history. To almost everyone's surprise, the president made the first major business of his second term a proposal for reforming the membership of the Supreme Court. Frustrated by a series of Court decisions in 1935–1936 that voided major New Deal laws, including the National Industrial Recovery Act, the Agricultural Adjustment Act, and the Guffey Coal Act, Roosevelt believed that the current Court would never allow the government to intervene in the economy to restore the country's economic health and assure a fair deal for labor.

Having been the first president since Andrew Johnson to serve a full term without a position opening on the High Court, and doubtful that any of the sitting justices would step down during his second four years, Roosevelt asked the Congress to empower him to add up to six new justices to the Supreme Court. His plan provided that, when any of the current nine members did not retire after reaching the age of seventy and a half, the president would be able to add a justice to the bench. Roosevelt considered the proposal as the only means by which he could assure a Court sympathetic to New Deal reforms.

But the president's manner of presentation—he consulted almost no one before sending his message on Court reform to the Hill—as well as the substance of the measure, led to a controversy that not only defeated the bill but weakened FDR's ability to lead during the following four years. Roosevelt's design to "pack" the Court, William E. Leuchtenburg says, "bore the mark of a proud sovereign who after suffering many provocations had just received a new confirmation of his power."

The proposal itself impressed most commentators as disingenuous, a smokescreen for an agenda that Roosevelt himself was initially unwilling to acknowledge. His public justification for the plan was that federal court dockets were so crowded that litigants suffered unnecessary delays and excessive costs; an increase in the number of judges on all the federal courts would relieve this burden. He made only oblique reference to his real intention—the need for younger judges to "vitalize" the courts by thinking in novel ways about current affairs. Reaction to the president's hollow argument was so hostile that he was soon forced to acknowledge his true motive in the matter.

But even Roosevelt's belated candor did not mollify his critics, who regarded his Court plan as little more than an assault on the constitutional principle of the separation of powers: by subordinating the courts to the executive, they argued, Roosevelt was attempting to make himself into a Nazi- or Fascist-style dictator. FDR's supporters scoffed at the vehemence of the opposition, which had unwarrantedly elevated the Court to an exalted state of infallibility, as well as the failure to see that five "Old Men" were nullifying the will of the people. Nevertheless, a majority of Americans accepted the proposition that the president's attack on the Court presented a genuine threat to the only institution that could assure their individual freedom and personal liberty.

At the start of the Court fight, few could imagine a Roosevelt defeat. The Senate, where division of opinion was more closely contested than in the House, was so heavily Democratic and filled with so many senators who owed their seats to the president that he seemed certain to win a showdown vote, however strongly people across the country might oppose his bill. Ironically, midway through the debate, a series of Court decisions upholding New Deal laws, as well as the unexpected retirement of one conservative justice, made Roosevelt's proposal seem moot. But deserted by his usual political acuity, he refused to give up the fight. If his defenders still argued that the Court might take another shift to the right if the president abandoned his reform fight, more astute observers predicted that the continuation of the struggle was likely to do the president more long-term harm than good. Indeed, by the end of the congressional session in August 1937, after the Senate rejected compromise proposals and shelved the president's bill, Washington political analysts wondered: "How did the president slide so far—so fast?" William Leuchtenburg concludes, "Because of the Court dispute, Roosevelt lost that overwhelming middle-class support he had mobilized in the 1936 campaign. Discord over the president's plan, coupled with other events, ended the brief era of great Democratic majorities."

Roosevelt's unyielding commitment to a battle that did him serious political damage is probably best understood as a product of his mistaken assumption that his landslide election gave him a mandate to do as he pleased. It may be that FDR saw the Court fight for what it was: a struggle to legitimize "the vast expansion of the power of government in American life." And even though that struggle produced a backlash against continued New Deal advances, it at least helped solidify the revolutionary changes of

1933–1937, which would be renewed in the series of Great Society laws fashioned thirty years later under LBJ. If the great victory of 1936 had blinded Roosevelt to political limitations that he had been more sensitive to in the past, his misjudgment would cost him dearly in his further attempts to achieve far-reaching domestic change. But history presented him with another opportunity to exercise his incomparable political skills, for the turn of events abroad would enable him to effect a transformation in American foreign policy as dramatic and ground-breaking as anything he had achieved at home.

Harry Truman, whose pragmatism in foreign policy helped him fashion a new consensus on international affairs at home and a stable anti-Communist alliance abroad, developed what seemed to be political myopia during the Korean war. Initially, Truman's decision to defend South Korea against North Korean Communist aggression shocked the nation. To most Americans, Korea was a remote place with little consequence for national security. Secretary of State Dean Acheson confirmed the popular opinion in January 1950 when he publicly indicated that South Korea had no significant priority in America's Asian defense plans.

But when the North took this announcement as license to invade the South, Truman and most Americans regarded the incursion as a test of U.S. resolve to defend free states from Communist encroachments around the globe. U.S. policymakers compared the attack to Hitler's assault on Czechoslovakia in 1938 and reminded the public that the failure to stop the Nazis immediately had led directly to World War II. American resistance to the current aggression would thus be a potent and necessary way to head off future Communist miscalculations, which, if unchecked, could provoke a third world war.

American public opinion quickly turned to support Truman's decision, and was even more strongly disposed to trust his leadership after U.S. forces repelled the attack and drove the invaders back across the 38th parallel into North Korea in less than five months. But Truman now made a grave error: despite warnings from Peking that an invasion of North Korea by U.S. and South Korean forces would bring China into the war, the president elected to carry the fighting north in an attempt to unify the Korean peninsula under a non-Communist regime. Truman's decision was partly based on General Douglas MacArthur's advice that, despite their threats, the Chinese would not enter the conflict because they lacked the capacity to fight effectively and understood that their real enemy was not the United States but the USSR.

Truman made two critical errors of judgment in following MacArthur's counsel to go north. First, he accepted that MacArthur, who had spent most of his military career in Asia, was exercising the sound judgment of his experience in arguing for China's reluctance to enter the war, and in predicting the likelihood of a quick end to the fighting in Korea. During a face-to-face meeting at Wake Island in October 1950, MacArthur had assured the president that Pyongyang, North Korea's capital, would fall within a week, and that all resistance would end by Thanksgiving. The United Nations could hold elections in the country by January, and U.S. troops would be able to withdraw entirely from the peninsula very soon thereafter. Truman and MacArthur also shared the conviction that if France could find an aggressive general to lead its forces in Indochina, they could make quick work of the Communists there as well.

But the military had never intimidated Truman, and MacArthur, for all his legendary stature, was no exception. "Have to talk to God's right-hand man tomorrow," Truman wrote irreverently on his way to Wake Island. And though he praised MacArthur warmly in public after their meeting as "a very great soldier" who was writing a "glorious new page in military history," Truman characteristically made up his own mind about the likely course of the Korean War, though relying on many of the same false assumptions held by MacArthur. Carried along by the euphoria of victory over North Korean forces, he believed that American success would do more to discourage than encourage Chinese intervention. Assuming that the Chinese were as pragmatic about foreign affairs as he himself had been, Truman blundered into a larger, more punishing conflict than the country wanted or needed to fight.

Truman also failed to anticipate the consequences to the United States and his administration from a drawn-out, unlimited war. After the Chinese crossed the Yalu into Korea in November, the fighting continued through the rest of 1950 and all of 1951. With no end in sight to the conflict and U.S. casualties reaching over twenty thousand, public sentiment turned against a president who seemed unable either to win or to negotiate a way out of a stalemate. Instead of being satisfied with having rescued the South from Communist aggression, Truman had overreached himself and trapped the country into a pointless conflict.

It would take another so-called limited war in Vietnam before a president learned that Americans will shed only so much blood on behalf of limited aims. George Bush scored a major victory in the Persian Gulf conflict, domestically and internationally, by knowing to call an end to the fighting when Kuwait regained its independence, at a minimal cost to the United States. The pragmatic lesson taught by Korea and Vietnam is that domestic political peace can be one of many casualties of a questionable foreign struggle, and that civil strife can in turn do even greater damage to the national well-being than acts of aggression abroad.

The Supreme Court's *Brown* v. *Board of Education* decision in 1954 ending segregation in the schools created a dilemma for Dwight Eisenhower that tested his political wisdom and foresight at a turning point in the United States' social and political history. By the fifties the legacy of racial bias that consigned African-Americans to second-class citizenship, especially across the South, where de jure and de facto segregation were inviolable mores, troubled great numbers of Americans. Locked in a struggle with totalitarian Communism, and concerned to honor rhetorical traditions of equal opportunity and individualism, much of the nation favored an end to the injustices that burdened the lives of its own citizens. The *Brown* decision was the most visible expression of a changing mood toward racial divisions in the United States.

Eisenhower, however, was not in favor of the Court's decision and reluctant generally to interfere in an issue on which feelings ran so strong. "I am convinced that the Supreme Court decision set back progress in the South *at least fifteen years*," he said privately. Unwilling or unable to empathize with the moral and legal case blacks had against the majority, he considered both civil rights protesters and violent defenders of the status quo as "extremists." For three years after the Court's decision, the president did little to enforce the new law of the land, and by 1957 not a single classroom had been integrated in the Deep South. Only when a federal court specifically ordered the desegregation of the Little Rock, Arkansas, schools and the city's Central High School accepted nine black students did Eisenhower feel compelled to act, and only then because Orval Faubus, the state's governor, had used the National Guard to turn away the black students and defy the rule of law.

Similarly, Eisenhower did not rise to the unarguable demand that, in a constitutional democracy, the federal government must assure black voting rights. In 1961 in Mississippi, where blacks made up 40 percent of the population, only 5 percent were registered to vote. The following year, when Fannie Lou Hamer tried to register in Indianola, the registrar demanded that she read and interpret a section of the state's constitution dealing with "de facto laws." "I didn't know nothing 'about no de facto laws," she replied, and Hamer and other applicants subsequently "flunked out." Literacy tests, poll taxes, and intimidation were standard weapons in excluding blacks from the polls.

The obvious record of southern disenfranchisement of blacks had led to 1957 and 1960 civil rights acts authorizing court action to give them the vote. But the laws were so hedged about with qualifications that they had little consequence, and in 1960, three-fourths of eligible southern blacks voters still remained off the rolls. This situation was partly the doing of a powerful southern bloc in the Senate, which relied on a traditional filibuster rule to protect their minority rights, but it was also the result of Eisenhower's reluctance to assign black rights a high priority on his political agenda. The vision of an America in which the "nation will rise up and live out the true meaning of its creed: ' . . . that all men are created equal,' " was left to Reverend Martin Luther King of the Southern Christian Leadership Conference to enunciate and foster.

Eisenhower remained essentially a passive figure in the great struggle of the 1950s for progress toward genuine civil rights. At the time, with many in the country ambivalent about the black struggle for equality, Ike seemed, as in so many other circumstances, to be the voice of moderation. He was viewed as the sane and sensible leader trying to take a middle ground between divisive voices and forces drawing the nation apart. But in fact, in this case his political and moral instincts simply failed him. He demonstrated neither vision nor political flexibility in refusing to take a sensible lead on the greatest domestic issue of his day. As developments in the 1960s would make clear, the country was ready for strong leadership on minority rights, and a president like Lyndon Johnson, ready to offer it, would reap moral and political gains as well as historical repute for accomplishments neither Eisenhower nor Kennedy had been able to achieve.

IV

Few developments in American political life have been more destructive to presidential authority than the rise of secret government. While doctrinaire adherence to an ideology, or a stiffbacked presidential personality like those of Andrew Johnson, Calvin Coolidge, and Herbert Hoover have been detriments to sensible, innovative leadership, so, too, has been the conviction of some chief executives that secret, unilateral actions could take the place of public debate. Without it, presidents have denied themselves the chance to consider alternative means of dealing with difficult problems. Moreover, when their machinations came to light, as they invariably did, they proved highly damaging to the president's credibility and his ability to govern.

The greatest of our presidential politicians established exceptional legislative records by quietly fashioning compromise agreements among competing congressional factions. These executives didn't invent the concept of a deal worked out in a smoke-filled room, but by their adroit use of it as a valid strategic tool, they demonstrated how determined political operators could turn private bargaining into public gain. This sort of behind-the-scenes maneuvering is, when responsibly deployed, a necessary and useful element in our periodic legislative advances. Once a deal is negotiated, however, it must still meet the test of democratic debate in the halls of Congress and before the press and the public. By contrast, the workings of a hidden government—the product of presidential arrogance that the head man and his principal aides should be free of democratic checks on executive action—have been injurious both to the president promoting them and to public confidence in the country's democratic institutions.

"I never think about politics more than eighteen hours a day," LBJ once said half-jokingly. Yet the most celebrated and admired of our chief executives have been precisely those who made honest political dealings the constant focus of their daily business. Those who even occasionally abandoned the hard work of political action for policy by presidential fiat ultimately made it more rather than less difficult for them to govern and lead.

Electoral politics and foreign affairs are two areas that have been especially vulnerable to overstepping by the executive branch. The destruction of the Nixon presidency through Watergate and the injury to Reagan's through the Iran-Contra scandal are two striking instances.

Nixon, the great presidential pragmatist, was also a great manipulator with little inclination to play by constitutional and political rules. The proposition by which he—and other practitioners of secret government—functioned is: where secret and often illegal arrangements can serve more effectively than open and ethical ones, there is no need for traditional political give and take. The primary advantage some presidents saw in this expedient was the freedom to bypass time-consuming debates and costly compromises.

From early in his career, Nixon had shown a strong impulse to win by whatever means necessary. Dirty politics—or at the very least a readiness to play fast and loose with the facts—had characterized his congressional campaign against liberal Democrat Jerry Voorhis in 1946 as well as his senatorial bid in 1950 against Helen Gahagan Douglas. Nixon depicted both Voorhis and Douglas as dupes or worse of sinister left-wing forces. As a congressman, he had built his reputation on an unholy war against Alger Hiss. The issue for Nixon was never whether Hiss was actually guilty, but how he could use the controversy surrounding the Hiss case to advance his own political career.

Eisenhower's secret foreign policy actions that helped elevate the Shah to power in Iran and topple Jacobo Arbenz in Guatemala; Kennedy's narrow victory over Nixon in the 1960 campaign by what Nixon believed were tainted votes in Illinois and Texas; Kennedy's secret campaign against Castro; and Johnson's imperious actions toward the Dominican Republic and Vietnam confirmed Nixon in his conviction that domestic and world politics were a dirty business that occasionally needed manipulation by other than straightforward means. When it came to the particularly difficult business of beating back the Communist threat and winning election to the White House, democratic politics was a luxury an effective politician could not always afford. The secret assault on Cambodia, the overthrow of Allende in Chile, and the Watergate scandal show Nixon at his apolitical, arrogant worst—a president with neither a moral nor a political compass to sustain him in office and assure his stature as the exceptional leader he aspired to be.

Shortly after taking office Nixon began secret, systematic bombing of Cambodian sanctuaries as a new means of cutting off North Vietnamese support of the Viet Cong rebellion in the South. In April 1970, when he announced formally an invasion of Cambodia to achieve what the hidden bombing had failed to do, he touched off a nationwide controversy about an undebated decision to widen rather than curtail the fighting in Southeast Asia. With protesting students being killed at Kent State University in Ohio and Jackson State in Mississippi and mass opinion deeply divided over the president's action, the Senate voted by nearly two to one to prohibit the use of funds for operations in Cambodia. Only after all U.S. forces had withdrawn from Cambodia did the House reject the Senate's resolution. But the episode did Nixon great political harm, and made it impossible for him to carry out his intentions in Cambodia.

Since Nixon believed that Cambodian neutralization was vital to an orderly U.S. retreat from Vietnam, it would have been far more judicious had he put his case before the Congress and the country for bombing and an invasion. Though a public forum would have risked his losing the freedom to implement a policy he considered essential, the alternative he chose proved ultimately ineffectual, for the unilateral expansion of the war into Cambodia did little to stop North Vietnamese cross-border attacks and supply shipments. Worse, it deepened U.S. domestic antagonism to an unwinnable war, further reduced the administration's ability to find an honorable way out of the conflict, and undermined public trust in a president who was already seen as less than scrupulous. Had Nixon paid heed to his better political instincts and made an aboveboard request to the Congress and the country to ratify his policy, he would at least have maintained some greater degree of credibility and support.

Though it did not gave rise to the same degree of controversy as Cambodia, the Nixon administration's dealings with the government of Salvador Allende in Chile added to the president's political problems in the United States. In opposing Allende's regime and then contributing to its downfall in 1973, Nixon viewed himself as being wisely pragmatic. While right-wing dictatorships in Latin America, Nixon told television interviewer David Frost in 1977, were little danger to the United States, left-wing governments intent on exporting their ideology to other countries in the hemisphere were a menace to our interests.

But Nixon's opposition to Allende was more the product of his residual anti-Communism than of genuine pragmatism. If he hadn't opposed Allende, Nixon also told Frost, Cuba and Chile would have turned Latin America into "a red sandwich, and eventually it [would] all be red." Nixon's covert efforts to destabilize and topple Allende's government, however, were superfluous and had untoward consequences in both Chile and the United States. Nixon's interference in Chile corroborated the belief in Latin America and among critics of U.S. foreign policy in the United States that his Chilean policy was nothing more than old-fashioned gunboat diplomacy imposed by an unscrupulous president with little genuine regard for self-determination. A more pragmatic plan would have been to leave Allende and Chile to their own devices. Allende was a largely ineffective leader whose hold on his country would likely have soon collapsed. But by aiding an unconstitutional right-wing regime under Augusto Pinochet to come to power, Nixon contributed to the creation of a repressive military dictatorship that lasted for sixteen years.

Cambodia and Chile, as so much else in Nixon's long political career, were only preludes to the climatic scandal of Watergate, the June 1972 break-in of Democratic headquarters at the Watergate apartments in Washington, D.C. Though the crisis did not reach its culmination until 1974, after Nixon had been reelected by one of the largest landslides in U.S. presidential history, the burglary eventually became the subject of criminal and Senate investigations that traced it to the president's inner circle of advisers at the White House. The discoveries made by skilled prosecutors and a Senate committee revealed a trail of corruption that can fairly be described as pragmatism run wild.

The most startling fact of the Watergate scandal is how unnecessary it was to assure Nixon a second term. Despite the evident advantage he held over South Dakota liberal Senator George McGovern in the 1972 campaign, the White House felt compelled to use every dirty trick it knew to assure the president's return to office. With the Vietnam war coming to an end, détente having established Nixon as a highly effective foreign policy leader, and a variety of domestic compromises showing him as a reasonable moderate, no Republican or Democrat seemed capable of toppling him from the presidency. Indeed, the only candidate at this point who could have destroyed Nixon's presidency was Nixon himself, which is, of course, exactly what happened. If he had followed his more sensible instincts, he would have overcome his desire for a record-breaking triumph for a more modest victory and built a reelection campaign based on traditional political efforts to persuade voters that he had earned another term. But he was so wed to disreputable means of destroying—not just defeating—opponents that he invariably turned to mean-spirited and illegal actions, which finally forced his unprecedented presidential resignation in August 1974.

While never the political cynic that Nixon was, Ronald Reagan did bring his administration to the edge of disaster by allowing aides to tie hidden arms sales with Iran to clandestine financial backing for the anti-Communist Contras in Nicaragua. At the time Reagan was eager to arrange the release of American hostages from Lebanon, where they were being held by Iranian-backed terrorists. His national security advisers tried to satisfy his wishes by offering to sell arms to Teheran in return for helping to free American prisoners. At the same time, the White House funneled some of the profits from the arms sales to "freedom fighters" (as Reagan liked to call them) battling the left-wing Sandinista government in Nicaragua.

Because Reagan had pledged never to make concessions to terrorists, and the U.S. Congress had forbidden support for the Contras, both elements of the White House arms sale strategy put the administration at political and legal risk. When a Lebanese newspaper published a story in the fall of 1986 revealing the terms of the arms dealings, Reagan was forced to commission a special investigation and to agree that a special prosecutor be allowed to ascertain the facts about the alleged scandal. The probes turned up abundant evidence of wrongdoing and led to convictions of national security officials, but they left open questions about the culpability of Reagan himself and Vice President George Bush.

While Irangate became a serious political scandal, a number of factors kept the president and vice president from being subjected to impeachment proceedings and possible prosecution in the matter. Most critically, there was no smoking gun to hold either man directly accountable, even though more than 50 percent of Americans believed that Reagan knew and approved of the transfer of funds to the Contras. Despite this, the country remained warmly disposed toward Reagan, whom it viewed as a great symbolic politician—or even American king—who took a limited part in daily affairs and left the administration of government to subordinates. After the presidential failures of Johnson, Nixon, Ford, and Carter, few Americans were ready for another bloodletting at the highest political level. Finally, however troubling the skulduggery and crimes, Americans were hesitant to bring a president before the law for trying to prevail over extremist regimes in Teheran and Managua, however unscrupulous his means.

Nevertheless, as a result of the affair, Reagan's popularity and historical reputation suffered damage from which it may never fully recover. Once he left office and Irangate was coupled with the realization that the Reagan presidency had been the occasion of a massive accumulation of national debt that jeopardized the country's economic future, Reagan's public standing began to plummet. In 1992, three years after his term had ended, his approval ratings in *New York Times* polls had fallen from 63 percent to 48 percent. Only LBJ's at 40 percent and Nixon's at 32 percent stood lower among presidents dating back to FDR. Gerald Ford, who had ended his term with a 53 percent rating, and Jimmy Carter, who held the support of only 34 percent of the country when he stepped down, had improved their standings to 55 percent and 50 percent, respectively.

Reagan's willingness to let high executive officials engage in the sort of secret actions that had caused serious political harm to some of his predecessors was yet another aspect of his affinity for unreasoning, dogmatic assumptions about the conduct of overseas affairs. Half evangelist, half political operator, Reagan embodied traits that in various combinations have both served and undermined our national chiefs. An old-fashioned believer in the assumptions about individualism and freedom that are the bases of the American dream, and a creature of the country's obsession with personality, and a man with a passion to be universally loved, Reagan was both an apolitical ideologue and a visionary pragmatist maneuvering toward the promised land. At his best, he was as successful a politician as any to hold the White House. At his worst, he was as unrealistic and obtuse a political leader as America has elected. In the long run, he will undoubtedly be judged as a standing example of advance and retreat, success and failure, all in one eight-year term—a model for those who want to understand how a president can be both effective and ineffective at the same time.

CHAPTER 3

E PLURIBUS UNUM: THE VIRTUES OF CONSENSUS

In the fifty-two presidential elections since the birth of the Republic in 1787, sixteen presidents have gained the White House with less than 50 percent of the popular vote. The list of minority chiefs includes John Quincy Adams; James K. Polk; Abraham Lincoln; Grover Cleveland (twice, in 1884 and 1892); Woodrow Wilson, with 42 percent of the vote in 1912, and 49 percent in 1916; Harry Truman with 49.8 percent; John F. Kennedy with a like percentage in 1960; and Richard Nixon and Bill Clinton with 43 percent in 1968 and 1992, respectively. Even most presidents who were elected with a popular majority have won less than 56 percent of the ballot. Only seventeen elections have produced decisive margins of more than 55 percent.

If they offer less than overwhelming support for a winning candidate, closely contested elections have had a salutary effect on America's democracy. Presidents without a mandate have been more attentive to popular sentiment and have usually recognized that their success in initiating a major policy has depended on assuring its support by a national consensus. Conversely, some of the worst presidential errors in judgment have come after landslide victories when overconfident recipients of popular mandates fell victim to political miscalculations. Harding after the 1920 election, FDR in 1937, LBJ in 1965, Nixon in 1972–1974, and Reagan

84

after 1984 all suffered largely self-inflicted defeats that more cautious judgments might have averted.

As a rule, presidents have understood how vital that consensual backing is to any far-reaching domestic or foreign policy. They have also appreciated how mercurial and unreliable the public mood has been and how difficult it can be to get the nation to sanction a presidential plan, especially if it represented a departure from customary patterns. Throughout its history, the United States has pledged itself to a set of core values that has kept it unified and enabled it to overcome regional, racial, ethnic, and religious differences. Individualism, democracy, freedom, opportunity, egalitarianism, and the rule of law have been imperishable tenets of America's national identity. But preaching these ideals has not necessarily made them more easily applied in the practice of everyday politics. The general public has had to be convinced and reassured that any novel idea would fit comfortably into traditional habits or would be a safely innovative means of fulfilling the familiar promise of American life.

Lyndon Johnson, a keen student of the country's values and the unpredictability of mass opinion, was especially aware of how difficult it was to sustain a stable majority for reforms in the law or new international commitments. Even after his massive victory over Goldwater in 1964, for example, he doubted that he had won a mandate for any specific legislative program. While he knew the country had given him implicit support for his intention to "move ahead," it hadn't endorsed a particular set of bills or given him its consent to push for the bold measures he sought to take. He believed there was "too much glib talk about the ease with which" he could get legislation passed, and was well aware that it would be "a hard fight every inch of the way." As he told his congressional liaison men in January 1965, "I was just elected President by the biggest popular margin in the history of the country—16 million votes," but warned them that Barry Goldwater's disappearance as a threat to New Deal reforms and international peace had already reduced that margin to 13 million. "After a fight with Congress or something else, I'll lose another couple of million," he added. "I could be down to 8 million in a couple of months." Johnson also expected the Senate and House to assert themselves against him in due course. "I've watched the Congress from either the inside or the outside, man and boy, for more than forty years," he told White House intellectual Eric Goldman, "and I've never seen a Congress that didn't eventually take the measure of the President it was dealing with."

Johnson also knew that even a consensus for one particular law or policy did not necessarily translate into public backing for other measures. Surges of national enthusiasm, whether for liberalism, conservatism, or the status quo, have never guaranteed public commitment to every proposal reflecting that outlook. The terms "Square Deal," "New Freedom," "New Deal," "Fair Deal," "New Frontier," and "Great Society" on the left, and the "conservatism" of Harding, Eisenhower, Nixon, and Reagan on the right, were only general labels describing what each of these twentieth-century administrations stood for; it was the principal programs enacted by each—programs that were the product of consensual agreements forged on their behalf—that gave them their unique character and substance.

A president's ability to win popular approval for his policies has also tended to fluctuate depending on whether the issues in question related to domestic or foreign affairs. Domestic developments have, understandably, always been uppermost in American minds, except, perhaps, in times of all-out war. Although the country has throughout its history been generally apolitical (often allowing a distinct minority of potential voters to elect candidates to high offices), it has kept an attentive eye on proposals promising major domestic changes. For that reason it has usually led the way or at least been ahead of its presidents in seeing what needed to be accomplished legislatively. In the area of domestic reform the role of presidents has often been to sense the national groundswell for altering domestic arrangements and to assume the role of leader by articulating the details of the country's general design. FDR is a perfect example, for as Richard Hofstadter said, he had "a sharp intuitive knowledge of popular feeling. Because he was content in large measure to follow public opinion, he was able to give it that necessary additional impulse of leadership which can translate desires into policies." In short, significant reforms at home have evolved out of the judgments a president has made about what best served the national well-being after long-term changes in the nation's conditions.

But as has been true of vision and pragmatic responses to shift-

ing realities, some presidents have been better at sensing opportunities for consensual backing than others. Success in
consensus-building on behalf of domestic change has likewise been
a function of political wisdom put into practice. Moreover, it has
always been inextricably linked to a sensible grand design: a national commitment to bold domestic reform has inevitably rested
on schemes served by political realism.

Innovations in foreign policy, in contrast, have generally been
more the result of executive forethought and leadership than is the
case in domestic affairs. Their isolationist tradition has made Americans far more reluctant to ponder U.S. actions abroad than to
confront difficult domestic issues, so that on matters of international war and peace, they have usually been content to follow the
lead of the president. While domestic consensus-building has been
subject to a presidential talent for reading and translating public
mood into concrete actions, foreign policy commitments have required presidential initiative to educate and sell the country on
topics of less immediate moment to people's daily lives. Would the
sacrifices required in World Wars I and II have been conceivable
without presidential attention to building public support for them
prior to 1917 and Pearl Harbor?

I

In the more than two centuries that have passed since the creation
of the Republic, American political life has undergone several defining sea changes. The Federalist or nationalist impulse which gave
birth to the nation in 1787 thrived only until 1800, when the
Democratic-Republicans or Jeffersonian-agrarians gained control.
The Democrats, as they came to be called by the 1820s, were
dominant until 1840, when a new nationalist Whig party began a
twenty-year period of sharing political control with Democrats.
The triumph of the modern Republican party in 1860 opened a
seventy-two-year period in which the Democrats never once gained
a majority of the popular presidential vote. The Great Depression
brought the next large-scale shift in national politics, with Democrats winning seven of the nine elections during the thirty-six-
year period beginning in 1932. In the twenty-eight years since

1968, the Republicans have staged a comeback, winning five of the seven presidential elections, with only one Democrat, Jimmy Carter, receiving more than 50 percent of the popular vote—a bare 51 percent majority.

The most successful presidential leadership has been exercised by individuals who were most attuned to the shifting political currents punctuating the last two hundred years. Andrew Jackson's awareness of a national wish for greater democracy in the 1820s and 1830s, Wilson's consolidation of the Progressive impulse between 1913 and 1917, FDR's leadership of a New Deal coalition built upon the ruins of the national economy, Eisenhower's receptiveness toward the post–New Deal desire for sustained government programs with less federal activism, LBJ's expression of public sympathy for equal treatment under the law for African-Americans and affordable health care for the elderly, and Reagan's sponsorship of a tax revolt and recognition of a national aversion to excessive federal intervention in people's lives made each of these presidents a model of how consensus politics can be exploited in the service of national renewal and a successful term in the White House.

Andrew Jackson was the first of our chiefs to convert a shift in national mood into a consensus for the enactment of specific legislation and for the consolidation of his own personal popularity. In the nine years after 1812, six western states entered the Union, increasing its membership from eighteen to twenty-four. At the same time, four of the older states lowered their voting restrictions to bring them largely into line with the more relaxed requirements of the more recent entries. As a result of these more liberal policies, this bloc of states tipped the balance of the electorate toward a more democratic faction demanding changes in government policies to accommodate their needs and ambitions.

It was this emerging democratic consensus that gave Jackson a base for both his election to the presidency in 1828 and his subsequent success in office. As so much of the recent scholarship on Jackson has revealed, the traditional image of Old Hickory as an early New Dealer battling economic royalists in behalf of labor is more myth than reality. While there is no question that Jackson spoke for the common man or ordinary citizen, as opposed to the more privileged elements of the society, his constituency was composed more of entrepreneurs or small farmers than laborers, more westerners than easterners, more aspirants to status as frontier aristocrats than as urban arrivistes. Jacksonians were Americans on the make, upwardly mobile, aspiring middle-class folks with their eye on the main chance. The age of Jackson—the 1820s and 1830s— was an era of liberal capitalism, a time when equality of opportunity rather than strict equality was the motive force in economic and political life. Given the chance, most everyone believed, the mass of Americans could rise above their station and make themselves and the country into a great success story. "Business is the very soul of an American," one commentator on the nation's life in the 1830s said. "It is as if all America were but one gigantic workshop, over the entrance of which there is the blazing inscription, 'No admission here, except on business.' " The Whig leader Daniel Webster had made much the same point a decade earlier when he described American Society as "full of excitement: competition comes in place of monopoly; and intelligence and industry ask only for fair play and an open field."

Jackson had no well-thought-out political philosophy, and he was not especially astute about the country's current and future economic needs: his policies, in fact, contributed to a banking panic in 1837 and a depression that gripped the country for almost five years in the early 1840s. But he did have a highly developed perceptiveness of the national political mood, which allowed him to turn to good account the country's contemporary faith in the worth of the ordinary citizen. The principal vehicle for Jackson's advancement of the national entrepreneurial consensus was his famous assault on the Bank of the United States (BUS) or National Bank. Economic realities aside, the Bank was regarded by the mass of Americans as a symbol of privilege, serving the interests of the few over the needs of the many. The commercial grievances of the period were directed less against employers and overseas influences (especially in Britain, where economic vicissitudes had a considerable impact on American prosperity) than at the credit and currency system dominated by the BUS.

In a veto message to Congress in 1832 in which he rejected legislation rechartering the Bank, Jackson demonstrated how well he understood the spirit of the times. The Bank, he pronounced, was an example of "the rich and powerful" bending "the acts of government to their selfish purposes." There was no such thing as pure equality: "Distinctions in society will always exist under every just government," he argued, and when favorable laws were added to natural advantages "to make the rich richer and the potent more powerful, the humble members of society—the farmers, mechanics, and laborers— . . . have a right to complain of the injustice of their Government." In dissolving the Bank, Jackson intended to ensure that the government confined itself "to equal protection, and, as Heaven does its rains, shower its favors alike on the high and the low, the rich and the poor."

Jackson's veto became a kind of touchstone to the age, a dramatic and inspiring statement of American beliefs that millions accepted as the very expression of national wisdom. The veto solidified Jackson's already strong hold on the public imagination and assured him of a decisive victory in the 1832 presidential campaign. His capture of more than 56 percent of the popular vote and 219 out of 286 electoral ballots was a remarkable improvement on his margins over John Quincy Adams in 1828, and left the National Republicans, led by Henry Clay and Daniel Webster, accurately convinced that they had suffered what one Democratic newspaper called a "Waterloo defeat." Jackson's undisputed dominance of the national political scene over the next four years earned him the enmity of the new Whig party opponents, who dubbed him "King Andrew the First" and compared him to France's "sun king," Louis XIV, around whom everything revolved. Whatever the merits of the Whig complaints, Jackson had shown that a chief executive in harmony with the current mood could establish himself decisively at the forefront of a national consensus, which, in combination with his vision of the country's future, practical political savvy, and charismatic personality, made him a legendary president in his day and ours.

Woodrow Wilson's initial ventures in public affairs suggested that, if elected to office, he would be a traditional conservative southern Democrat, favoring rugged individualism and supporting the great business and banking combines as efficient instruments of modern capitalism. Wilson's nomination to the presidency, a conservative editor announced in 1906, "would be a good thing for the country as betokening a return of his party to historic party ideals and first principles, and a sobering up after the radical 'crazes' " of William Jennings Bryan and the Populists. In 1907, when Wilson prepared a "Credo" of his political views, it was, in biographer Arthur Link's words, "conservative to the core."

But Wilson's adherence to traditional homilies all but disappeared over the following three years, for a rising tide of progressive sentiment demanding strict limits on the economic power of corporations and the political influence of corrupt machines worked a profound change in his outlook. Seizing upon middle America's yearning for a "new morality," he became a national spokesman for ending fraud in the country's politics and excessive concentration of wealth in the hands of trusts and robber barons. Wilson comfortably placed himself at the head of the battle for progressive advance through a return to greater democracy and equality of opportunity. As the president of Princeton University in 1910, he called for the democratization of American colleges as a prelude to making the country's churches and political parties less the bastion of privileged interests than of the "people."

New Jersey political bosses, believing Wilson a conservative opportunist who could talk like a progressive but would take up the causes of corporations and the state's party machine when called upon to do so, made him their candidate for governor in 1910. Adopting the progressive agenda of a direct primary, a corrupt-practices law, workmen's compensation, and a regulatory commission overseeing the railroads and public utilities, Wilson won nearly 56 percent of the vote and led his party to victory in the state's typically Republican lower house. Once in office, Wilson gave the bosses a lesson in pragmatic politics, for having relied on their endorsement to advance his gubernatorial candidacy, he now waged a two-year war against them to serve his presidential ambitions. He helped defeat Democratic party boss James Smith, Jr.,'s bid for a U.S. Senate seat and won passage of his four-part progressive agenda. Wilson commented that while some people saw his achievements "as little less than a miracle in the light of what has been the history of reform hitherto in the State," he himself understood that they were more the result of constant pressure on

the legislature at a time when "opinion was ripe on all these matters."

If Wilson had taken these steps simply to position himself to win
his party's presidential nomination and the presidency, he could
not have been more politically astute. Though the party's convention was the occasion for a fierce struggle between conservative
and progressive opponents, Wilson had enough of a hold on both
camps to gain the prize on the forty-sixth ballot. His subsequent
campaign was another adroit balancing act between Taft's conservatism and TR's advanced progressivism in the form of New Nationalism. Taking up a proposal from the jurist Louis D. Brandeis
that he advocate the "New Freedom," a program of regulated
competition that would reduce corporate dominance of business
and promote greater economic and political democracy, Wilson
found a theme that resonated strongly with voters. Because they
were loath to continue with Taft's traditional ideas and were reluctant to commit to TR's plan of expanded federal control over
domestic affairs, which impressed them as more a threat to than
an expansion of freedom, the electorate turned to Wilson's progressive program as the most acceptable expression of the national
will. Wilson succeeded in winning 43 percent of the popular vote
in a field that included Taft, TR, and socialist Eugene V. Debs.

During the next four years, Wilson did not disappoint public
hopes for a new era in government. In a dramatic appearance before a special session of Congress in April 1913, the first president
to address the two houses in person since John Adams one hundred and thirteen years earlier, Wilson dramatically demonstrated
his eagerness for cooperation with the legislative branch. Over the
next eighteen months he won passage of the first downward revi-
sion of the protective tariff since the Civil War, a measure reducing
the cost of living for lower- and middle-income Americans, the
creation of the Federal Reserve to reform the nation's banking and
money system, and the Clayton Antitrust and Federal Trade Commission acts to assure the regulation of big business, a measure
that most Americans believed essential to a better life.

Though he announced an end to his reform efforts in November
1914, Wilson soon resumed the fight for progressive change, mo-
tivated by a turn to the left in the congressional elections, the
pressure to build a national majority for his reelection in 1916, and

his belief that a "great movement" toward social justice required him to battle for additional reforms or risk becoming "a back number." The result was a series of laws that included federal support of farmers and workers, and higher taxes on affluent Americans. Wilson's electoral victory that year as the leader of a minority party attests to his continuing effectiveness in leading a national consensus.

Wilson's success was achieved without the sort of crisis which gave FDR almost carte blanche to deal with the national economic disaster of the 1930s. Wilson's leadership was a subtle demonstration of presidential wisdom in turning a national impulse into concrete reforms expressing a desire for direct action against festering problems undermining public confidence in an American future as great as its past.

FDR's New Deal was a masterful response to the greatest domestic crisis in the country's history since the Civil War. This is not to say that the president's catalogue of reforms solved the problems of the Depression and eased once and for all the travails of an advanced industrial society. Critics on the left then and since have pointed out many of the New Deal's limitations, complaining that it didn't truly overcome the Depression, or significantly reduce poverty by redistributing income, or advance the cause of racial equality. At the same time, critics on the right have maintained their own inventory of New Deal failings, although they, too, argue that it never restored economic prosperity. But in its attempts to do so, conservative critics maintain, it created a welfare state, which made millions of Americans dependent on federal handouts and stifled initiative by burdening society in general and business in particular with unnecessary regulations and costs.

In answer to such objections, New Deal defenders have pointed to a record of accomplishments that neither left nor right can reasonably dismiss. In 1983, fifty years after FDR launched his administration, William E. Leuchtenburg made the case for the program's contributions:

What then did the New Deal do? It gave far greater amplitude to the national state, expanded the authority of the presidency, recruited university-trained administrators, won control of the money supply, established central banking, imposed regulation on Wall Street, rescued the debt-ridden farmer and homeowner, built model communities, financed the Federal Housing Administration, made federal housing a permanent feature, fostered unionization of the factories, reduced child labor, ended the tyranny of company towns, wiped out many sweatshops, mandated minimal working standards, enabled tenants to buy their own farms, built camps for migrants, introduced the welfare state with old-age pensions, unemployment insurance, and aid for dependent children, provided jobs for millions of unemployed, created a special program for the jobless young and for students, covered the American landscape with new edifices, subsidized painters and novelists, composers and ballet dancers, founded America's first state theater, created documentary films, gave birth to the impressive Tennessee Valley Authority, generated electrical power, sent the Civilian Conservation Corps boys into the forests, initiated the Soil Conservation Service, transformed the economy of agriculture, lighted up rural America, gave women greater recognition, made a start toward breaking the pattern of racial discrimination and segregation, put together a liberal party coalition, changed the agenda of American politics, and brought about a Constitutional Revolution.

New Deal achievements rested on Roosevelt's partiality for the middle ground, for standing firmly at the center of American politics, where the great majority of voters wished to see him. Charges that he should have tacked much more decisively to the left, nationalizing banks and public utilities and restructuring the social order through redistribution of wealth and empowerment of the chronically poor, seem wholly misguided when viewed in the context of the country's overall history and of the majority sentiment in the thirties. Had Roosevelt adopted the left's proposals for radical reform, it is doubtful that he could have remained in power or, more to the point, that he could have won national backing for the material changes in the nation's economic and social affairs embodied in the New Deal.

As it was, Roosevelt's agenda of moderate reform raised suspicions of a hidden fascist or socialist agenda, and not just from the Right. The 1938 clash over government reorganization, for example, reached "a point of near hysteria," with congressmen and groups as diverse as the Catholic Church and American Federation of Labor warning against the coming totalitarianism. This largely innocuous bill, which aimed to promote greater government efficiency, was more a continuation of FDR's prior commitment to expand government powers to meet the economic crisis than the sign of any inclination, or a substantive means, to establish a dictatorship.

The actual right-wing critiques of FDR have been no sounder than those of the left. Had Roosevelt chosen not to act, repeating Hoover's impulse to let the business cycle runs its course, he would have confronted charges of failing to address immediate and long-term national problems. Worse, the hardship and social divisions that would have resulted from such a political strategy would have left the country in a shambles, if not even more vulnerable to a new cycle of economic collapse, in which massive numbers of Americans, lacking the safety net put in place by FDR's humanization of the country's industrial system, would have suffered further privations. Likewise, the class warfare that right-wing critics feared these reforms boded was, to say the least, highly unlikely, for however far-reaching FDR's policies, they never threatened an end to free enterprise or the creation of a state-controlled command economy. Only a program of more pronounced change would have made a reality of what the left favored and the right dreaded.

Roosevelt's success as a reform leader was greatly aided by his appreciation of his role as spokesman for the great bulk of the country, which wished to see traditional habits survive, even in somewhat altered form. His experiment in government, as he saw his program, was a middle-ground effort to do "the greatest good for the greatest number." The New Deal catered to neither radicals nor standpatters but to progressives from across the political spectrum convinced that the nation had to use "government as an active instrument of democratic change to meet the needs of the day without violence or upheaval."

The economist John Maynard Keynes articulated the meaning of Roosevelt's leadership for the United States after only nine months into his first term. "You have made yourself the trustee for those in every country who seek to mend the evils of our condition by reasoned experiment within the framework of the existing social system," Keynes told him. "If you fail, rational change will be gravely prejudiced throughout the world, leaving orthodoxy and revolution to fight it out." The historian Sir Isaiah Berlin echoed the point later when he wrote that Roosevelt's "moral authority, the degree of confidence which he inspired outside his own country . . . has no parallel. . . . Mr. Roosevelt's example strengthened democracy everywhere." FDR's New Deal leadership rested on a consensus not only in his own country, but in democratic states and peoples around the globe.

By the beginning of the 1950s, after almost twenty years of government activism in domestic and foreign affairs, a majority of Americans were ready for less federal influence and control over economic and social relations. At the same time, however, few were ready to abandon the advances the New Deal had introduced and revert to the less regulated world of the 1920s and earlier.

Polling data from the 1950s is a valuable index of this shift in attitudes. Between 1951 and 1956, some 60 percent of Americans wanted to see sharp curbs on government spending and significantly reduced taxes. Proposals to limit taxation to 25 percent of an individual's income and make across-the-board cuts in federal programs found consistent favor with large numbers of voters who feared the government might spend the nation into bankruptcy. In contrast, proposals that U.S. authorities take over the country's banks and railroads met with almost universal opposition. Though the Democrats largely continued their domination of Congress during the decade, losing control of both houses only from 1953 to 1955, party affiliation was more evenly divided than in the previous twenty years. Moreover, Ike's commanding electoral majorities—thirty-nine states to nine states in 1952, and forty-one states to seven states in 1956—destroyed any assumptions that the South would remain solidly Democratic, and restored two-party competitiveness to presidential politics.

Yet at the same time, the greater part of the country not only continued to hold New Deal programs in high regard but also wanted to see some modest additions brought to the welfare state. In the midst of a 1954 recession, for example, half of a sample poll favored 1930s-style public works programs to relieve unemployment. In 1953, a decisive 60 percent supported a government increase in the minimum wage from 75 cents an hour to $1 an hour. Fifty-six and 57 percent of those polled said they wanted the government to add a secretary for health, education, and welfare to the president's cabinet; a majority of those with an opinion on the issue supported federal aid for school construction; while 68 percent of Americans opposed a constitutional amendment that would have permanently placed a ceiling of 25 to 35 percent on individual and family income taxes. Fully aware that sudden crises could require more revenue for government programs, most Americans preferred a degree of flexibility in tax policy to any rigid scheme for keeping rates low.

When asked which group of Republicans they preferred—"Liberals like Eisenhower, Dewey, Nixon, and Lodge, who want . . . to keep social security and welfare programs" or "conservatives like [Herbert] Hoover, [William] Knowland, [Joseph] McCarthy, and other followers of the late Senator [Robert] Taft" who want "to cut down or reduce many social security and welfare programs"— 74 percent of the country replied "Liberal Republicans." Mass sentiment favored not a national shift to the left or the right but a general policy midway between liberal labor groups and conservative business ones.

In the eyes of most Americans (55 percent of Republicans, 54 percent of Democrats, and 70 percent of Independents), Eisenhower was an ideal embodiment of this principle: a blend of liberal and conservative, a middle-roader who had won election as a Republican president but stood "somewhere in between" the two parties. Unlike the Roosevelt and Truman administrations, which aroused considerable partisanship, Ike's maintained a kind of above-the-battle posture, which satisfied public longing for a period of less political strife. As surveys on Eisenhower demonstrated, people regarded him less as a Republican or a Democrat than a patriotic American doing his duty for the good of the nation as he had during his service in World War II.

Eisenhower also fulfilled the nation's hopes for a more passive presidency and less government. He resisted suggestions that he set the legislative agenda for Congress, explaining that he had no wish to "nag them" or infringe upon the prerogatives of another sovereign branch of government. He declared his aversion to costly federal programs that would increase national deficits and undermine the country's free enterprise system. His preference for giving American business freer rein than in the recent past was reflected in his appointment of corporate executives to most of his cabinet posts and to regulatory agencies.

Liberals complained bitterly about Ike's method of running the government. *The New Republic*, for example, described his cabinet as "eight millionaires and a plumber," the latter being the secretary of labor, a former president of the plumbers' union who stayed in the cabinet for only eight months. After Defense Secretary Charles E. Wilson, a former president of General Motors, declared that "what was good for our country was good for General Motors, and vice versa," and compared the jobless to "kennel-fed dogs," critics retorted that Wilson had invented the automatic transmission so that he would always have one foot free to stuff in his mouth. Most Americans, however, did not take exception to so pronounced a business presence in the government: fifty-one percent thought it a good idea, 20 percent had no opinion on the issue, and only 29 percent objected.

Yet Eisenhower carried nothing to an extreme, balancing his affinity for conservative aides and less government with substantial increases in Social Security benefits, expanded unemployment coverage, a higher minimum wage, and the establishment in 1953 of a Department of Health, Education and Welfare (HEW). Moreover, in spite of his antagonism to farm subsidy payments and public ventures like the Tennessee Valley Authority, these policies and most other New Deal commitments to less advantaged Americans remained in place. For all the discussion by the president and his spokesmen of cutting government, the Eisenhower administration presided over a near doubling of the government's annual budget from $39 billion to $76 billion.

Eisenhower's presidency may have been "mastery in the service of drift," as one critic observed, but it was "drift" congenial to public temper. The consideration of this administration, which remains notable for being one of the least activist governments in this century, raises the question of whether a president who principally reflects current mood can, in fact, be judged a successful leader. The answer is yes and no. Yes, if one accepts the proposition that democracy is an expression of shared majority sentiment at any given moment in time, and that one can sing only at the high-

est note for so long. No, if one assumes that effective leaders
consists mainly of prescience and the courage to take an unpopular
but foresightful stand on matters of vital importance to the country's future.

If history has not been especially kind to Eisenhower's centrist
consensual politics, it is worth recalling that the American political
experience has traditionally depended on periods of stasis as a preparation for any new forward surge. And unlike the era's reaction-
aries, who dismissed the public desire for the status quo and hoped
to reclaim an earlier idyllic time, Eisenhower consolidated support
for what was and temporarily calmed the country's anxieties in
preparation for what would be. Between the bold, innovative leaders like Wilson and FDR and the militant conservatives believing
an earlier Eden was theirs to command, stood the cautious moderates like Eisenhower, taking one step forward and one step back.
They have been and will remain the truest representatives of an
American public that sees more virtue in social incrementalism than
in occasional revolutionary advances.

II

Unlike the articulators and makers of consensus, presidents who
failed to identify and express the public mood have at times managed to do damage not only to their own careers but to the country
as a whole.

John Quincy Adams is a first case in point. A man of exceptional
intelligence, cultivated taste, and vision, Adams was also a poor politician with little feel for the nation's political climate. After his election in 1824, he spoke of his goal of bringing about a shared
American perspective free from "the baneful weed of party strife."
But at a time when America's "second-party system" of Democrats
and Whigs was just emerging with force, the president couldn't have
made a graver miscalculation about the course of national politics.

Similarly, Adams's conception of a federal government setting a
national agenda, while in theory forceful as a grand design, was
the wrong plan at the wrong time. In his first message to Congress
in 1825, one of the great state papers of U.S. history, he proposed
federal financing of roads and turnpikes, canals, education, science,

urged a protective tariff to foster the development
industry, a national banking system issuing a common
regulating credit, and a national university. "The
the institution of civil government," he declared,
vement of the conditions of those who are parties to
the s   mpact." He proposed to multiply and facilitate "the
communications and intercourse between distant regions and mul-
titudes of men" in pursuit of the ideal of one nation advancing
toward a better life for one and all.

With such proposals Adams proved himself a great visionary, but
his bold plans fell victim to political conditions he didn't understand and couldn't control. The circumstances of his election alone
should have provided a cautionary note for his subsequent policies.
In a contest between himself, Andrew Jackson, Treasury Secretary
William H. Crawford of Georgia, and Kentucky's Great Compro-
miser, Speaker of the House Henry Clay, Adams won only 30 percent of the popular vote and 84 out of 261 electoral votes. Though
43 percent of voters cast their ballots for Jackson, who received a
99-electoral-vote plurality, the election was ultimately decided in
the House of Representatives, where an Adams-Clay deal gave Adams the presidency. Demonstrating some capacity for pragmatic
politics, Adams kept his promise to make Clay secretary of state, but
the new president paid a heavy price for the arrangement. Jackson
supporters declared it "a corrupt bargain" and dismissed Adams's
reputation for integrity and high-minded politics as a fiction.

Under constant attack as a monarchist with no regard for the
people, Adams lacked the character for the grassroots politics just
then emerging in the country. Unlike Jackson, who united a national coalition through rhetorical assaults on the privileged interests who were denying equal opportunity to aspiring
entrepreneurs, Adams appealed to ideas of nationhood and dreams
of progress through material and intellectual advances that were
simply too abstract for the average American of the 1820s to grasp.
If anything, Adams impressed his countrymen as a latter-day Federalist more tied to the assumptions of his president father, John
Adams, and Alexander Hamilton than to modern notions of helping common folk seize the main chance.

With little appreciation of the transformation marking national
politics from Monroe's relatively benign era of good feelings to the

sharply divisive class antagonisms of the 1820s, Adams found himself without any base of support, and his plans for the country came to little. His reelection bid in 1828 resulted in a defeat on a level with the beatings other one-term presidents like Taft, Hoover, Carter, and Bush suffered in the twentieth century. The 44 percent of the popular vote and 31 percent of the electoral ballots that he received was one of the most one-sided loses suffered by an incumbent in American history.

If Adams's failure to create a national consensus was more a personal loss for himself than a tragedy for the country, which found in Jackson a successor who more faithfully reflected its current outlook, the same cannot be said for the presidency of James Buchanan. Sixty-five years old when he ran for the highest office in 1856, Buchanan, who had served for ten years in the House, another decade in the U.S. Senate, five years as minister to Russia and to Britain, and four years as secretary of state, was known as "Old Public Functionary." Yet twenty-nine years of public service did not endow him with the vision, pragmatism, or political sense to become an effective president, especially in a time of national crisis when only great statesmanship could have preserved the nation from a threatened civil war.

Buchanan's victory in a three-way race between himself; former Whig president Millard Fillmore, who ran as the American or Know-Nothing party candidate; and John C. Frémont, the first nominee of the new Republican party, rested on a coalition of southern states and the lower northern states of Pennsylvania, New Jersey, Indiana, and Illinois. In the North, where a remarkable 83 percent of voters went to the polls, interest in the danger of disunion was so high that commentators saw the region as "on the tiptoe of Revolution." A veteran of six presidential campaigns observed "a solemn earnestness that is almost painful." While Buchanan won only five of the sixteen northern states, receiving just 36 percent of the region's popular support, his triumph turned on the decisions of thousands of former Whigs to back him or Fillmore against Frémont out of concern that a Republican victory would destroy the Union. Though 56 percent of Buchanan's popular votes were cast in the South, where he won all eleven of the future Confederate states, he in fact owed his success to swing voters in the North eager to preserve a United States of America.

But with war looming Buchanan managed to lose whatever small chance that remained to sustain a North-South consensus for one nation indivisible. The sectional division over slavery could only have been resolved by strong leadership, which would have averted the greater conflict and, as the wisest political commentators at the time believed, would have allowed slavery to die an inevitable, natural death. As Lincoln warned in a famous 1858 speech, "A house divided against itself cannot stand. I believe this government cannot endure, permanently half *slave* and half *free*." Lincoln and other reasonable Republicans assumed that preventing the spread of slavery into the territories would place the institution on the path to "ultimate extinction."

Buchanan was in a position to encourage that result. At the start of his term in 1857, a bloody struggle over extending slavery into Kansas had been under way for three years. It was clear that a majority of Kansas settlers favored entering the Union as a free state, and Buchanan's initial impulse was to settle the problem in accordance with fair dealings and the rule of law. He appointed Robert J. Walker, a courageous Mississippian, as territorial governor and backed his insistence on an honest election, which would have given free-soil Kansans control of the state. But when southerners denounced Walker and threatened Buchanan with secession, the president yielded and allowed an unrepresentative group of pro-slavery settlers to write a constitution and seek admission for Kansas to the Union as a slave state.

Buchanan's capitulation to the South split northern Democrats and led to a defeat in Congress for the proposal to give statehood to a Kansas controlled by a minority attempting a political swindle. When Democrats objected that a slave-state Kansas would be "a vile fraud, a bare conceit," Buchanan defended himself by arguing that any other result would lead the southern states either to "secede from the Union or take up arms against him." But at the time Buchanan's fears seem unjustifiable. In 1858 the South was not simply guided by warmongers spoiling for a fight but also by pragmatists who recognized that opposition to an honest vote in Kansas would have been an unconvincing pretext for secession. With a pro-southern Democratic president and a tradition of

North-South compromises during the period from 1820 to 1854 as precedent for a national compromise, the makings of a national consensus to head off civil war were very much in place.

But Buchanan lacked the political imagination to seize an opportunity that might have rescued the country from the terrible ordeal of national bloodletting. To the contrary, he added to the likelihood of a fratricidal outbreak by facilitating a seven-to-two decision in the Supreme Court's 1857 Dred Scott case denying both citizenship to African-Americans and Congress's right to prohibit slavery in a territory. To give even greater legitimacy to the conclusion that the U.S. government had no right to impede the expansion of slavery (a principal aim of the new Republican party), Buchanan and Chief Justice Roger Tawney sought one or two northern justices to join their five southern colleagues in supporting this opinion. In a breach of tradition that violated the separation of branches, Buchanan brought "highly improper" pressure to bear on Justice Robert Grier of Pennsylvania, who eventually "succumbed."

Buchanan's policies fueled the North-South crisis, further undermined the Democratic party in the North, and opened the way to a Republican victory in 1860, which made a civil war all but inevitable. Though he belatedly made a spirited effort to prevent secession in the interregnum between November 1860 and Lincoln's inauguration, he could not stem the crisis he had helped bring about. In the judgment of one expert on this era, "Few Presidents have entered office with more experience in public life, and few have so decisively failed."

A like judgment could be made against Herbert Hoover, for despite his lengthy and generally successful national and international service, he showed a want of political sense once elected to the presidency. He was not only too rigid about the wisdom of his beliefs but he also failed to see that in the midst of the Great Depression public opinion was moving in directions he would have done well to follow. Whether he was tied too strongly to a set of outworn ideas, which he mistakenly believed the public also remained bound by, or whether he failed to understand how essential public backing is for presidential effectiveness, he paid little heed to the emerging consensus for a humane and innovative response to the country's economic collapse.

Only after his humiliating defeat at Roosevelt's hands did Hoover belatedly recognize that the nation had moved beyond him. He hoped, nevertheless, that a dose of FDR's New Deal would bring it to its senses: "When the American people realize some ten years hence," he said privately in December 1933, "that it was on November 8, 1932, that they surrendered the freedom of mind and spirit for which their ancestors had fought and agonized for over three hundred years, they will, I hope, recollect that I at least tried to save them." Although Hoover's misjudgment can be attributed to an excessively evangelical faith in the wisdom of his opinions, at the center of his failing was also an arrogant belief that his opinions were unquestionably superior to those of his constituents, and that to accept current public sentiment as a sensible guide was not leadership but demagoguery.

Hoover's response to the Bonus march on Washington in the spring and summer of 1932 illustrates his lack of both wisdom and responsiveness as a leader. The march was initiated in Portland, Oregon, by a group of unemployed, impoverished World War I veterans who wanted the federal government to make early payment of a bonus that had been promised for 1945. Some twenty thousand veterans from across the country ultimately joined in support and came to Washington in May and June. Settling in a marshy area across the Anacostia River and in some abandoned buildings along Pennsylvania Avenue, the veterans waited patiently for Congress to decide the fate of a bill granting their request.

As the Bill moved toward defeat, President Hoover refused even to meet with any of the veterans, and no one from the White House gave them the slightest nod of sympathy. To the contrary, the administration intended to make a show of force that might convince the marchers to go home until it was dissuaded by the District's superintendent of police, a former Army brigadier-general unwilling to dismiss the veterans' cause or to provoke them into violence. But after the Congress rejected a bonus bill mandating early payment and most of the veterans refused to accept a government loan to help them return home, the president and Patrick Hurley, his secretary of war, spoiled for a chance to assert the embarrassed administration's authority.

In late July, after a clash between the protesters and police oust-
ing them from the abandoned buildings cost two veterans their
lives, Hoover and Hurley responded to a request for help from
local authorities by sending U.S. Army forces. Four troops of cav-
alry, a column of infantry with fixed bayonets and supplies of tear-
gas bombs, and six tanks took the measure of the unarmed men
in the downtown buildings and in the Anacostia flats, where their
wives and children also resided. Under the command of General
Douglas MacArthur, the troops gassed and burned out the helpless
men, women, and children who symbolized the suffering of millions afflicted by the Depression.

If many in the country were unsympathetic to increasing the
government's debt by funding a bonus it could not then afford to
pay, most Americans objected more to a president who seemed to
be so indifferent to citizens who had fallen on hard times through
no fault of their own. As the drama in the capital unfolded, the
villain in the piece came to be seen as the cold-hearted president.
"What a pitiful spectacle," the Washington *News* declared, "is that
of the great American Government, mightiest in the world, chasing
unarmed men, women and children with Army tanks. . . . If the
Army must be called out to make war on unarmed citizens, this is
no longer America." Or, as the November election shortly made
clear, it was no longer Herbert Hoover's America. The country
was ready for something Hoover simply couldn't give: a presidential administration ready, at least in part, to free itself from the
dead hand of the past.

Sixty years later George Bush made a comparable miscalculation in
failing to take into account the seriousness of the nation's economic problems. Unlike Hoover, however, Bush faced a recession,
not a depression, and in 1992 there was little of the sense of crisis
that had beset the country sixty years earlier. Nevertheless, in the
nineties, public frustration over unemployment, debts, deficits, and
a general decline in middle-class living standards caused some two-
thirds of Americans to see the country as "fundamentally on the
wrong track." A twenty-year trend toward greater income disparity
between the bottom 10 percent of workers (whose annual earnings
had dropped by 24 percent after inflation) and the top 20 percent

(whose earnings had increased by 10 percent) left Americans convinced that the economy had settled into a disturbing pattern of stagnant incomes and growing inequality; indeed, the widest of "any modern democratic nation."

Although Bush's defeat in 1992 with only 38 percent of the vote revealed how poorly he had assessed the public's mood on these issues, he was not the only victim of the country's discontent with its economic plight. A substantial trend in American politics away from the established parties and toward independents who seemed to promise novel approaches to long-standing problems began to gain momentum. As the country moved toward the 1996 presidential campaign, General Colin Powell; Bill Bradley, who announced his retirement from the Senate with slams at both parties; and Ross Perot, who captured renewed public attention with a United We Stand conference in Dallas in August 1995, appealed to millions of Americans as more effective potential leaders than Bill Clinton or any of the Republicans bidding for his job.

Clinton's weak standing in public opinion from 1993 to 1995 stemmed not only from a lack of vision but also from his inability to establish himself as a national spokesman on a major issue that mattered to people and made them feel he was responding to their deepest concerns. Polls indicated that his initial failure on this count was a result of his efforts on behalf of gays in the military, which seemed to put him too visibly on the side of a minority interest. He suffered an even greater setback when he missed the opportunity to provide universal health care insurance, for which there had been a consensus in the summer and fall of 1993.

After fifty years during which public health experts and liberals unsuccessfully pressed the case for medical insurance guaranteeing health care for everyone, a national majority finally began to favor such a reform in 1990. Disturbed by escalating doctors' fees and hospital costs and by diminished access to health care for 37 million uninsured and millions of additional underinsured, 69 percent of Americans favored either fundamental or partial restructuring of the country's health delivery system. Even most insured Americans, who were satisfied with their coverage and doctors, feared they could end up in the ranks of the uninsured if they lost their jobs or costs were not brought under control. At the same time, however, opinion surveys indicated that the 69 percent who approved health care change were "either ambivalent or undecided about what that change should entail." In the summer of 1991, two public opinion analysts concluded that "although the general picture of public support for national health reform is becoming more clear, there is still no public consensus on the specifics of such a proposal."

By 1993 the desire for health care reform was reaching a peak. A *Wall Street Journal* article in March described "stunning backing for an overhaul . . . 78 percent of the public believe that the current health-care system doesn't meet the needs of most Americans, and 74 percent say a complete overhaul is needed to cover everyone and control costs." The *Journal* also noted "a surprising willingness to accept some sacrifices." Sixty-six percent of those surveyed were receptive to small tax increases to assure universal coverage, while 52 percent were even willing to "accept limits on the right to choose their own doctors." Eighty-seven percent thought government limits on doctor and hospital charges were an acceptable trade-off for universal coverage, while 71 percent were willing to see "more government involvement in the health-care system."

Nine months later the *New York Times* noted that 90 percent of the country had a "sense of urgency" about completely rebuilding or substantially changing the system, with 61 percent ready to pay higher taxes for such measures. Eighty-three percent believed universal coverage was "very important"; 67 percent felt the same about long-term care for the disabled at home; and 73 percent saw preventive care as vital to such a plan. Sixty-three percent favored requiring employers to provide basic insurance for workers and wanted the federal government to provide subsidies to small businesses to help them cover the costs. Large majorities favored additional liquor, beer, and cigarette taxes to help finance such far-reaching reforms.

Health care advocates could hardly believe that, after decades of struggle, their goal seemed to be within reach. Skeptics among them, however, circulated an anecdote about the advocate who after a lifetime of fighting unsuccessfully for reform arrived at the Pearly Gates. Granted an audience with the Lord, the advocate asked, "Will there ever be fundamental health-care reform in the United States?" After a long moment, the Lord replied, "Yes, but not in my lifetime."

Unfortunately, such skepticism proved to be well advised. Despite the national consensus and a nine-month effort led by First Lady Hillary Clinton, the president could not find the right formula to satisfy congressional and public demands for a workable plan. In September 1993, a detailed Clinton proposal won 2 to 1 backing from the public, which accepted his contention that "maintaining the status quo would be more risky than dramatic change." It also rejected conservative complaints that Clinton's plan would lead to "excessive government intrusion" into the workings of the private sector. The one factor on which the country remained "extremely tentative" was what one journalist described as a "numbingly complex proposal." A majority found the 1,300-page plan impenetrable and they doubted that it would assure them of future health coverage; even if it did, 50 percent believed that it would be at greater cost to them than under current arrangements.

The initial uncertainties grew stronger as more details of the proposal were examined over the next several months. By the summer of 1994 the bill was all but dead, the victim of scrutiny by the public, which had finally decided that the complexity of the White House's "competitive market approach" made its proposal unworkable. Despite its provisions for coupling traditional fee-for-service medicine paid for by private insurance with managed care groups or health maintenance organizations, the Clinton plan seemed to offer only "another big government program," taking over 17 percent of the private sector, with impossibly bureaucratic regulations that would eventually confound everyone. The tentative consensus for reform that had emerged in the fall of 1993 had been lost in a year-long battle over the implementation of its specific details. "Because we had failed to edit the plan down to its essentials and find familiar ways to convey it," Paul Starr, one of the architects of the plan, explained, "many people couldn't understand what we were proposing. There were too many parts, too many new ideas, even for many policy experts to keep straight."

No one familiar with the intricacies of designing a viable means of assuring affordable health care to 255 million Americans can fault Clinton for failing to find the ideal solution to so formidable a problem. But unlike his greatest predecessors, who faced challenges at least as demanding, Clinton was not even able to introduce incremental change, which could have opened the way to additional future reforms. As one of the great missed opportunities of recent domestic history, the health care debacle strikingly displayed the limits of Clinton's presidential leadership—and how political practice has the potential to make a telling difference in the nation's domestic life.

III

Throughout our country's history presidential leadership in war and peace has been an even greater test than the conduct of domestic affairs. Because Americans have generally attended less to foreign events, presidents have been left freer to respond to them as they saw fit. Ironically, once they have acted in defense of the national security, they have enjoyed a degree of popular support rarely granted policies affecting internal concerns. But, on the whole, presidents have found it difficult to sustain a national consensus for any long-term, substantial expenditures of human lives and defense budgets. Unless the war is relatively short and involves limited casualties as in the Spanish-American and Persian Gulf conflicts, the White House has had to assure that a clear understanding and commitment preceded involvement in drawn-out warfare.

Our most successful wartime presidents have been those who systematically built a consensus in the Congress, the press, and the country before taking up arms, just as the most ineffective leaders have been those who tried to impose a military policy on the nation in which it didn't believe. The freedom allowed America's chiefs in the making of war and crafting of peace has also burdened them with considerable risks, and it is in this arena that the reputations of some of the country's most and least successful presidents have been made.

As with so many considerations in the history of the presidency, Lincoln's administration is an ideal place to begin when assessing presidential effectiveness in the struggle to assure national backing for an agonizing war. Upon Lincoln's election in November 1860 seven Deep South states seceded from the Union, and for the time being, Arkansas, North Carolina, Tennessee, and Virginia refused to follow their lead. When he assumed the presidency on March 4, 1861, Lincoln searched for a means to hold these states in the Union and woo the others back from a rebellion that he knew would in time compel a military response.

The issue he seized upon to effect this goal was the status of Fort Sumter in South Carolina's Charleston harbor. As Lincoln made clear in his Inaugural Address, he would not assail slavery where it existed; southern property rights would be preserved. But these assurances did not give any states the right to leave the Union, and it was his constitutional duty to assure their adherence to the laws of the land. As part of that duty he intended to "hold, occupy, and possess the property and places belonging to the government," which meant he would not abandon U.S. forts in the South to seceding states. As he shrewdly perceived, the forts, and particularly Fort Sumter, which was located in a state leading the charge toward secession, were both symbolic and substantive manifestations of the crisis.

Yet having clearly stated his policy, Lincoln faced a political dilemma. If he took the initiative to reclaim the forts then under occupation or threatened with it, he would provoke bloodshed that would serve to unite the South, including the states that had not yet decided to withdraw from the Union. Such a plan also seemed certain to divide the North, which did not want to bear the burden of having started the war. On the other hand, if Lincoln gave into southern pressure and relinquished Sumter and the other forts, he would likewise split Union opinion by implicitly acknowledging southern independence. To give up Sumter, one cabinet member told him, meant giving up the Union.

Lincoln, holding the same view, wished to take a firm line without inciting a battle and its predictable repercussions. His solution was to announce a resupply expedition to Sumter, which would involve no military action against South Carolina's secessionists. The strategy was brilliantly devised to give Lincoln the moral and political upper hand in any possible war. If the secessionists attacked the unarmed Union ships bringing "food for hungry men," the onus of war would fall upon the South and create a northern consensus to meet the Confederate challenge. If the South did not attack, Lincoln would have won a significant symbolic victory. "[His] conception of the supply undertaking was a stroke of genius," James McPherson writes. "In effect he was telling Jefferson Davis, 'Heads I win, tails you lose.' It was the first sign of the mastery that would mark Lincoln's presidency." In one stroke he had declared his determination to preserve the Union and the future of constitutional rule, shown himself to be a resourceful pragmatist capable of formulating a workable policy to meet an unprecedented crisis, and assured himself of broad support for the most demanding commitment a president can ask of his people.

Theodore Roosevelt was as artful as Lincoln in dealing with matters of war and peace. Although he never faced the sort of crisis over which Lincoln prevailed, TR was exceptionally effective in meeting the foreign policy predicaments of his day. Convinced that nineteenth-century isolationism could not assure America's twentieth-century security, Roosevelt devised means to exert U.S. influence abroad without provoking excessively hostile objections at home. Believing that America's population, wealth, and potential military power gave it unavoidable responsibilities in the Western Hemisphere, he acted to secure its position in Central America and the Caribbean through acquisition of the Panama Canal route and his Corollary to the Monroe Doctrine. In both instances he mustered widespread public support for his actions not by speechmaking on behalf of power politics—the principal motive behind both policies—but by stressing the moral and economic necessities for acting as he did.

TR was confident that acquiring the rights to and building a Panama Canal would be "from the material and constructive standpoint one of the greatest bits of work that the twentieth century will see." The canal, as he described it, was to be "one of the future highways of civilization" bringing benefits to peoples around the globe. Equally true—if unstipulated—was the fact that it would enable the United States to move freely its naval forces between the two great oceans bordering its shores; that it would offer indirect encouragement to Panamanians seceding from Colombia, a violation of international law; and that Colombians viewed the Hay-Herran Treaty of 1903, which granted the United States rights to build a canal, as an abuse of their sovereignty. TR saw these matters as neither material obstacles nor worthy of public debate in the United States. The acquisition and construction of a canal was essentially and indisputably a step forward for America and all the world.

Unsurprisingly, TR's actions did provoke both domestic and international criticism. The New York Evening *Post,* for example, condemned "this mad plunge of ours [as] simply and solely a vulgar and mercenary venture, without a rag to cover its sordidness and shame." Yet on the whole, though he was accused (as he would be throughout his life) of being a gunboat diplomatist or Yankee imperialist who held nations to the south in contempt, he enjoyed widespread support in the United States for what he and most Americans saw as "our duty, when it becomes absolutely inevitable, to police these countries [in Latin America] in the interest of order and civilization."

Roosevelt's dealings in East Asian affairs rested on similar unstated concerns with national self-interest, but, as he had in the Western Hemisphere, he presented them in ways that assured widespread public support. His descriptions of American intentions in East Asia struck idealistic chords that thrilled the country. Roosevelt was deeply committed to assuring an open door for U.S. commerce and influence in the region generally and in China in particular. America's presence in Hawaii, the Philippines, Guam, Wake Island, and Midway had made it a Pacific power, and it was now eager to assure a balance between nations competing against its interests in the area.

The struggle between Russia and Japan for dominance in Manchuria especially concerned TR. He and Secretary of State John Hay understood that the U.S. public would strongly oppose any commitment to side with one or the other of the parties in the conflict or to use American military might directly to assert its influence. "The bad feature of the situation from our standpoint," the president told Hay in May 1903, "is that as yet it seems that we cannot fight to keep Manchuria open. I hate being in the position of seeming to bluster without backing it up."

To forge a consensus for U.S. interference in East Asia, Roosevelt had to create the impression that he was acting strictly in the name of high-minded principles or of the interests of peace and international law. He insisted that Americans "stand upon [their] own feet and try to look into the future as clearly as may be," and in 1904 urged them to recognize that "We have become a great nation . . . and we must behave as beseems a people with such responsibilities." He knew that any direct appeal to arrangements entailing alliances, spheres of influence, balances of power, or any other conventional diplomatic tool would undermine rather than advance a national resolution for involvement abroad. If he were to win public backing for an activist policy in East Asia, it would have to be, as he announced, in the name of helping "every movement which will tend to bring us into more friendly relations with the rest of mankind."

In the summer of 1905, as he mediated a settlement in the Russo-Japanese war, he gave masterful expression to public statements of idealism which nonetheless masked selfish American interests. From the commencement of his presidency in 1901, Roosevelt had devoted a large part of his diplomatic efforts to inhibiting Russian expansion in Manchuria, arguing, "For years Russia has pursued a policy of consistent opposition to us in the East, and of literally fathomless mendacity," he said. When Japan staged a surprise attack and destroyed the Russian fleet in Port Arthur in July 1904, TR declared privately that the Japanese were playing the same game as America.

As the mediator in the conflict, he aimed to create in China a rough balance of power between Tokyo and St. Petersburg, for a Russo-Japanese deadlock would inhibit both of them from actions inimical to U.S. interests in Manchuria. Though his efforts to bring the warring parties together drove him "nearly mad," TR persuaded them to meet at the American naval base in Portsmouth, New Hampshire. The negotiations themselves tested the president's endurance even further, but the month-long talks, in which he successfully played the honest broker, brought a settlement that won him worldwide praise and the 1906 Nobel Peace Prize. While Americans celebrated the accomplishment of their leader as a milestone in the search for enduring global peace, Roosevelt saw his achievement in a different light: he had used the presence of the Japanese and Russian delegations in Portsmouth as an occasion to show off America's battle fleet, delivering the not-too-subtle message that the United States had the power and determination to play a shaping role in East Asian affairs. Moreover, he knew that the Portsmouth Conference would help condition Americans to think of their country as an influential force on the world scene. Indeed, the assumption TR instilled in American minds was that even if its weapon was no more than moral suasion, the United States would, from then on, have a central part to play in overseas affairs.

No modern U.S. president was more adept at the politics of foreign policy than FDR. The defeat of Wilson's peace plans in 1919 made an indelible impression on him, for he learned that no leader could ignore the vital connection between domestic opinion and conduct of international relations. As president, he lived by the proposition that an effective policy abroad required a supporting consensus at home. The greatest test of this axiom came in 1939–1941, when a clear majority of Americans favored fascist defeat while also opposing involvement in the war.

Roosevelt had never had any doubt where U.S. interests lay in the conflict between the Axis and the Allies. He was eager to do all he could to break fascist power, even if it meant that the United States would enter the conflict. From the outbreak of the war in September 1939 until his declaration of a national emergency in May 1941, he counted on the ability of Britain and France, and then Britain alone, to neutralize German and Italian power with the help of American supplies. Because U.S. public opinion still believed that American loans and munitions to the Allies were responsible for its role in World War I, a decision it had come to regret, the country was reluctant to make the same "mistake." To address this concern, Roosevelt proposed a policy of "cash and carry," which would prevent involvement through loans or German submarine violations of American neutral rights, the conditions most Americans believed had drawn us into World War I. As he announced repeatedly at this time, "cash and carry" was the best means to keep America out of the fighting.

After the collapse of France in June 1940, Britain's need for greater U.S. aid manifested itself in a request for World War I destroyers, which could help deter a Nazi invasion of the British Isles. Churchill described them to FDR as "a matter of life or death." Since such a commitment seemed certain to bring America closer to full participation in the conflict, Roosevelt searched for a way to assure public approval of the transfer while not jeopardizing his campaign for an unprecedented third term. His solution was to exchange the destroyers for ninety-nine-year leases on naval and air bases in seven British Western Hemisphere possessions. Though he feared an executive agreement on destroyers for bases might "raise hell with Congress" and subject him to charges of being a " 'warmonger' and a 'dictator,' " he believed it essential to act. When he did, he emphasized that obtaining the bases was "the most important action in the reinforcement of our national defense . . . since the Louisiana Purchase." Though most Americans dismissed the analogy to Louisiana as political hyperbole, they felt reassured that Roosevelt had received excellent value for the old destroyers. "You can't attack a deal like that one," one opposing senator declared, and the country agreed.

At the end of 1940, when Britain ran out of cash to pay for supplies, Roosevelt was forced to confront another foreign policy dilemma. A request to Congress to revoke or revise laws barring loans and requiring cash for munitions impressed the president as a poor idea; it seemed certain to resurrect the issues that had prompted such legislation in the first place. His solution, therefore, was the strategy of Lend-Lease. Roosevelt's plan involved increasing U.S. arms output and then telling the British, "We will give you the guns and ships that you need, provided that when the war is over you will return to us in kind the guns and ships that we have loaned to you." Eager, as always, to assure public backing for a potentially controversial action, Roosevelt explained to the press and the public that his plan was comparable to one neighbor's lending another a garden hose to put out a fire in his home. "What do I do in such a crisis?" the president asked at a press conference. "I don't say . . . , 'Neighbor, my garden hose cost me $15; you have to pay me $15 for it.' . . . I don't want $15—I want my garden hose back after the fire is over." Roosevelt's homey analogy won over the public, and because Americans were eager to help Britain defeat the Nazis, no one questioned FDR about what use all the newly manufactured arms and munitions would be after the war. Lend-Lease was a device for supplying Britain with the wherewithal to fight at a time when Americans were still reluctant to take a direct hand in the conflict. Roosevelt's presentation of Lend-Lease created a partnership with the public in support of a larger goal on which they agreed.

By the spring of 1941, Nazi victories in the Mediterranean and North Atlantic persuaded Roosevelt that direct American involvement in the fighting was now necessary to defeat Berlin. Yet even with these incursions the country remained painfully divided about entry into the war. In May, 68 percent of Americans said it was more important to help Britain than to stay out of the conflict. At the same time, however, 79 percent of the country expressed a desire to avoid involvement in the bloodletting. The conflicting messages persuaded FDR that forceful leadership on his part would be insufficient to assure a unified response to America's joining the Allies. If the country was to take a role in the conflict with a minimum of dissent, he understood, it would be not because he persuaded it to do so but rather as an unavoidable response to events overseas.

None of the incidents that took place in the Atlantic between June and December of 1941—neither the sinking of the U.S. freighter *Robin Moor* nor an exchange of fire between a German sub and the U.S. destroyer *Greer*—impressed the president as a legitimate casus belli, and it was only the all-out attack on Pearl Harbor on December 7 that convinced him he had the provocation to ask for a declaration of war. However terrible the cost in men and ships, the Japanese assault relieved Roosevelt of a political burden he could not throw off on his own. No one should assume that he turned a blind eye to the attack as a way to solve his political problem. Pearl Harbor was a genuine surprise. But it gave the president the impetus he needed to carry the country through a long and costly war: a national consensus that America was fighting for the preservation of its own democratic way of life.

Once America joined the fighting, Roosevelt turned his attention to winning the war and assuring U.S. postwar commitments to maintaining the peace. If past experience was any guide, a victory on the battlefield seemed more achievable than any satisfactory postwar arrangements. Throughout the conflict Roosevelt was diligent in promoting a new national consensus in favor of long-term

U.S. involvement in international affairs, for he sought to head off another return to isolationism, as had occurred after World War I.

His device for winning this internationalist consensus was to convince Americans that the fighting would inexorably lead to Wilsonian or universalist commitments to postwar peace. He encouraged the belief that a new world league would replace traditional power politics with collective security. Democracy, the rule of law, and concern for international well-being, as opposed to selfish national interests, would dominate the world of the future.

Roosevelt knew that this scenario was in large part fated to remain only a fantasy. In January 1945, before leaving for the Yalta conference with Churchill and Stalin, he met with a bipartisan group of senators, who complained that recent European developments suggested that the future would, in fact, resemble in many respects the past. FDR candidly told them that spheres of influence were a reality that America could not abolish. "The idea kept coming up," he said, "because the occupying forces had the power in the areas where their arms were present and each knew that the other could not force things to an issue. He [Roosevelt] stated that the Russians had the power in Eastern Europe, that it was obviously impossible to have a break with them and that, therefore, the only practicable course was to use what influence we had to ameliorate the situation."

Roosevelt's public pronouncements on the shape of the postwar world gave no hint of such concerns, for he believed that he could only bring about a revolutionary shift in American foreign policy by appealing to idealistic hopes. His depiction of an effective United Nations organization, as well as a state of harmonious relations with cooperative allies—a benign Soviet Union and a stable, democratic China—was meant to disarm isolationist fears of an America corrupted and ruined by commitments to traditional power politics or sphere-of-influence diplomacy.

Roosevelt saw that the key to bringing the country through the war in a mood to participate in world affairs was its belief in the possibility of friendly dealings with Russia, even though he himself had serious doubts about Soviet intentions after the fighting. To guard against possible Soviet aggression, he joined Churchill in signing a covert aide memoire in September 1944 agreeing not to share the secret of atomic power with Moscow.

In public, however, the president not only never wavered in his support for his Soviet ally, but he made every effort to encourage the impression that the Soviets were becoming similar to Americans. In 1943, conservative publicist Henry Luce featured an article in *Life* magazine describing the Russians as "one hell of a people . . . [who] to a remarkable degree . . . look like Americans, dress like Americans and think like Americans"; the piece went so far as to characterize the NKVD as "a national police similar to the FBI." At the same time, Wendell Willkie, the Republican candidate in the 1940 presidential campaign, published *One World*, a book describing a global trip he had made at FDR's request. Selling over a million copies and distributed to U.S. troops gratis, the book portrayed a Soviet Union that remarkably resembled the United States. The grain crops running to the horizon were reminiscent of Texas; the irrigated valley near Tashkent looked like southern California; the stately manors along the Volga could have stood along the banks of the Hudson. Russian farmers reminded Willkie of his ancestors on the Indiana and Iowa frontiers, and the leader of the Republic of Yakutsk in Siberia was a young go-getter who "talked like a California real-estate salesman."

Roosevelt fostered the view that Moscow was abandoning totalitarianism and sphere-of-influence diplomacy for American democracy and universalism. After the Teheran conference in December 1943, he told the nation: "I got along fine with Marshal Stalin. I believe he is truly representative of the heart and soul of Russia; and I believe that we are going to get along very well with him and the Russian people—very well indeed." Asked his impressions of Stalin, Roosevelt answered: "I would call him something like me . . . a realist." Similarly, after Yalta in February 1945, the president declared his conviction that as a result of the conference the world could look forward to a future without "the system of unilateral action, the exclusive alliances, the spheres of influence, the balances of power, and all the other expedients that have been tried for centuries—and have always failed." He urged the Congress and the American people to endorse a universal organization made up of "all peace-loving Nations" and promising "a permanent structure of peace."

Although Roosevelt fully understood that potential postwar difficulties with Moscow could leave him vulnerable to charges of naïveté and worse, he felt compelled to sustain wartime illusions about Russia and international politics as a prelude to American leadership of a devastated world. Though the Cold War would give the lie to his optimistic statements about cooperation and peace and would tarnish his historical reputation for great leadership, he did, in fact, largely achieve his foreign policy goal of an America centrally involved in international affairs. If the world "structure of peace" turned out to be substantially different from what he intended, the post-1945 consensus accepting responsibility for stability abroad represented a transformation in national mood for which he deserves significant credit.

Forty-five years after Roosevelt helped bring about a revolution in U.S. foreign policy, George Bush tried to create a post–Cold War consensus he described as "the New World Order." With East-West tensions dissolved and Americans confused about their country's future role in a tumultuous world, Bush, a "foreign policy president," urged the country to continue to see itself as an international policeman leading the community of nations in opposing aggression and preserving global and regional peace.

This policy faced its severest test when Iraq invaded and occupied its oil-rich neighbor, Kuwait. Arguing that unopposed aggression by Saddam Hussein would not only endanger Saudi Arabia and world oil supplies but would tempt other Third World dictators to strike at weaker neighbors, Bush initiated economic sanctions against Baghdad and led a coalition of nations in giving Iraq an ultimatum to withdraw or face an American-led attack. Because he appreciated the importance of enlisting congressional and public backing for such a course, he asked the Congress to vote on the question of waging war or continuing embargoes. When the House and Senate gave him narrow votes of support for war, if he thought it necessary, he had won the sort of official commitment that neither Truman nor LBJ had obtained when leading the country into the politically divisive Korean and Vietnam conflicts.

Apart from the Spanish-American war in 1898, the Persian Gulf struggle was the most popular limited war in U.S. history, in large part because it lasted merely six weeks and cost only 350 American lives, half of them in noncombat accidents. Bush's wisdom in establishing national and international support for an American military action of this magnitude provided an instructive contrast to the many instances of twentieth-century gunboat and secret diplomacy, which did more to erode confidence in the country's democratic institutions than to advance the national interest.

IV

The two greatest presidential failures in making peace and war were the Johnsons, Andrew and Lyndon. Andrew was not only unable to reconstruct the Union but also destroyed his political power and became the only president in American history to have been impeached. Lyndon not only did not overcome the Communist insurgency in Vietnam but also had to abandon office and bear the onus of being the only president to have "lost" a war.

Miscalculations of the process of bringing the South back into the Union, on one hand, and in preserving a pro-Western regime in South Vietnam on the other were central factors in the downfalls of the Johnsons. But their greatest missteps were in believing they had national support for, or could proceed without assuring themselves of, the public backing needed for their policies.

Andrew Johnson was a paradoxical character who initially seemed well-suited to the presidency. With long experience in public life and a capacity to survive the rough and tumble of both Tennessee and national politics, where he had served as an alderman, a state legislator, a congressman, a governor, a U.S. senator, and a vice president, Johnson might seem to have been eminently prepared for the requirements of high office. But he was in fact a rigid, dictatorial martinet who could not bend to political realities at odds with his own ideas and aims. "As governor," the historian Eric Foner says, "Johnson failed to work effectively with his legislature; as military governor he proved unable to elicit popular support for his administration. Hardly a political novice, he found himself, as President, thrust into a role that required tact, flexibility, and sensitivity to the nuances of public opinion—qualities Lincoln possessed in abundance, but that Johnson lacked."

Johnson's primary objective as president was to restore the South to a position of equality in the Union as quickly as possible. A strong believer in states' rights and an opponent of black equality, he had little patience for majority opinion in the North. Despite intense feelings of antagonism toward southerners who had provoked a horribly costly war in lives and money, northerners were not intent on a radical reconstruction depriving southern states of self-rule, or on compelling full social and political equality for blacks. At the same time, they were not prepared to accept Johnson's indulgent approach to the former Confederate states.

Instead of acknowledging that he needed to accommodate himself to congressional and popular opinion in his plan for reconstructing the South, Johnson plunged ahead and launched a fight with congressional opponents which he seemed to relish. Instead of forcing a congressional compromise on reconstruction policies by playing radical Republicans off against moderates, he united them in opposition to himself by stubbornly insisting on a Johnson policy or no policy at all. In 1866, for example, after the Congress passed a Freedmen's Bureau bill and a civil rights bill guaranteeing minimal rights to all citizens, Johnson vetoed both laws. Moreover, when the Congress responded by passing the Fourteenth Amendment to the Constitution, Johnson urged the states to reject it. More a compromise measure than an expression of any revolutionary design, the amendment barred only former government officials from holding office in the reconstructed South, and granted no additional powers to the federal government to enforce civil liberties; instead, it prohibited the states from making or enforcing any law that abridged the privileges and immunities of U.S. citizens, deprived them of due process, or denied them equal protection under the law.

Johnson's battle with the Congress reached a climax over the Tenure of Office Act. Fearing that he intended to build an independent political party by removing Republicans from federal jobs and replacing them with officials loyal to him, the Congress required that the Senate give its approval to any dismissals the president chose to make. When Johnson defied the Congress by firing Secretary of War Edwin M. Stanton after the Senate refused to ratify his removal, the House impeached him, though a reluctance to destabilize the political system persuaded the Senate to defeat conviction by a single vote.

Johnson was eager to construct a new party of southerners, northern Democrats, and moderate Republicans to help elect him president in 1868 and endorse his reconstruction plans. But he was simply out of touch with mainstream northern sentiment, as the results of the 1866 congressional elections and his own failure to win another term made clear. In the end Andrew Johnson did more to extend the period of national strife than to speed the reconciliation for which a majority of Americans now yearned.

It is difficult to understand today how so effective a politician as Lyndon Johnson could have so misjudged the need for creating an effective consensus on an issue as fraught with controversy as Vietnam. As a congressman, he had witnessed firsthand FDR's performance in easing the country toward involvement in World War II. Moreover, he had seen the political damage done to Truman over his neglecting to build a national commitment for an extended war in Korea.

If these historical precedents were not sufficiently enlightening to give Johnson pause, he also had the benefit of the warnings of senior administration advisers. In February 1965, for example, before he began the systematic bombing of North Vietnam, termed Operation Rolling Thunder, and the subsequent introduction of massive ground forces, Vice President Hubert Humphrey urged Johnson to remember that "American wars have to be politically understandable by the American public. There has to be a cogent, convincing case if we are to enjoy sustained public support. In World Wars I and II we had this. In Korea we were moving under United Nations auspices to defend South Korea against dramatic, across-the-border, conventional aggression. Yet even with those advantages, we could not sustain American political support for fighting Chinese in Korea in 1952." Humphrey also cautioned that protracted fighting in Vietnam could cost Johnson his public backing and play havoc with his domestic reforms. National Security Adviser McGeorge Bundy made an equally impassioned case to Johnson for assuring popular backing for Vietnam and quietly resigned when he could not convince the president to let him pursue this goal.

But LBJ found a number of reasons to ignore the historical and contemporary admonitions against escalating the war without firm public support. The examples of FDR and Truman in fact encouraged rather than deterred Johnson from pursuing his Vietnam policy, for he viewed both of them as bold statesmen doing what had to be done to preserve U.S. security rather than waiting for the ratification of public opinion. During a visit to the FDR Library in Hyde Park, New York, for example, Johnson paused before an exhibit of Roosevelt's 1937 "Quarantine" address in the country's isolationist heartland to comment on his predecessor's courage in challenging the public to recognize the dangers from international aggression.

Johnson also believed that he had at least implicit congressional backing for his Southeast Asian strategy from the Gulf of Tonkin Resolution passed in August 1964. Apparent attacks on U.S. destroyers conducting electronic espionage in the Gulf persuaded Johnson to make retaliatory strikes against North Vietnamese military targets. Though he was aware that the second of these "attacks" may have been the product of a destroyer crew's imagination (in 1995 North Vietnamese General Vo Nguyen Giap denied that such an incident had occurred), Johnson asked the Congress to authorize him to take "all necessary measures to repel any armed attacks against the forces of the United States and to prevent further aggression." The resolution, however, was hardly a blank check, for although it won unanimous House endorsement and all but two votes in the Senate, it was passed in the midst of a presidential campaign against the hawkish Barry Goldwater, and made no provisions for expanding the air war and beginning a massive land war over the following year.

Johnson's subsequent escalation of combat was accomplished by presidential fiat and without significant debate in the Congress, the press, or among the people. Convinced that the national interest required him to fight in Vietnam, the strong-willed president saw little value in encouraging a national debate that might persuade the Vietnamese Communists that America was too divided to hold its ground. Johnson and most Americans, at least until the beginning of 1968, were also confident that the Communists would eventually succumb; it was accepted wisdom that they could not hold out forever against U.S. power. Therefore, all Americans had to do was patriotically endorse the president's war policy and patiently wait for Hanoi and the Vietcong to negotiate a settlement. Johnson believed that the great majority of Americans would come to accept the burdens of the war because, like him, they understood that there was no choice but to fight, for not taking a stand in Vietnam seemed likely, if World War II had taught any lesson, to lead to a wider, more destructive war. As far as the president was concerned, the consensus for fighting in Vietnam had been formed in the early years of the Cold War and was sufficient for his current policies if only shortsighted dissenters did not discourage mass support at home and encourage the Communists in Vietnam to await an American political collapse.

But domestic political divisions were exactly what Johnson could not prevent. In February 1968, when the North Vietnamese and Vietcong mounted a Tet offensive, which belied repeated administration predictions of a "light at the end of the tunnel," Johnson felt compelled to acknowledge that the public had lost faith in the war. Announcing on March 31 that he would not send additional troops, would limit the bombing, and would not run for another term, he conceded that he lacked a consensus for what he still considered an essential strategy in Vietnam. Whatever the wisdom of the massive military effort, public inability to comprehend a war engaging over half a million troops and involving more tonnage of ammunition than had been used in all of World War II cost Johnson his ability to sustain the fighting and his presidency.

From a century apart the two Johnsons remind us that control over war and peace, as with so much else in America's democracy, ultimately rests not with the executive but the people from whom he derives his power.

CHAPTER 4

THE POWER AND LIMITS OF PRESIDENTIAL PERSONALITY

From the early days of the Republic parties and personalities have tended to have a stronger hold on the American public imagination than dialogues over specific issues. During election campaigns, candidates have long understood that the less they discussed complicated economic, social, and international questions the better their chances of winning votes. Aspirants to the presidency who have looked and acted "presidential" have usually had an advantage over more cerebral opponents overly concerned with formulating substantive solutions to domestic and world problems. Public figures who fervently appeal to American shibboleths about flag, family, liberty, fair play, and all our other cherished national values have been especially attractive to the electorate. In times of crisis, of course, people want to hear more concrete proposals about how office seekers plan to cure the country's ills, and the ratio of public interests changes. But by and large, it is the photogenic, hail-fellow, well-met sort of candidate with an appealing sales pitch who is the more likely to command voter support.

And once in office, as the most astute chiefs have understood, the president takes his place among the divinities of our national mythology, a privileged actor on the stage of history, someone "almost more than human." "The media bring across the president," presidential analyst James David Barber says, "not as some neutral administrator or corporate executive to be assessed by his production, but as a special being with mysterious dimensions.'' We have always wanted to place our faith in presidents as virtuous, noble citizens incapable of lying or self-serving actions contrary to the national well-being; we have been eager to make them anointed bearers of sacred symbols, vessels of "Americanism" embodying our most precious ideals.

Such uncritical hero worship has, of course, not withstood the test of reality. Intense public focus on presidential personalities has invariably turned up idiosyncrasies, flaws, and weaknesses. Also weakening the power of the halo effect are equally strong traditions of political partisanship and fierce egalitarianism, which, in proclaiming that no one—not even presidents—deserved to be elevated above the rest of the populace, assured that, in the final analysis, America's chiefs would be judged as ordinary men with common limitations. In short, an affinity for demythologizing presidents has been as strong a national impulse as any inclination to endow them with exalted traits.

To the people they govern, American presidents have most resembled Janus, the two-faced Roman god who peered from gates and doorways in opposite directions at the same time. Given how often presidents have attempted to be all things to all people, it is not surprising that they have come to be regarded as alternately wise and foolish, honest and devious, lovable and contemptible, exalted sovereigns and flawed mortals. Bound up as they must be with our dreams and hopes, our disappointments and frustrations, presidents have inevitably been accorded the stature of our greatest heroes and our most despised scoundrels. On one hand, they have triumphed as citizen-kings rescuing their charges from terrible crises of war and depression. They have been celebrated as decent, well-meaning public servants advancing the national interest as ably as they could. On the other, they have been pilloried as foolish, ineffectual, and destructive—architects of economic disasters including joblessness, poverty, national debts, inflation, and lower living standards; ill-considered domestic social programs undermining our self-reliance; unproductive foreign wars and interventions; and other policies that ultimately did more to blight than to advance our futures.

"Presidential ratings," which have lately become as favored a form of national entertainment as the World Series or the Super Bowl, are one notable demonstration of our love-hate attitudes toward our chiefs. We have become accustomed to keeping score cards on presidential triumphs and defeats, tracking winners and losers, charting the ups and downs in historical reputations as revisionist estimates of individual terms have been published.

For all its mythmaking about presidents and impulses to overstate both their positive and negative influences, the public has maintained a healthy pragmatism about the impact of their policies. For the most part, the mass of Americans have admired and disdained their chiefs for legitimate reasons, usually measuring them by standards of common sense that have served the national well-being. They have been armed with sufficient political savvy to discern when presidential actions have advanced or retarded prosperity, provoked military clashes or preserved peace, exhilarated or demoralized the nation.

Yet however much presidents have understood the value of personally engaging the public and however eager Americans have been to respect and esteem their leaders, mutual affection has never been an easily attainable goal. While all presidents have had some initial attraction to voters, or they never would have gained the Oval Office in the first place, some have been much more proficient than others at exploiting their personal appeal to advance their agendas. Washington, Jefferson, Jackson, Lincoln, the two Roosevelts, Ike, JFK, and Reagan had uncommon charismatic qualities which mesmerized their contemporaries and subsequent generations as well. While none of the other thirty-two men who served in the presidency have possessed quite this degree of personal chemistry, figures like Madison, Monroe, Polk, Grant, Cleveland, Wilson, Truman, the second Johnson, and Nixon have at least been resourceful practitioners of the politics of personal leadership, though in the case of the latter group their personalities have served as often to undermine as to aid them in the pursuit of their goals.

Presidents have succeeded and failed in proportion to their effectiveness in making themselves into popular figures: those best able to reduce the distance between themselves and the people by diminishing the impersonality of the office or by using their personal appeal to excite public interest and affection have tended to be our most memorable executives. How some managed and others failed to do so is a puzzle worth considering; how some first attracted and then repelled the mass of Americans during their presidential terms presents yet another challenge to historical understanding.

I

The country's first great mythic and charismatic chief, George Washington, "already stood for an entire people," Garry Wills writes in his brilliant study of Washington's leadership, "before some observers suspected there *was* a nation—before there was any symbol of that nation (a flag, a Constitution, a national seal)—there was Washington. Even when . . . a flag did appear, and a Constitution, they did not have the long tradition behind them. . . . But Washington was still there, steadying the symbols, lending strength to them instead of drawing it from them."

As our first president, Washington set a standard to which the country has always aspired. He gave contemporary meaning to classical conceptions of political heroism and republicanism. By three acts of public selflessness—resigning his commission as commander-in-chief at the close of the Revolutionary War; sponsorship of the Constitution in 1787, which risked his reputation for honorable service to the nation; and his Farewell Address of 1796, surrendering the presidency—he identified himself with Cincinnatus, the heroic Roman who left his plow to rescue Rome and returned to it when danger had passed. "Washington's charisma," Wills says, "came from a prominently displayed eagerness to transcend it; he gained power from his readiness to give it up."

It was through this pattern of shunning power that Washington not only gained it but afforded himself the opportunity to use it. Washington the reluctant general, Constitution maker, and president put his popularity in the service of democracy and the rule of law, teaching by example that Caesarism—dictatorial control—had no place in America's constitutional system. He had fought the revolution against Britain not as a rebellion against lawful authority but as a means of restoring "the rights of Americans" or redressing grievances in a legally sanctioned way. He had supported the constitutional reforms of 1787 not as a means of usurping powers conferred by the Articles of Confederation but as a way to make them more effective, or to give the confederation of states a more stable and workable democracy. He had assumed the presidency not to elevate his personal standing or to enjoy the trappings of high office but to assure against arbitrary rule and promote the development of a unified, cooperative government.

Despite the strength of his iconic status none of Washington's hold on the public's imagination was accidental, for he worked at fostering it as carefully as modern politicians design a national campaign. To quote Wills again: "Washington was constantly testing public opinion and tailoring his actions to suit it. . . . This constant attention to the mood of the people—to the receptivity, as it were, of his audience—deterred him from unrealistic projects, from grandiose schemes hatched more to satisfy his ego than to accomplish what was needed." He "realized . . . that winning the people's long-term confidence is a more solid ground for achievement than either pandering to their whims or defying their expectations."

No president after Washington lived up to the exalted standards set by the man who was "first in war, first in peace, and first in the hearts of his countrymen." But myth and reality do not have to intersect to sustain larger-than-life ideals. Despite the more transparently flawed men who succeeded Washington, the country has clung to hopes of finding other Cincinnati to fill the office. The myth of presidential sanctity has remained as potent a symbol of America's nationhood as the Constitution, the flag, the White House, and the spread eagle.

The three nineteenth-century successors to Washington who most nearly achieved legendary status during their own presidencies were Jefferson, Jackson, and Lincoln. The power of Jefferson's personal influence is made particularly interesting by the fact that he was a painfully shy man who disliked publicity and shunned political station. Afflicted with a speech defect, he hated public speaking and abandoned the tradition that Washington and Adams had established of delivering State of the Union messages to Congress in person. "He had not the temperament of an agitator, hardly even of a leader in the qualities that leadership requires under modern democracy," Richard Hofstadter has written. "Not once did he deliver an exciting speech. His private life was one of enormous variety and interest, and there were many times when he would have been happy to desert public service to enjoy his farm, his family, and his books."

But as long as his country needed him, he performed public service, a duty that consumed most of his adult life: he was a member of the Virginia House of Burgesses, governor of Virginia during the Revolution, a member of the Continental Congress, minister to France from 1785 to 1789, secretary of state under Washington, vice president under John Adams, and president for eight years, 1801–1809. "Nature intended me for the tranquil pursuits of science, by rendering them my supreme delight," he once said. "But the enormities of the times in which I have lived have forced me to take a part in resisting them, and to commit myself on the boisterous ocean of political passions."

Part of Jefferson's considerable public appeal rested, like that of Washington, on his very reluctance to wield power. But even more than his predecessor, Jefferson was a standing symbol of the country's faith in practical democracy. His authorship of *A Summary View of the Rights of British America* (1774), the Declaration of Independence, and the Virginia Statute for Religious Freedom, and his founding of the University of Virginia made him the country's foremost spokesman for the "natural rights of man" and the Enlightenment belief in majority government or the people's right to self-rule. His diplomatic service in France and visits to other European countries, including England, intensified his commitment to democracy as a far more desirable system of governance than any devised by kings, noblemen, and priests, whom he described as "fools" and "idiots."

However much he valued it, Jefferson had no illusion that democratic governance would automatically lead to social justice or result in wise rule. He accepted the inevitability of the public's continuing to make poor choices and to act intemperately. Although he feared "an elective despotism," he believed it would be restrained by institutional checks and balances. Whatever errors might then occur under a democratic system could be no worse than what societies had already experienced under self-serving aristocrats. Jefferson had an abiding faith in the capacity of mass education, free speech, and freedom of the press to correct democracy's wrongs, and he would have readily accepted Winston Churchill's observation that democracy is the worst possible system except for all the rest.

Although he was passionately devoted to the idea that a politically healthy America was one that would not be administered through a Hamiltonian federalism in which the government played a central part in encouraging a manufacturing economy, he refused to ruthlessly overturn policies that had already been in place for almost twelve years and had achieved an undeniable measure of success. Instead, he declared, "We are all republicans—we are all federalists," and pursued a course of political conciliation and economic compromise.

Jefferson's preference for the mechanical arts over politics also strongly endeared him to his contemporaries. His fascination with husbandry, agriculture, architecture, the weather, practical devices like the swivel chair and dumbwaiter, and any mechanical advance from plows to steam engines, metronomes, thermometers, and elevators that might improve people's lives demonstrated his interest in everyday matters of greatest importance to his constituents. John F. Kennedy once aptly quipped on greeting a group of Nobel laureates at the White House that they represented the greatest collection of minds ever assembled there except for when Thomas Jefferson dined alone.

Jefferson's leadership rested decisively on the public's regard for him as a man devoted to their well-being, and few doubted that "life, liberty, and the pursuit of happiness" were the foundation for all he did. He had no appetite for "frequent and untried changes in laws and institutions," as he admitted toward the end of his life. But he did believe that "laws and institutions must go hand in hand with the progress of the human mind. As that becomes more developed, more enlightened, as new discoveries are made, new truths disclosed, and manners and opinions change with the change of circumstances, institutions must advance also, and keep pace with the times." He saw "nothing . . . unchangeable but the inherent and unalienable rights of man." During and after his presidency, Jefferson the man was a living monument to America as a great republic, an eminent and abiding experiment in national democracy.

* * *

Like Jefferson, Andrew Jackson was, in the words of John William Ward, a "symbol for an age." But the early nineteenth century, Ward argues, should not actually be considered "the age of Jackson," for: "Through the age's leading figure were projected the age's leading ideas. Of Andrew Jackson the people made a mirror for themselves. . . . The age was not his. He was the age's."

Nevertheless, it was in his person that the era's hopes and beliefs, and the highest good that Americans sought to achieve, found a magnificent vessel. Even if Jackson did not consciously invent a persona or fashion himself and his program to meet the needs of the time, he understood that his background and natural attributes made him a national icon who could capitalize on his personal appeal to advance economic and political policies he and most Americans judged essential to the country's well-being.

At his death in 1845 one eulogist asked, "What *was* Andrew Jackson, and what did he do, that he should receive such honors while living . . . ? He was the embodiment [*sic*] of the true spirit of the nation in which he lived." His contemporaries saw "in him their own image. . . . The spirit that has burned in their own bosom. . . . Because his countrymen saw their image and spirit in Andrew Jackson, they bestowed their honor and admiration upon him."

What, precisely, were this "image" and "spirit"? As Ward describes them, they were a belief in the power and central influence of Nature, Providence, and Will. Americans like Jackson, dwelling on the raw western frontier, removed from the corrupting influences of European cities, had the strength of character and purity of purpose to triumph over both their environment and nations like Britain that were intent on harming them. Jackson and his countrymen were also the chosen people, fulfilling a lofty calling and favored by Providence in the pursuit of their goals. "Because it was believed that America had a glorious destiny," Ward says, "a mission, which had been ordained by divine providence, the immensity of the task facing the nation and each citizen was bathed in a glorious optimism." Finally, there was the matter of will, which might also be thought of as ambition or purpose. Like so many others of his time, Jackson was enamored of the ideal of the self-made man. "The unchecked development of the individual," Ward summarizes, "was the chief implication of the ideas of nature, providence, and will. It is in this respect that the figure of Andrew Jackson most completely embodies the spirit of his age."

But Jackson was no merely passive conduit through which flowed the temper of the times. Certainly his frontier origins in the Carolinas and Tennessee, along with his military career as an Indian fighter and victor in the 1815 battle with the British at New Orleans, helped to make him a popular hero, and his reputation for plainspoken democracy and vocal opposition to privileged capitalists added to his luster as an American everyman. But his popularity was also a product of his concerted effort to fashion himself as a tribune of the people—a vehicle steadfastly dedicated to the popular will. And that will fixed, of course, on the maintenance and protection of freedom or individual liberty—"America's most prized possession," and the "single most important heritage from the Revolutionary age."

"The essence of Jackson's political leadership of this country," biographer Robert V. Remini has written, was the preservation of freedom. "Everything else—banking, internal improvements, tariffs, even slavery in a strange and peculiar way—was secondary. Individual liberty. That was the basic question."

And Jackson never abandoned that conviction. Throughout his political career, whether running for the House of Representatives, the Senate, or the presidency, he never wavered from his cherished principle that his will and the will of the people must remain one and the same. His election in 1828 was a vote for "the restoration of morality and virtue to civic life, and a reform of those practices that had corrupted officials, expanded government, and endangered freedom. As Remini asserts, "It represented a reaffirmation of the republican doctrines of the Revolution." "I now commend you, fellow-citizens, to the guidance of Almighty God . . ." Jackson declared in his first annual State of the Union message in 1829, "with an earnest supplication that whatever errors it may be my lot to commit in discharging the arduous duties which have devolved on me will find a remedy in the harmony and wisdom of your counsels."

During the most trying moments of his presidency it was this assurance that he was the sole representative of all the people that sustained him. When he vetoed the Bank bill, for example, he came under fierce partisan attack for allegedly having sought despotic power, and no less an opponent than Daniel Webster accused him of annulling the will of the Congress and the courts. The nine presidential vetoes that had occurred prior to 1832 had all been applied against bills the chief executive had seen as violations of the Constitution. But Jackson's Bank veto was aimed at an institution he declared a menace to the country's economic and social life, and as such his action implicitly asserted the unprecedented doctrine of a presidential right to legislative leadership. Jackson claimed for the president, Webster complained, "not the power of approval, but the primary power of originating laws."

Jackson himself did not deny it, for he interpreted this policy not as a presidential abuse of democracy and the Republic but rather as a legitimate advance toward gaining greater freedom. As the one officeholder capable of speaking for all the people, he regarded himself as the party best able to defend their freedoms. "In the difficulties which surround us and the dangers which threaten our institutions," he said in his Bank message, "let us firmly rely on that kind Providence which I am sure watches with peculiar care over the destinies of our Republic, and on the intelligence and wisdom of our countrymen. Through *His* abundant goodness and *their* patriotic devotion our liberty and Union will be preserved."

Like Washington, Jackson also established a powerful connection to his constituents by promoting and manifesting an ideal of self-sacrifice. In Jackson's case, however, it was not inspired by his relinquishing high office, but by the empathy the public had for his physical suffering, which plagued him throughout his time in the White House. Remini records that Jackson "suffered physical pain practically every day of his life from 1821 until his death twenty-four years later." Two bullet wounds, one in his chest and the other in his left arm and shoulder, resulted in a pulmonary abscess, which was followed by lifelong respiratory infections, incessant coughing, and racking pain from osteomyelitis. Bouts of dysentery, malaria, decaying teeth, a worsening condition of rheumatism, periodic hemorrhages from his gunshot wounds, and episodes of headaches drained his physical stamina and made his life a daily struggle to fulfill his professional obligations. Jackson's assumption of the presidency when he was already sixty-five years old and in a debilitating physical condition helped solidify his reputation as a great patriot whose love of country transcended personal needs. He was more than a symbol for an age; his contemporaries saw him as a national hero who would inspire all Americans for all time.

Abraham Lincoln is an example of a president who achieved a legendary stature only after his assassination in 1865 rather than in response to his achievements during his four years in office. In death, Lincoln was far more popular than he was in life, to the point that, as David Donald has expressed it, "the Lincoln cult is almost an American religion." A half-century after his passing, Illinois schoolchildren celebrated the great man's birthday by chanting in unison as they stood facing the state's capitol in Springfield: "A blend of mirth and sadness, smiles and tears; / A quaint knight errant of the pioneers; / A homely hero, born of star and sod; / A Peasant Prince; Masterpiece of God."

In his martyrdom Lincoln was even ascribed the characteristics of Christ. "It is no blasphemy against the Son of God," one minister asserted, "that we declare the fitness of the slaying of the second Father of our Republic on the anniversary of the day on which He was slain. Jesus Christ died for the world, Abraham Lincoln died for his country." Other worshipful portraits of the sixteenth president praised his virtues as a self-made man, a preserver of the Union, and a liberator of the slaves. "This Lincoln," Donald says, "has the outlines of a mythological hero; he is a demigod. Born in obscure circumstances, he rose over hardships, became President, was lawgiver to the Negro people, won a tremendous victory, and was killed at the height of his power. By his death he expiated the sins of his country." As summed up by one early fashioner of the myth, Lincoln was "President, savior of the republic, emancipator of a race, true Christian, true man."

Though the circumstances of his death would contribute greatly to Lincoln's mythic standing, his personal history and qualities of character had already captured the public's imagination and laid the groundwork for the idolatry to come. "The first author of the Lincoln legend and the greatest of the Lincoln dramatists," Richard Hofstadter asserts, "was Lincoln himself." While no one should discount the extent to which Lincoln was held in contempt by some contemporaries, who declared him a "huckster," a "second-rater," the *most dishonest politician that ever disgraced an office in America,* the Lincoln magic, the charisma—which won him the presidency in 1860, helped hold the Union together during four years of unprecedented bloodletting; aided him in winning a second four-year term in 1864; and ultimately made him the most celebrated and beloved man in presidential history—was a compelling feature of his whole political career.

As president, Lincoln was already perceived as a kind of Christ figure who, in one apt description, bore "the torments and moral burdens of a blundering and sinful people, suffers for them, and redeems them with hallowed Christian virtues." Preaching "malice toward none and charity for all" as the postwar plan for healing national wounds, he invoked the compassion of Christ's fundamental teachings, and by so doing lifted himself to a station far above the actions of ordinary presidents, politicians, and citizens.

A central aspect of Lincoln's religious appeal was his seeming capacity to suffer for the entire nation. His very appearance and demeanor gave eloquent expression to the grief the war had inflicted on him and millions of Americans on both sides of the line. Lincoln was notable for an extraordinary brooding detachment, which convinced some contemporaries that he alone was capable of bearing the sorrows of the conflict. His was "a dry, weary, patient pain, that seemed to some like insensibility," Harriet Beecher Stowe said after meeting him in the White House. "I never saw so gloomy and melancholy a face in my life," one friend recalled. ". . . His face would become so despondent, his eyes so full of anguish, that it would hurt to look at him," another said. It was impossible to describe "the strain of intellect and the anguish of soul he endured," his secretary John Nicolay remembered. Lincoln was not "ungainly plain," one supporter asserted, for though "grave was his visage . . . no cloud could dull the radiance from within that made it beautiful."

Those who puzzled over how this man of despair and tears could also be a punster, a ribald storyteller, found an answer in the suggestion that his gift for comedy was a way of curtailing his "ceaseless dole." "Humor was his opiate—a device 'to whistle down sadness,'" one friend believed. Lincoln was "the laughing man of

sorrows," David Donald states. Lincoln himself sav
therapy, saying, "Some of the stories are not so nic
be, but I tell you the truth when I say that a funn
the elements of genuine wit, has the same effect on
suppose a good square drink of whiskey has on an old toper; it
puts new life into me."

Lincoln indeed needed his sense of humor, as for him the presidency was scarcely less than a chamber of horrors. There were
thirty-one rooms in the White House, his biographer Carl
Sandburg observed, and Lincoln never felt at home in any of them.
Told to rest by a friend, Lincoln replied: "I suppose it is good for
the body. But the tired part of me is inside and out of reach." The
office he had worked so hard to attain became a place of "ashes
and blood." "I don't know what the soul is," Lincoln confessed,
"but whatever it is, I know that it can humble itself." "The great
prose of the presidential years," Hofstadter believes, "came from
a soul that had been humbled. Lincoln's utter lack of personal
malice during these years, his humane detachment, his tragic sense
of life, have no parallel in political history."

But more than suffering tied Lincoln so powerfully to his contemporaries, for as with Jackson, he was distinguished by his ambition, by his up-by-the bootstraps career, which made him the
quintessential self-made man. Fully aware how appealing this side
of him was to the American people, Lincoln never failed to remind
them of his humble origins, giving expression to his modesty in
public and private. As a superb politician, he recognized that his
greatest personal asset was not his identification with any particular
policy—"My policy," he liked to say, "is to have no policy"—but
the drama of his life story, the rise of a common man to the country's highest political position. As such, it was the fulfillment of the
American dream, a saga that promised that native intelligence and
unquenchable ambition could bring the reward to which every na-
tive-born, white American male in the mid-nineteenth century believed himself entitled.

II

The first of our twentieth-century presidents to achieve the degree of heroic status enjoyed by the four great nineteenth-century chiefs was Theodore Roosevelt. His public allure, however, differed from that of his predecessors by being less an expression of mythic principles, sacrifice, or tragedy than of popular fascination with a charismatic personality who reignited national hopes for a unified America that would share common goals at home and effectively asserting national ideals abroad.

Roosevelt was our first modern media president who used his talents as an early public relations expert to fashion himself into one of the most popular leaders in U.S. history. At a time when rapid industrialization had created concentrated wealth and poverty, and massive immigration from southern and eastern Europe had opened up divisions along ethnic and religious lines, the country yearned for the restoration of a more harmonious nation in which traditional verities about equal opportunity and honest dealings prevailed. Above all, it craved a national leader who could transcend current domestic conflicts by reaffirming the supremacy of old-fashioned American values.

In that respect, TR proved to be the right man in the right place at the right time. He was a great American activist, a doer who preached "the strenuous life" and was the very incarnation of American capability—surmounting every obstacle, winning every battle, conquering every challenge in the fight to advance personal and national fortunes. The president, one commentator quipped, wanted to be the preacher, bride, and bridegroom at the wedding. TR once described every man's mission in life as to "work, fight, and breed." "I cannot say that I entered the presidency with any deliberately planned and far-reaching scheme of social betterment," TR declared in 1913, but he did have "strong convictions" about how to make "the government the most efficient possible instrument in helping the people of the United States to better themselves in every way, politically, socially, and industrially." "After McKinley's grey respectability," the historian Lewis L. Gould comments, "Roosevelt seemed a roman candle of exuberance and fun. Becoming the president in the first year of a new century also helped Roosevelt convey a symbolic sense of change and vitality."

When he ran for election to a full term in 1904, Gould continued, the presidential race became less a contest between two political parties than a personal referendum on Roosevelt himself. TR was our first celebrity president whose daily comings and goings, as well as those of his wife and six children, became the stuff of ongoing popular discussion. Even after he left the White House in 1909, Roosevelt's decision to make a hunting trip to Africa, where he thought he might kill some rhino, buffalo, and antelopes, and possibly get a shot at a lion, caught the public's imagination in ways that a predictable round-the-world tour of foreign capitals couldn't have. While the personalities of the men running for and serving in the presidency had always been instrumental in shaping American politics, TR gave a new meaning to the term "personal influence" as a description of how presidents could use the office to advance a political agenda and alter the direction of national affairs.

Roosevelt made his mark on the White House not simply by turning himself into a celebrity whom millions of Americans admired, but by identifying himself with a progressive and romantic nationalism that promised to bind the country together and make it a force for law and order on the world scene. During the national coal strike of 1902, for example, he took center stage by summoning union leaders and mine owners to the White House, where for the first time a president used his influence to obtain a negotiated settlement in a labor dispute. His intercession gave rise to the depiction of his administration as a Square Deal, a federal government devoted to putting the general or national interest above the special interests of capital or labor. During the 1904 campaign, after he refused to accept a $100,000 contribution from the Standard Oil Company, he announced that he would remain "unhampered by any pledge" and guaranteed that "every man has a square deal, no less and no more."

During the final two years of his term, TR became even more convinced that the federal government, and the executive in particular, had to assume the role of national arbiter of disputes between the country's various factions. Without such intervention, he believed, the country might well tear itself apart. His New Nationalism, as his reform stance of 1910–1912 became known, reflected both his understanding of what the country wanted and his conviction that it would increase his popularity and return him to the White House in 1913. Though mere personal appeal could not overcome the obstacles to an independent candidacy in 1912, TR did have the satisfaction of easily surpassing Taft in the popular and electoral votes and of seeing Woodrow Wilson embrace much of TR's own program in his 1916 reelection campaign.

But there was a limit to the political value of TR's personal appeal. Unlike Washington and Lincoln, he had no clearly delineated crisis with which to deal—no fundamental testing of domestic cohesion, and no war against which to preserve the nation. To be sure, national discontent was considerable. Had opinion polls asked, as they now do, whether people thought the country was on the right track, it seems safe to assume that a majority would have said no. But a dispirited public is not the equivalent of a nation that is faltering or jeopardized. While effective, there was so strong a quality of boosterism to Roosevelt's leadership that it could not outlast his time in office. Indeed, the national divisions between conservatives and progressives provoked by Taft undermined TR's credibility as a great unifier, transforming the presidency into a force for cohesion. Not only was Taft Roosevelt's handpicked successor, but TR's decision to oppose him in 1912 and make the election a three-way race also helped repudiate his personal standing as a great political reconciler.

Although the limits of TR's charisma were acknowledged in the biographies and historical studies produced in the three decades following his death in 1919, he has since then made an unquestionable comeback as the first modern president to have "wove the office into the fabric of daily life." While he guaranteed his popularity by asking "some of the right questions about conservation, the control of corporations, the welfare of the average American," the nature of a just society, and the obligations of world power, his presidency also demonstrated that rhetorical bombast can engage public attention for a time but can never truly substitute for the sort of binding ties that grow between public and president when long-term national security and stability are at stake.

Franklin Roosevelt was his cousin Theodore's most attentive student, but one who ultimately eclipsed not only his teacher but all his twentieth-century predecessors and successors in the White House. No modern president has wielded his personal influence more effectively than FDR. Two great crises, the Depression and the Second World War, gave him exceptional opportunities to impress himself on the country, to the point that people born in the late 1920s and early 1930s could not imagine anyone else as president. Twelve years of dynamic leadership during which the nation witnessed the rise of the welfare state, the greatest foreign war in U.S. history, and the collapse of traditional isolationism gave Roosevelt unsurpassed national and international visibility. Partly driven by his charm, ebullience, and natural self-confidence, he established an unmistakable hold on people everywhere. His actions and programs, which led to unprecedented transformations in American life, gained some measure of their credibility from the broad-shouldered, smiling, buoyant optimist with the up-tilted head offering reassurance that the nation would endure and prosper. Few misunderstood what commentators meant when they said that FDR's concept of the presidency was Franklin Roosevelt as president.

Initially, many doubted Roosevelt's abilities as a chief executive in such demanding times. Walter Lippmann spoke for the skeptics when he observed that Roosevelt was "a pleasant man who, without any important qualifications for the office, would very much like to be President." But even before he worked his personal magic from the Oval Office, Roosevelt had established an unspoken personal rapport with the electorate that would serve him brilliantly throughout his presidency. His paralysis, which immobilized him from the waist down and confined him to a wheelchair, or compelled him to wear steel braces or walk with metal crutches, was a fortuitous link to the public in a time of national suffering. Though photographers respected the president's privacy by not focusing on his disability, and Roosevelt himself did everything in his power to divert attention from his physical limitations, including cheerfully telling visitors he ushered out of his office, "Well, I'm sorry, I have to run now," his infirmity had great symbolic force. Afflicted by a crippling Depression, Americans took psychological hope from a president who, after losing the use of his legs, had surmounted his handicap to become governor of New York and president of the United States.

Roosevelt's bonds to the country were further strengthened by his expertise in the art of communication. Well before Ronald Reagan, FDR was notable for his abilities as a "great communicator." His most effective device for reaching the populace was the radio, particularly the Fireside Chats, which brought him into millions of homes, and during which he "used to talk to me about my government," as one man later told Eleanor Roosevelt. "He talked like a father discussing public affairs with his family in the living room," William Leuchtenburg agrees. "As he spoke, he seemed unconscious of the fact that he was addressing millions." His secretary of labor, Frances Perkins, described how "his head would nod and his hands would move in simple, natural, comfortable gestures. His face would smile and light up as though he were actually on the front porch or in the parlor with them."

His prowess at press conferences was equally remarkable. He instituted twice-a-week meetings with reporters whom he called by their first names and with whom he joked. These appearances were like exercises in well-crafted theater. He would strike dramatic poses and play to his audience with wit, charm, sarcasm, amazement, curiosity, and mock alarm. Though he might begin with a coy announcement that there was no "particular news," as James MacGregor Burns describes, reporters could always tell "from his airs—the uptilted cigarette holder, rolled eyes, puffing cheeks, bantering tone—that something was up." By the time he finished, the journalists knew they had a front-page story, a tactic that allowed FDR to get himself and his programs before the public while at the same time countering the hostile editorials conservative publishers used to attack him.

In the midst of the Depression and the global contest between democratic and totalitarian societies, Roosevelt's optimism and confidence were national tonics. From his First Inaugural Address, when he had warned against fear as the only thing the American people had to fear and called for prompt and unwavering action, to his final, draft speech of a Jefferson day address, where he described "the only limit to our realization of tomorrow" as "our doubts of today," and urged the country to "move forward with strong and active faith," he was a dispenser of hope and courage in uncommonly troubled times.

His buoyant personality often combined with his intuitive feel for how to encourage positive thinking. Churchill said that meeting FDR for the first time was like opening a bottle of champagne. In his first Fireside Chat, the president eased a national crisis by declaring a "bank holiday." Avoiding an emphasis on the country's troubles or a focus on its failings he instead offered a time for relaxation from public woes and economic ills. His rhetoric worked an immediate change in national mood that ended the panicky run on banks. Through his words and self-assurance in his powers as a leader, Leuchtenburg says, Roosevelt "made his greatest single contribution to the politics of the 1930s: the instillation of hope and courage in the people. He made clear that the time of waiting was over, that he had the people's interests at heart, and that he would mobilize the power of the government to help them."

Roosevelt also used his gifts to give the country a renewed sense of shared national purpose. In the 1920s, regional, ethnic, religious, and racial tensions were dividing the country. The reappearance of a Ku Klux Klan preaching anti-Catholic, antiblack, anti-Semitic, and antimodern sermons; the famous Scopes "monkey" trial in Tennessee pitting rural America against the rising influence of newer, urban, forward-looking citizens; and the passage of a National Origins Act favoring "old-stock" immigration were all symptoms of cultural strains that, if unchecked, threatened civil strife.

Roosevelt, the upstate New York, Protestant patrician, made diversity a central aim of his presidency. He tied himself to the country's urban political machines and brought ethnics of every kind into his administration. At the same time, he identified himself with traditional small-town Americans, especially in the South. In so doing, he created a farmer-labor, rural-urban coalition of north-south, east-west citizens that guaranteed his hold on the presidency and, more importantly, gave the country a fresh sense of its common values and purposes.

Roosevelt's public standing did, of course, have its share of ups and downs during his twelve-year term. In the late 1930s, the Court-packing fight, a severe economic downturn, and a bitter series of election battles in 1938 shook his hold on the country. FDR himself slyly recalled F. P. Dunne's comic character Mr. Dooley's observation that people build triumphal arches out of brick so that they would have something handy to throw at their heroes when they passed by.

Yet even in the face of such adversities Roosevelt's average approval ratings during his third and fourth terms was an astonishing 75 percent. If many in the country had doubts about his policies, his operating methods, and his advisers, they almost uniformly loved the man. For example, in the spring of 1938, a politically troubled period for his administration, Roosevelt's personal standing with Americans remained impressively high. Eight out of ten people across the country said they liked Roosevelt personally; only one out of ten disliked him. Minority and labor affection for a president seen as their advocate was no surprise. But "most remarkable of all," Burns explains, "not a single occupation group— not executives, nor professional people, nor proprietors—'voted' for the presidential personality by less than three-quarters of that group." People referred to Roosevelt as "our president," the man in the White House who was on their side, working for them.

In 1990, after ten years of conservative Reagan-Bush dialogues about the imperfections of federal authority and the need to reduce government programs dating from the 1930s, FDR's approval rating remained at 75 percent. Whatever the shortcomings of his New Deal policies and wartime diplomacy, the country continues to judge Franklin Roosevelt as among the greatest of its presidents.

The first of Roosevelt's successors to sustain the power of his personal public appeal through an entire presidential term was Dwight Eisenhower. Although Harry Truman had his winning moments with the public, especially in 1948, and in recent years his reputation has profited from comparisons with most of his successors, his personality was often too abrasive, a bit too forthright, for millions of Americans who wanted more harmony and less of the domestic controversy and international conflict that Truman regularly gave them.

The paternal, largely nonpartisan "Ike," who was neither decidedly Republican nor Democrat, neither self-righteously conservative nor liberal, appealed to the country as a moderate, sensible patriot more concerned to serve the national interest as a whole than to cater to any of its constituent groups. Exhausted by the partisanship of the previous twenty years, and especially by the furor over the internal Communist threat engineered by Joseph McCarthy, the public welcomed an unobjectionable leader with a talent for smoothing over differences and bringing people together. One of Eisenhower's principal attributes as a candidate in 1952 and later as president was his proven ability to stand above the fray and disarm antagonisms. His reputation as a World War II general partly rested on his facility in mediating differences between Allied military chiefs as well as between Roosevelt, Churchill, and Charles de Gaulle. His status as a man who was more a military hero than a politician with strong party affiliations made him attractive to a country that had had its fill of domestic strife.

As president, he took pains to mute "the excesses of political rhetoric and partisanship. He managed to achieve that goal," biographer Stephen Ambrose explains, "by not dismantling the New Deal, as the more conservative Republicans wanted to do. Under Eisenhower, the number of people covered by Social Security doubled as benefits went up. The New Deal's regulatory commissions stayed in place. Expenditures for public works were greater than they had been under FDR or Truman. . . . Eisenhower, in effect, put a Republican stamp of approval on twenty years of Democratic legislation, by itself a major step toward bringing the two parties closer together."

Eisenhower's appeal, like FDR's, also derived from a genial personality and unaffected naturalness. An infectious smile, a steady optimism about the country's future, and an easygoing likableness made Ike one of the most popular presidents in American history. With a 65 percent average approval rating during his eight years in office (which has increased in recent years to 70 percent), he stands second only to FDR among long-term-serving presidents in this century.

Decency and integrity were other essential ingredients of Ike's charisma, and particularly appealing was his life's work as a soldier who hated war. He often quoted Robert E. Lee's observation: "It is well that war is so terrible; if it were not so, we would grow too fond of it."

When some of his advisers urged him to strike the Soviet Union with nuclear weapons and destroy it before the Soviets could match our military strength, he responded by encouraging a decent regard for international opinion. "I want you to carry this question home with you," he told the Joint Chiefs. "Gain such a victory, and what do you do with it? Here would be a great area from Elbe to Vladivostok . . . torn up and destroyed, without government, without its communications, just an area of starvation and disaster. I ask you what would the civilized world do about it? I repeat, there is no victory except through our imaginations." Similarly, he refused to order a nuclear strike to rescue the French at Dien Bien Phu. "You boys must be crazy," he told the National Security Council, which was pressuring him on this measure. "We can't use those awful things against Asians for the second time in less than ten years. My God."

His integrity was a strong factor in his coming to despise McCarthy, whose abusive attacks on honorable citizens he considered a disgrace that he was eager to end. Some advisers urged him to confront the Wisconsin senator directly, especially after McCarthy had attacked General George Marshall as a traitor, but he dismissed such a showdown as a poor tactic: a president going after a senator would do more to enhance than weaken the man's influence. Instead, he waited patiently until McCarthy overreached himself. When the senator tried to force administration officials to testify in the Army-McCarthy hearings, Eisenhower declared it an invasion of executive prerogative, a violation of presidential privilege that would undermine the effectiveness of the office. It was a forceful defense of the executive against congressional authority, which people across the country applauded.

Likewise, when Governor Orval Faubus of Arkansas defied the Constitution by refusing to follow federal court directives on integrating Little Rock schools, Eisenhower sent troops there to enforce the orders. Ambrose calls the decision to dispatch troops to Little Rock "the great moral and character test of the Eisenhower presidency. . . . It was a brilliant stroke and the action of a man of principle. It settled forever the question of whether the federal government would use force to break down segregation."

Surprisingly, Ike was an opponent of the Supreme Court's 1954 *Brown* v. *Board of Education* ruling on desegregation of schools. He himself was a segregationist, privately siding with southern whites in their outrage at the Court's attack on their traditional mores. But the law was the law, and his sense of propriety compelled him to stand behind the Court's decision. "There must be respect for the Constitution—which means the Supreme Court's interpretation of the Constitution—or we shall have chaos," he wrote a friend. "We cannot possibly imagine a successful form of government in which every individual would have the right to interpret the Constitution according to his own convictions, beliefs, and prejudices. Chaos would develop. This I believe with all my heart—and shall always act accordingly."

Since Eisenhower, the two most attractive presidential personalities have been John F. Kennedy and Ronald Reagan. Both men had an almost mystical hold on the country, less as a result of what they accomplished in public affairs before and during their White House terms than because of their personal styles. To be sure, Kennedy's effectiveness in the Cuban missile crisis and the nuclear test ban negotiations made him a respected foreign policy leader, and Reagan's tax cuts and breakthrough in arms-limitation talks with the Soviets substantiated his claim to have altered domestic and international affairs. But unlike FDR and Eisenhower, whose successes in office justified their claims to popular regard, JFK and Reagan ultimately had less substantial achievements to recommend them to the electorate.

Nevertheless, they closely rivaled and continue to rival their two esteemed party predecessors in public appeal. Kennedy came to office as a kind of fabled prince, a handsome, rich, intelligent, and intrepid character whose storybook life engaged Americans across class, regional, ethnic, racial, and gender lines. His charm, wit, courage, boldness, and family advantages excited national admiration and, if the polls are to be believed, made him the most popular president since FDR. The average approval rating of 71 percent he received during his thousand days in office has since been dwarfed by the 84 percent of the polling sample who have nothing but praise for his presidential performance. Obviously, his assassination at the age of forty-six, cutting short the promise of the New Frontier, as he described the vision of his administration, made him into a martyr and boosted his public standing. But Kennedy's grip on the public largely rested on the evident excellence of his character and his genuine regard for national traditions of freedom, opportunity, and public service or civic duty, virtues that were reflected in his presidency. While programs like the Alliance for Progress in Latin America and the Peace Corps in Third World countries, for example, may have had more rhetorical than substantive significance in international affairs, they were symbolically powerful expressions of American ideals and helped identify JFK with the best of the country's customs.

Even more than Kennedy, Ronald Reagan was a kind of national monument to many of the ingredients that had gone into creating the American character. A blend of Catholic and Protestant, small-town boy and famous entertainer, Horatio Alger and P. T. Barnum, traditional moralist and modern media celebrity, Reagan declaimed old values in current terms. His career as an up-by-the-bootstraps sportscaster and movie and television celebrity who had been divorced, had problems with his children, and only occasionally went to church, despite authentic religious beliefs, made him an entirely understandable and familiar character with whom most Americans could feel comfortable. His oft-stated attachments to an earlier, idealized America of hard work, small towns, family, church-going, and star-spangled, Fourth-of-July patriotic oratory recommended him all the more to an America that viewed him as a representative figure or recognizable contradiction in terms—a hero of the consumer culture preaching the Protestant ethic.

But, as they had to JFK, the country granted Reagan its good will largely in response to charismatic elements in the man's makeup. Humor, charm, good looks, an intuitive feel for public concerns, and an extraordinary ability to speak persuasively to millions of people were principal elements of Reagan's popularity as president. Moreover, like Washington and Eisenhower, he was widely perceived as a reluctant president, a citizen politician more concerned for the good of the country than ambitious for himself or his political party. To many, he is our modern Cincinnatus who left the beauty and comforts of his Santa Barbara ranch for the travails of the presidency. His speechwriter Peggy Noonan expressed this sentiment when she said, "There were things bigger than *staying* in office for Reagan. He didn't need power, which contributed to his power with the people—they could tell he didn't need it, and so felt free to give it to him." The recent revelation that he is suffering from Alzheimer's disease, which had begun taking a toll on him years earlier, only reinforces this image of him as a selfless patriot who habitually put the country's needs ahead of his own.

As president, he generated a surge of popular exuberance rarely seen during the last thirty years. His response to being wounded in a March 1981 assassination attempt made a powerful impression on millions of Americans. Shrugging off the attack, he quoted Churchill's observation that there was nothing so exhilarating as to be shot at without effect. "Honey, I forgot to duck," he told his wife. "I just hope you're Republicans," he joked with doctors as they wheeled him to an operating room. "Today, Mr. President, we're all Republicans," one doctor replied, speaking for the entire country. In 1984, in the midst of excitement over U.S. success in the Olympic games staged in Los Angeles, national television ads proudly proclaimed "the pride is back" and boasted that products were "Made in the U.S.A."

There can be no doubt that expanding national economies under each of their presidencies, as well as limited loss of American lives in overseas conflicts, contributed greatly to Kennedy and Reagan mystiques. But like all their great popular predecessors from Washington forward, JFK and Reagan profited most from the quality of their own characters, which was finally the most effective means of recommending them to their compatriots.

III

For better or worse, presidents who were not blessed with personal magic far outnumber the nine men described above. The majority of these less attractive chiefs were too rigid or unimaginative or aloof or insensitive to human yearnings to be emotionally engaging political leaders who won significant popular regard. They were generally too unsure of themselves and devoid of that special quality that earns the confidence of the people, who will always be more responsive to a president who seems willing to bear their burdens and answer their wishes for a better future. While it is tempting to contemplate how most of our elected one-term presidents—the two Adamses, Van Buren, Pierce, Buchanan, Hayes, Benjamin Harrison, Taft, Hoover, Carter, and Bush—won in the first place, this is more accurately a separate consideration, one suggesting that an effective national campaign does not necessarily translate into a successful presidential term. Of course, nine of our presidents—William H. Harrison, Tyler, Taylor, Fillmore, Andrew Johnson, Garfield, Arthur, Harding, and Ford—either died before they could complete a single term or served less than four years after succeeding to the office through the death or resignation of a predecessor. None of these nine, however, received high marks for their abilities during these abbreviated presidencies, and certainly not for achieving any significant degree of popularity with voters.

Presidents whose reputations reached impressive highs and fell to crippling lows during their White House years are far more interesting to chart than the men who largely stumbled through unsuccessful terms. Four in particular—Grant, Truman, Lyndon Johnson, and Nixon—deserve a closer examination.

Ulysses S. Grant was, for a time, the most successful of the country's post–Civil War presidents until TR. In the tradition of Jackson and Lincoln, Grant was a self-made man who had overcome great personal adversity—alcoholism, and failed careers in business and the pre–Civil War military—on the path to triumph and fame as a Union general. Winning victories at Vicksburg, Mississippi, and Chattanooga, Tennessee, in 1863, and against Robert E. Lee's Army of Northern Virginia in 1864–1865, Grant was rewarded with appointments as lieutenant general and supreme commander of the Union armies. He emerged from the war as the country's preeminent military hero and patriot.

During Andrew Johnson's unhappy time in office, Grant, as head of the army, steered a neutral course between Johnson and the Radical Republicans. As dissatisfaction with Johnson mounted, Grant's stock as a potential successor increased. One wartime staff associate, who spoke confidently about the people's "temper," described Grant's public image in 1866 as that of "a latter-day George Washington: 'He is the country's best hope in Peace, as he has been in War!' " By that time, Grant biographer William S. McFeely says, "Everyone in Washington talked of the general as the next President." During a floor debate in the House that had first considered raising Grant's rank to general, Pennsylvania radical Thaddeus Stevens declared his readiness to advance "this Marlborough, this Wellington," to "a higher office whenever the happy moment shall arrive." "It looks to me as if General Grant was to be the rising man," Associate Supreme Court Justice David Davis said. "The people love military glory and renown and love to honor it."

In a time of continuing national strife, after the worst bloodletting in American history, Grant seemed to promise a period of tranquility and a return to shared national purpose. In May 1868, when two delegations of veterans brought him news of his nomination for president, he replied: "I shall have no policy of my own to interfere against the will of the people." McFeely adds: "He had almost said that he would have no policy at all; almost too well he had suggested that he offered the nation a clean slate." In a written statement of acceptance, he included his well-known slogan, "Let us have peace," reflecting the country's perceived need for a recovery from the ordeal of civil war and now its first presidential impeachment and trial.

Grant's 1868 presidential campaign was notably devoid of content. On questions of enfranchisement for blacks, which agitated voters in the North as well as the South, and monetary policy, which divided conservative creditors and liberal debtors, Grant adopted a studied silence. "There was, in fact, no issue he cared about deeply," McFeely remarks, "no cause in the furtherance of which he sought the presidency. He did not introduce into the campaign any issue of personal concern to him." Though one Radical complained, "It is a bad sign when we take men instead of principles," Grant's passive approach worked perfectly with an electorate eager for quieter times and leadership by a president they admired and trusted and considered the embodiment of victory and virtue. Spending the campaign at his home in Galena, Illinois, from which he wrote a supporter, "A person would not know there was a stirring canvas going on if it were not for the accounts we read in the papers," Grant won a solid 53 percent of the popular vote, making him one of only two presidents (along with McKinley) in the eight elections of the late nineteenth century to reach the White House with popular majorities.

Domestic debates over tariffs, civil service reform, corruption, the annexation of the Dominican Republic, and the resolution of tensions with Great Britain over claims arising from damages caused by the British-built Confederate frigate *Alabama* marked

Grant's first term. Massachusetts Senator Charles Sumner, who wanted the Dominican Republic as the center of a black West Indian confederation, effectively defied and humiliated Grant in his fight for annexation. The Crédit Mobilier scandal of 1872 also undermined the president by revealing the role of Vice President Schuyler Colfax. A construction firm controlled by the directors of the Union Pacific Railroad, who enriched themselves at the expense of both companies, the Mobilier tried to fend off public investigation by giving Colfax and other politicians corporate shares paid for by later dividend earnings.

Yet neither episode, when balanced against Grant's ability to find compromise solutions to other problems and to promote national unity through both symbolic and more tangible expressions of patriotism, inflicted much damage on his public standing. Indeed, in the 1872 election, despite opposition from Liberal Republicans as well as Democrats, Grant won reelection by a decisive 55 percent of the vote. Distancing himself from any hint of personal corruption and depicting his opponents as elitists indifferent to the concerns of farmers and ordinary workingmen, Grant strengthened his power over the populace, receiving the largest majority votes in any presidential election between 1836 and 1892. "I was the worst beaten man that ever ran for that high office," his Democratic opponent Horace Greeley complained. The fervor of support for Grant and opposition to Greeley moved him to remark that he had been "assailed so bitterly that I hardly know whether I was running for president or the penitentiary." He went out of his mind and died a few weeks after the election. Grant himself saw the election as a vindication of "his private character, which had been assailed during the campaign."

Yet inevitably Grant's high standing fell victim to his personal limitations and changes in national circumstance. His second term sullied his reputation for honest dealings as a result of a series of scandals involving leading members of his administration, but more permanently damaging was the longest economic depression in U.S. history, which undermined his popularity and ultimately led to his being one of the least well-thought-of presidents in American history. Scandals in the Navy, Treasury, and War departments involved Grant appointees who received payoffs respectively from shipbuilding companies for lucrative contracts, importers for favorable treatment by customs officers, and merchants chosen to sell goods to Indians and soldiers at frontier posts. The extent of the corruption suggested that Grant was a man of lax standards all too ready to accommodate himself to subordinates who had no moral compass.

But the most severely compromising scandal—that involving the Whiskey Ring—was yet to come. Grant's personal secretary Orville E. Babcock was accused of helping a number of whiskey distillers avoid excise taxes and of receiving gifts and favors in return. Though Grant met news of the affair with the admonition, "Let no guilty man escape," he subsequently did all he could to protect his associates from investigation and prosecution. He gave a deposition on behalf of Babcock, which attorneys used successfully to defend his integrity at a trial. Babcock's acquittal received Grant's approval, and his continuation in the administration was assured.

Even more critical than the misdeeds of his staff in shattering Grant's heroic image was his passivity toward the suffering caused by the Panic of 1873 and subsequent depression. The collapse, which lasted six years, reduced daily wages of city workers by 25 percent. With no government support programs available to help the unemployed, more than a million workers subsisted on meager handouts from private charities. "It would be anachronistic to expect Ulysses Grant to have become the spiritual cheerleader that Franklin Roosevelt made of himself in a similar period sixty years later," McFeely observes. "Still, it is curious that Grant could not stretch his imagination" to fight for better conditions for farmers and workingmen. But Grant was paralyzed by his inability to free himself from the need for deference from America's "better" people, which he had won by cautious conservative monetary and economic policies. The depression revealed him to be not a man of the people, but a social climber who lacked the courage to risk his political ties to wealthy Americans by becoming an advocate for those who most needed his help. Grant's second term largely put an end to his authority as a leader by showing him to be all too human—a man of limited talents governed more by self-serving concerns than greater national needs.

*   *   *

Harry S. Truman's personal appeal to the country ran a very different course in the periods during and after his presidency. Succeeding FDR in the White House put Truman at an immediate disadvantage, for in 1945 no American political leader could eclipse, let alone equal, the standing of the longest-serving president in U.S. history. In addition, Truman had always been seen as a relatively minor figure, and what was known about him did little to encourage public confidence that he would heroically rise to the situation. Although he had served courageously in World War I and had gained considerable notoriety from his Senate committee's wartime investigation of the national defense program, nothing in his background generated much conviction that he had the makings of a great president.

FDR's selection of him as vice president over Henry Wallace on the left and Jimmy Byrnes on the right had earned Truman the label "the second Missouri compromise," while his physical stature at five foot nine, alongside FDR and generals like George Marshall and Dwight Eisenhower, made him "the little man from Missouri." He wasn't an exceptional orator; he had no significant social connections comparable to those of TR, FDR, or JFK later. "He is the only president of our century who never went to College," David McCullough says, "and along with his clipped Missouri twang and eyeglasses thick as the bottom of a Coke bottle, he had that very middlewestern plainness of manner that, at first glance, made him seem 'ordinary.' "

After enjoying a honeymoon period of sympathy for a fledgling president unexpectedly burdened with difficult postwar dilemmas, Truman suffered a steady eclipse. Where 87 percent of Americans had approved of his performance in the summer of 1945 and 82 percent echoed that sentiment in October, his approval rating slipped to 63 percent by January 1946 and tumbled to 43 percent by June. By September the number was down to 32 percent and in November, after the Republicans gained control of Congress for the first time since 1928, 79 percent of Americans expected the Republicans to win the White House in 1948. In February 1947 the public listed Truman in fourth place behind Douglas MacArthur, Eisenhower, and Churchill as the men they most admired. Over sixteen months later, in June 1948, his approval rating still stood at only 39 percent. Straw polls during the year indicated that he had little chance of winning election to the White House in his own right. In the month before the vote, New York Governor Thomas Dewey held a five-point lead over Truman, and two out of three Americans predicted that Dewey would be the next president. The watchword on HST's White House tenure had become "To err is Truman."

But, paradoxically, faced with this adversity, Truman was freed to be himself, to act on his own instincts without regard for comparisons to FDR or the pressure to pander to public sentiment. "I'm doing as I damn please for the next two years and to hell with all of them," he told his wife after the 1946 congressional defeat. "I wonder how far Moses would have gone, if he had taken a poll in Egypt," he also commented. When people were asked what they liked best about Truman, they responded, "His honesty, sincerity, and friendliness." They also liked "the fact that he is doing the best he can under present circumstances."

He was at his most effective with the public when he was simply the straightforward Harry Truman, whether leveling with the country and the Russians or using his common sense to guide him through extraordinary undertakings like the Truman Doctrine, the Marshall Plan, the Berlin Airlift, the recognition of Israel, and enforcing civil rights for blacks. Firing General Douglas MacArthur, the most unpopular decision of his presidency, "wasn't difficult for me at all," he admitted later: it was a simple matter of obeying the constitutional requirement of civilian control over the military.

Despite the polls' prediction of his failure, the 1948 campaign marked the high point of his romance with the nation. Running as an underdog against powerful, selfish interests and a humorless opponent, Truman transformed himself into a kind of folk hero who carried off the greatest upset in American presidential history. Using the back platform of a train for a whistle-stop campaign, he lambasted the Eightieth Congress as indifferent to the people's interests. "You're a bunch of damn fools and ingrates if you vote Republican," he told voters, as he reminded them of all that Roosevelt and the New Deal Democrats had done for them in the previous sixteen years. When audiences urged the president, "Give 'em hell, Harry," he promised to defend the country's national and international well-being by offering a Truman Fair Deal and a continuing commitment to contain the Communist threat. He also took advantage of Tom Dewey's detached style, which made him appear, as Truman gibed, like "the little man on the wedding cake." When the final tally was counted, the uncharismatic, predictable Tom Dewey won 2 million fewer popular votes than HST and only 189 electoral ballots to Truman's 303.

But Truman's newfound popularity was short-lived, the casualty of Korea and corruption. Initially, the decision to enter the Korean war in June 1950 was warmly supported by the mass of Americans. Once again, Harry Truman impressed people as an independent-minded leader who had made a tough decision without regard for his public standing. Ignoring politics and what people might say about his judgment, Truman judged the defense of South Korea from Communist aggression as essential to the national well-being. But public approval for the Korean war turned to frustration and antagonism when Truman agreed to cross the 38th parallel. Committing the country to topple North Korea's Communist regime and unify the peninsula under a pro-Western government turned out to be a serious blunder, which resulted in a larger war with China, threatened to become a nuclear conflict with Moscow, and alienated Americans unwilling to accept thousands of additional casualties in a limited war.

Korea now became known as "Harry Truman's war," and the tough-mindedness that had impressed his supporters earlier was reexamined and judged to be stubbornness and wrongheadedness. The president had plunged the nation into a conflict he wasn't prepared to win, and both his disinclination to support Mac-Arthur's proposed plan of victory and his own inability to end the fighting once again made him an unpopular leader without national backing. A series of scandals, real and imagined, further damaged his standing and left him with only a 31 percent approval rating as he retired from office. Of course, although Truman would have been the first to complain about measuring his presidential merit by the results of opinion polls, he was well aware that popular approval and disapproval had a significant impact on his ability to govern effectively. The Fair Deal proposals of his second term failed enactment when he lost his hold on the Congress and the country, and he found himself trapped in an unwinnable war when his capacity to stiffen the national resolve to sustain an expanded conflict in Korea all but disappeared.

But history has been kind to Truman's reputation, and the 31 percent at the close of his term and the average 41 percent during his nearly eight years in office had grown to a 68 percent approval rating by 1990; after David McCullough's critically acclaimed and widely read biography appeared in 1992, Truman's standing rose probably higher than ever.

His public esteem today seems to rest more on memories and feelings about the man than admiration for any particular set of policies he backed. With hindsight, containment and the Korean fighting can be judged as wise actions that contributed vitally to American victory in the Cold War. Truman's stand on civil rights and his support for national health insurance can likewise be considered prescient. But it is really Truman himself—the jaunty, smiling, irascible, courageous character—who has become a standing example of principled effectiveness in the White House. Harry Truman is no George Washington or Abraham Lincoln or Franklin Roosevelt; he is not thought of as a president who rescued the country from a dire crisis. His leadership in the early Cold War is remembered as essential to the national security, but it is not equated with the greatest challenges in our history. Harry Truman is a different sort of hero: an extraordinary ordinary man who demonstrated that an American from the heartland, with good values and a thick skin, could lead the nation along the right track.

Where Harry Truman's personal appeal largely derived from his plain-spoken, aboveboard manner, Lyndon Johnson's rested on his mastery of Washington politics and compassion for the needs of middle-class and poor Americans. Johnson is held in such little regard now that it is difficult to remember that he commanded large majorities during his first two years after JFK's death and had overall approval ratings of 56 percent during his five-plus years in the White House, bettering six of the nine other post-1945 presidents in that respect.

Johnson was as complicated a man as ever to have served in the presidency. He was Winston Churchill's puzzle inside a riddle wrapped in an enigma. He was, in the words of one associate, an octagonal figure, and in the judgment of another, a man who left you with "the most baffled wonderment." Johnson was an example of what the Japanese call the contradiction of opposites. Driven, tyrannical, crude, insensitive, humorless, and petty, he was also empathic, shy, sophisticated, self-critical, uproariously funny, and magnanimous.

New York Times columnist Russell Baker remembers Johnson as "a human puzzle so complicated no one could ever understand it. . . . Johnson was a flesh-and-blood, three-volume biography, and if you ever got it written you'd discover after publication that you missed the key point or got the interpretation completely wrong and needed a fourth volume to set things right." Johnson, Baker concluded, "was a character out of a Russian novel, one of those human complications that filled the imagination of Dostoyevsky, a storm of warring human instincts: sinner and saint, buffoon and statesman, cynic and sentimentalist, a man torn between hungers for immortality and self-destruction."

In time, Johnson's contradictions would destroy his public standing and capacity to lead and govern. But initially his grandiosity and insatiable appetites served him brilliantly in the White House. He was possibly the most grandiose man ever to serve as president. "I understand you were born in a log cabin," German chancellor Ludwig Erhard allegedly said during a visit to the president's ranch. "No, no," Johnson replied. "You have me confused with Abe Lincoln. I was born in a manger." In September 1965, when William E. Leuchtenburg interviewed Johnson for an article about the Great Society, LBJ's bombastic nature astonished him. Johnson seemed to think that his accomplishments as president were unparalleled in American history. "He held a conviction of his own centrality in the universe bordering on egomania," Leuchtenburg commented.

After his landslide victory in 1964 and the election of the most liberal Congress in American history, Johnson believed that he had license to carry out his vision of a renewed America. The first session of the Eighty-ninth Congress became "the Congress of accomplished hopes . . . of realized dreams": voting rights; medicare; medicaid; aid to elementary, secondary, and higher education; clean air and clean water; departments of Housing and Urban Development and Transportation; highway, automobile, tire, fire, gas pipeline and mine safety; aid to small businesses; fair immigration; national endowments for the arts and the humanities;

National Public Radio and Television; truth in lending, packaging, and securities; product safety; model cities; fair housing; and freedom of information were the forward-looking policies that formed the core of LBJ's reform program.

Johnson's accomplishment may also be interpreted as a response to his own inner sense of emptiness. He couldn't stand to be alone, and needed constant companionship, attention, affection, and approval. He had gargantuan appetites: for work, women, food, drink, conversation, and material possessions. All were in the service of filling himself up—of giving himself a sense of validity or self-worth. In Johnson's mind, his Great Society made him a great man, and perhaps even the greatest president in the country's history; the Great Society was in no small measure an expression of his need to salve his ego. Such a reading does not diminish Johnson's achievement, but rather reveals a great deal about the centrality of presidential personality in shaping public affairs.

Johnson's neediness also translated into a compelling desire to aid the country's least affluent citizens. It was as if providing federal largesse to the poorest Americans, with whom he identified, could fill what one associate described as that gaping hole in his ego. "Some men," he told Doris Kearns, "want power simply to strut around the world and to hear the tune of 'Hail to the Chief.' Others want it simply to build prestige, to collect antiques, and to buy pretty things. Well I wanted power to give things to people— all sorts of things to all sorts of people, especially the poor and the blacks."

The president's compassion for the needy and confidence in what federal domestic programs could achieve in relieving national ills was infectious. Though a majority of Americans were skeptical about the possibility of "curing" or ending poverty, they were receptive to combating it by the sort of fresh programs fashioned under LBJ. Like the faithful in a national crusade or evangelical drive against sin, Americans took their cue from a president who spoke so confidently of overcoming economic want principally by creating rather than redistributing wealth.

Johnson's goal of curing poverty would not outlive his administration, and the false hopes generated by his promises would play their role in diminishing his political power. But it was his own character flaws, which helped lead him astray most dramatically in his dealing with Vietnam, that would play an even larger part. Because Johnson believed that America's preservation of an independent South Vietnam was essential to world peace, he felt justified in expanding U.S. commitments in Southeast Asia without full congressional and public consultations. Likewise, when opposition to the fighting became vocal and insistent, Johnson, who considered such dissent in time of war unconscionable and harmful to the war effort, made every effort to stifle it, asserting that when boys were dying other Americans should not encourage the enemy with indications that we would not stay the course.

But his response to war opponents was also strikingly, and typically personal. Criticism wounded and enraged him. He could not separate himself from attacks on his policies; he felt individually assaulted by them. He, and not the policies, was almost always the issue. Though he understood that differences played a vital part in the complexion of politics, he could never distance himself from objections to his public actions, especially by people he counted as allies and friends. When Hubert Humphrey privately raised questions about the wisdom of fighting in Vietnam, he became persona non grata, and Johnson exiled him to the fringes of his administration, where he found himself in "limbo," with his access to the president "limited" and his "counsel less welcome." When Canadian Prime Minister Lester B. Pearson publicly opposed the war, Johnson almost assaulted him in a later meeting between the leaders, complaining about the "ignorant liberals, the 'know nothing' 'do gooders' who were troubling his sleep and making him 'feel like a martyr; misunderstood, misjudged by friends at home and abroad.' "

By 1967 and 1968, the war, which was being fought by his "boys," with his planes, his helicopters, and his guns, had made Johnson less than rational. When Leonard Marks, his old friend and director of the U.S. Information Agency, privately suggested that the president follow Vermont Senator George Aiken's advice that he declare victory and withdraw, Johnson, who had always treated Marks with consideration and respect, threw him out of the White House. During the same period, Senator Richard Russell of Georgia could not bear to see Johnson alone in his office, because the president would cry uncontrollably. The journalist William S.

White had similar memories of LBJ weeping when reading casualty reports.

The war brought out Johnson's propensities for overbearing, high-handed control and imperiousness, which is so often displayed by insecure characters threatened by any challenge to their power and stature. Though the public did not know the full story of LBJ's erratic behavior during his presidency, it did become increasingly aware of his manipulativeness and morbid determination to sustain a questionable war in Vietnam. With growing public doubts about the wisdom of the war, especially after the Tet offensive in February 1968, a majority of Americans lost confidence not only in the need for an ongoing struggle against Communism in Southeast Asia but also in a president who seemed too inflexible, too devious, and too unreliable to warrant their support. The Johnson of 1963–1965, whose credentials as a professional politician and a compassionate reformer had won him widespread admiration, had become the mean-spirited, intemperate war leader of 1967–1968. By then, he could not travel freely around the country without being exposed to expressions of rage at a president whose poor judgment and questionable character had offended the country's sense of decency and made him a lame-duck chief.

Recriminations over character also contributed to the downfall of Richard Nixon's administration. Journalist and Nixon biographer Tom Wicker suggests that mistrust shadowed Nixon from his first day in office, for his public persona had always been contrived: "He was an intellectual appealing to a public that puts low value on eggheads." He was also a politician who disliked campaigning or pressing the flesh, as LBJ described it. Nixon was essentially a shy, introverted man who preferred to spend time alone or engaged in cerebral activities. On the hustings, as Wicker writes, he "always seemed somehow ill at ease. His gestures when he spoke—the counting of points on fingers, the arms upstretched in the victory sign or sweeping around his body like a matador flicking a cape before a bull—the body language always seemed a little out of sync with what he was saying, as if a soundtrack were running a little ahead of or behind its film."

Nixon had, of course, earned the animus of liberals in the forties and the fifties by his ruthlessness on the campaign trail, especially his unrestrained use of anti-Communism to both attack Democrats and to build a national reputation, through which he ultimately gained the vice presidency and later the presidency itself. But even people who liked and supported him considered him enigmatic, someone who was never quite genuine or was so inclined to posturing that it was never clear precisely what lay behind the Nixon facade. It is this quality that led opponents to describe him as "the new Nixon," when he ran for president in 1960, and "the new, new Nixon" in 1968, when he declared himself eager to end the divisions of the sixties.

Yet, as Wicker persuasively argues, whatever doubts the man gave rise to, he also enjoyed considerable popularity. Nixon was the only candidate in American political history other than Franklin Roosevelt to have been nominated by a major party on five national tickets: as vice president in 1952 and 1956, and as president in 1960, 1968, and 1972. He also had an impressive tenure of four years in the House of Representatives, two in the Senate, eight as vice president, and five and a half years as president, in which office he was one of only fourteen chiefs in American history elected twice, and one of only five out of eighteen so far in the twentieth century. Moreover, his reelection to the White House in 1972 with nearly 62 percent of the popular vote and only 17 electoral ballots cast against him stands as one of the greatest landslides in presidential history.

Nixon's appeal rested in part on his skill in communicating with millions of Americans who considered him "one of us." While every candidate for high office takes pains to wrap himself in the flag and identify himself with those verities of American life that no politician can ignore in statewide and national campaigns, Nixon had an ability to utter these familiar pieties about flag and nation, family and religion, freedom and democracy with uncommon conviction.

He positioned himself as an aggressive "have not," a man who brilliantly spoke for the "silent majority" of ordinary working-class stiffs without special connections or wealth or even personal charm to sell themselves to the world. Nixon did have a legitimate claim on the mass of Americans in this respect, for his impoverished childhood in southern California, attendance at Whittier College, inability to connect with a prestigious law firm after earning a Duke University law degree, and his attacks on wealthy establishment figures like Jerry Voorhis, Helen Gahagan Douglas, Alger Hiss, Adlai Stevenson, and Dean Acheson were all powerful testaments for the many Americans who shared his class resentments. Nixon's first major presentation of himself as a self-made man was in his famous 1952 "Checkers" speech, in which he called attention to Pat Nixon's plain cloth coat and invoked the image of the little cocker spaniel beloved by his family. He scored again in his much-publicized "kitchen debate" with Nikita Khrushchev in 1959, when, zealously defending the virtues of American consumerism, he expressed the sentiments of ordinary Americans convinced of the superiority of their own political system to that of the Soviets.

Nixon, Wicker argues in his biography *One of Us,* gave Americans an image of themselves not as they wished to be but as "they knew they were. . . . They could have recognized in Nixon their own sentimental patriotism and confidence in national virtue, their professed love of God and family, their . . . preference for action over reflection . . . and their vocal if not always practiced devotion to freedom and democracy. They also might have seen reflected in the ambiguous figure of Richard Nixon—even in his reputation for sharp practice and his transparent presentations of himself—their own melancholy knowledge, hard-earned in a demanding world, that ideals sometimes had to yield to necessity." In this view, Nixon's cunning and his questionable morals were partly a comfort to the mass of Americans, who perceived in the man traces of their own instincts to cut corners, to lie or cheat a little, in a harshly competitive world in which they were trying to get an edge. Nixon himself seemed to understand the process of identification involved here. "You've got to be a little evil to understand those people out there," he told Hugh Sidey of *Time.* "You have to have known the dark side of life to understand those people."

Yet he was able to carry underhanded tactics only so far. His affinity for secrecy and for unethical dealings, regardless of legal and constitutional niceties, made his downfall in a society founded upon law, likely, if not inevitable. Watergate, the break-in at the Democratic headquarters by Nixon-campaign operatives, and the White House cover-up that followed were, historian Stanley Kutler says, "rooted in the tumultuous events of the 1960s in the United States and abroad, and in the personality and history of Nixon himself, going back to his first presidential term and earlier."

To Nixon, Kutler adds, "Watergate was essentially one more episode in a series of wars and clashes with long-despised enemies." As Nixon himself put it, "I had thrown down a gauntlet to Congress, the bureaucracy, the media, and the Washington establishment and challenged them to engage in epic battle." Nixon may have given the most insightful explanation of the origins and outcome of the crisis when he told aides as he was resigning the presidency: "Always remember, others may hate you, but those who hate you don't win unless you hate them, and then you destroy yourself."

"It was just such corrosive hatred, however, that decisively shaped Nixon's own behavior, his career, and eventually his historical standing," Kutler concludes.

There is no need to revisit the details of the Watergate crisis. Its importance here is as a cautionary tale—a demonstration of how character, or what we in the late twentieth century call personality, helped build and destroy the political career of an intelligent, determined, troubled man. Driven by inner demons of resentment to show the world and especially himself that he was the best, that no one could beat him at anything he turned his mind to, Nixon viewed his life as a struggle to overcome adversity by whatever means were at hand. If he gave constant lip service to honoring the rules of the game, he knew that many—indeed, some of the most successful men he met in his political journey—chose not to live by them. And because he lacked the advantages some of those men—like the Kennedys—enjoyed, he felt entitled to manipulate the truth and anything else that might stand in the way of his reach for status, control, and power.

Some people believe that if Nixon had owned up to the facts at the start of the Watergate affair, he would have saved his presidency. But, to quote Wicker again, this argument "ignores the fact that the man Richard Nixon was by 1972 *couldn't come clean*. . . . With his view of life as battle and crisis as challenge, his determination to prove his worth, particularly to himself, his consequent inability to 'give up' and his reluctance to show weakness, as well as his conviction that through 'personal gut performance' any height could be scaled," he saw no alternative but to "stonewall" his enemies.

Nixon, like Johnson, was carried to great heights and then broken on the wheel of his own ambition. Yet their failures were not simply the consequence of flawed personalities but also of lost credibility or diminished public trust in men expected to honor the highest office with honest dealings that showed a proper respect for traditions of accountability and democracy. How public trust can be as essential as vision, and pragmatism, and consensus, and charisma to effective White House governance deserves a discussion of its own.

CHAPTER 5

IN PRESIDENTS WE TRUST

It is a truism of American history that presidential campaigns are rough affairs, in which the candidates viciously attack one another's characters. While their innuendoes and even outright allegations of wrongdoing have provided much amusement, they have occasionally offered valuable insight into the lives of the men who asked their fellow citizens to honor them with the White House.

Lest anyone assume that character assassination through negative advertising and similar tactics is a modern contrivance spawned by television, consider the tone of the contest between the Democratic-Republicans and Federalists at the start of the Republic. Declaring Washington "the source of all the misfortunes of our country," an opposition newspaper editor wrote of his departure from office in 1797: "If ever there was a period for rejoicing, this is the moment. Every heart in unison with freedom and happiness of the people ought to beat high with exultation that the name of Washington from this day ceases to give a currency to political iniquity and to legalized corruption."

The Federalists gave as good as they got. During the 1800 election, they denounced Jefferson "as an atheist, an 'intellectual voluptuary,' and the progenitor of the mulatto children upon his plantation." Should Jefferson be elected, "the just vengeance of insulted heaven" would be visited upon the United States, with "dwellings in flames, hoary hairs bathed in blood, female chastity violated . . . children writhing on the pike and halberd." A vote for Jefferson was a vote against God, since it would put "a howling atheist . . . at the head of the nation," signaling that the Lord "had utterly forsaken the United States."

As for John Adams, Jefferson's opponent in 1796 and 1800, he was a man of "disgusting egotism," "distempered jealousy," "ungovernable indiscretion," and "vanity without bounds," and this was only, the Jeffersonian Democrats emphasized, what Alexander Hamilton, his Federalist rival, had to say about him.

Like party platforms and campaign promises, however, most partisan rhetoric has been quickly consigned to the dustbins of history after the voters spoke. Though echoes from such verbal assaults sometimes remained, especially in the minds of those relentlessly subjected to them, most presidents-elect were quick to forgive and forget. Andrew Jackson may have promised retribution against those circulating "the most base calumnies" about him, his wife, and "pious Mother . . . held to public scorn as a prostitute," but the great majority of chief executives were all too eager to let the "slanders" of the contest fade away.

And with the close of campaign seasons, newly minted presidents have also generally enjoyed the trust of the country. From Washington to Clinton, whatever assertions had been made during a campaign about an aspirant's bad character did little to affect his capacity to govern at the outset of his term. Even where there was good reason to find some measure of truth in the criticisms made of the new chief, the public was inclined to give the president the benefit of the doubt and let him get on with the more important business of governing the nation. All but one president, then— including the sixteen occasions when the office was won with a plurality rather than a majority of the popular vote—have begun their administrations with their credibility largely intact. Only Lincoln, in whom the South refused to entrust its future, entered office without a viable degree of national confidence in his ability to provide acceptable leadership.

But the initial trust invested in presidents carried no guarantees about how long it might last. It is the nature of the job that presidents have had to work at sustaining their credibility with a citizenry that remains attentive to their principal public actions.

Presidents who fared best at keeping the public—or at least a majority of voters—on their side have been those whose policies conformed most closely to what the mass of Americans believed essential to the national well-being. However isolationist and antimilitarist the country generally was before the Cold War, for example, the country's leaders have been able to maintain public trust only by aggressively defending the national interest as they did when it was seriously threatened in 1812, 1917, and 1939–1941.

Presidents who have lacked vision, a talent for practical compromise promoting consensus, or personal appeal have understandably made the country less sure of their leadership. Others have more directly caused the loss of the mandate when they acted in ways that broke with accepted standards of national governance, as occurred during the John Adams, Andrew Johnson, Harding, FDR, and Ford presidencies. Others, including TR, Wilson, Hoover, LBJ, Carter, and Bush, damaged their credibility by promising more than they could deliver. And presidents who deceived or seemed to be deceiving the country, as had FDR, LBJ, and Nixon, paid a heavy price in political influence and/or historical standing for their actual or alleged transgressions. Indeed, observing traditional rules, fulfilling avowed goals, and keeping to a standard of truthfulness have all been crucial tests of presidential effectiveness. In most instances, the public has repudiated executives who failed these tests. "Trust is the coin of the realm," as former Secretary of State George Schulz said, and so, as with vision and pragmatism, consensus and charisma, credibility or trust has proved to be a vital element in helping or hindering presidential performance.

I

Madison, McKinley, and Truman were three presidents whose difficult decisions in foreign policy matters went far to build trust in their capability to lead the country. While it is tempting to interpret their actions as principally examples of consensus-building, what they achieved in each of these cases was even more fundamental: at defining moments in their administrations they encouraged the country to accept their authority as leaders acting in the national interest.

James Madison, despite his brilliance as a Constitution-maker and genius in defending the document in the Federalist papers, was not one of our most popular presidents. Shortest of any president (5'4") and unimpressive as a personality, he did little to excite the country's imagination. "Jemmy Madison, poor Jemmy, he is but a withered little apple John," one critic said.

The central dilemma facing Madison from the onset of his presidency in 1809 was the Anglo-French war. The European conflict had led to violations of American neutral rights, including the impressment of U.S. seamen, but had also incited hopes of United States expansion into the Northwest and Southwest, where "war hawks" demanded elimination of British, Spanish, and Indian power. Like Jefferson, Madison had little zeal for a conflict that might undermine republican principles by increasing the national debt, compelling new taxes, enlarging executive powers, and encouraging the growth of an army and a navy potentially hostile to democratic rule. To avoid war, he tried to sustain Jefferson's policy of "peaceful coercion." Because Jefferson's Embargo and Nonintercourse Act had reduced American exports and stifled the national economy, Madison favored instead a policy of trading with both belligerents, while promising that if either country ended its assault on U.S. shipping, he would reinstate nonintercourse against the other power.

Although Napoleon largely deceived the U.S. government into thinking that he would honor Madison's request, the French continued to violate American rights almost as flagrantly as the British. "The Devil himself," one congressman asserted, "could not tell which government, England or France, is the most wicked." While many in the United States considered it impossible to challenge both the British and French simultaneously, there was plenty of sentiment for fighting them individually, with Britain favored to receive the first drubbing by American military power. At the same time, however, many in the northeastern part of the United States preferred not war but trade with England, which they believed would restore prosperity to their hard-hit region. Nevertheless, after mustering pro-war votes of 79 to 49 in the House and 19 to

13 in the Senate, Madison led a divided country into the War of 1812.

But support for the war was more widespread and intense than the congressional votes suggested. Indeed, after a decade of neutral rights violations and Indian assaults inspired partly by British indifference to U.S. sovereignty, a war against England had become an irresistible imperative. Though the declaration of war listed American grievances as impressment, violations of U.S. territorial waters (including unlawful seizures), injuries to U.S. commerce through Orders in Council, and frontier barbarities by British-backed Indians, the conflict was also viewed as a second war of independence, a renewed defense of popular self-government against monarchical Britain. "We are going to fight for the reestablishment of our national character," Andrew Jackson declared. The surge of patriotic backing for the military campaign and the popularity Jackson gained from his January 1815 victory over the British at New Orleans suggested that most Americans regarded the war as he did.

In asking for war against Britain, Madison saw himself as rescuing not only republican institutions from Britain's anti-American incursions but also his administration and his party from defeat. By 1812, Madison recognized that if he resisted a direct conflict with England, he would lose the public's trust—one unspoken issue in the decision for war was preserving national confidence in his and the Republican party's commitment to a defense of American freedoms. When John Adams told Jefferson in 1817 that Madison had "established more Union than all his three predecessors," he was referring to this very episode.

American victory in the War of 1812 resulted not only in British defeat but also in the end of the Federalists as a viable political force. Their antiwar actions had alienated them from the rest of the nation and all but done away with their acceptability as a party capable of defining the country's best interests. In the presidential race of 1816 between James Monroe and Rufus King, the Federalist share of the electoral vote fell to 15.5 percent. Monroe's uncontested reelection in 1820 marked what Jefferson called the "complete suppression of party" and the triumph of the Era of Good Feelings. Despite his own personal limits and the lack of a consensus for war, Madison used a conflict with England to convert his vision of an independent America into a groundswell of national trust.

Eighty-three years later William McKinley found himself in much the same situation. McKinley had initially showed little enthusiasm for a war with Spain over Cuba, and his caution had moved Theodore Roosevelt to complain privately about the president's unsuitability for stewardship of a great nation. Alongside of TR, McKinley was admittedly a relatively weak leader with almost none of his successor's personal flair and passion for grand national and international designs. But McKinley's cautious approach to war in April 1898 found approval with an America that had reservations about abandoning traditional isolationism for adventures abroad.

During the ten-year insurrection that had roiled Cuba from 1868 to 1878, Americans had opposed any direct intervention in the conflict, despite some angry outbursts over Spanish repression and violations of the rights of U.S. citizens. Steering clear of overseas involvements continued to be the watchword of foreign policy in the 1870s, 1880s and early 1890s to the point that newspapers periodically called for the abolition of America's diplomatic service as a waste of taxpayer monies. But in 1895, when Cuban economic suffering exploded in another rebellion, the United States was more receptive to freeing the island once and for all from the Spanish yoke. Many factors contributed to the growth of imperial sentiment in the United States, which lay behind the impulse to now oust Spain from Cuba, but suffice it to say that by 1898 a consensus had emerged to take action.

The only significant reservations about entering the struggle came from U.S. commercial interests. Fearful that a war would impede an economic recovery from the panic and slide of 1893–1897, businessmen counseled McKinley to avoid an all-out clash. As a loyal supporter of American business and as a Civil War veteran who saw little appeal in hostilities of any kind, the president tried to hold back the national tide toward war. In March 1898, after the battleship *Maine* blew up in Havana harbor, he set conditions that could have averted a conflict, asking Spain to grant Cuba's insurgents a temporary armistice, to end its policy of herding rebels into concentration camps, and to accept withdrawal from

Cuba. Though it hedged on withdrawal, Madrid largely acceded to McKinley's proposals, but the president found it impossible to contain the press-inspired domestic pressure for an end to Spanish rule on the island.

On April 11, the president asked Congress to allow him to intervene in Cuba if Spain did not settle the Cuban upheaval and permanently end a disturbance that menaced the peace of the United States. Congress seized upon McKinley's message to demand Spanish withdrawal from Cuba and independence for the island. Should these conditions not be met, McKinley would respond with American military might, and the United States pledged not to annex Cuba. "By the spring of 1898," historian Thomas A. Bailey has written, "the pressure of herd hysteria had become so overwhelming that it could not have been stemmed by an ordinary mortal. The American people, whipped to a white heat by the yellow press, were determined to have their war to free Cuba—and they got it. McKinley was determined to free Cuba, and war seemed to be the only solution. His views coincided with those of an inflamed and fight-thirsty opinion."

Opting for war was a decision McKinley saw as a clear-cut political necessity. With even pacifists like William Jennings Bryan, his leading Democratic opponent, militating for an independent Cuba, McKinley did not relish the prospect of a Democratic presidential campaign in 1900 trumpeting "Free Cuba" and "Free Silver." More immediately, he feared a Democratic victory in the congressional campaigns of 1898 and the humiliating prospect of a Republican Congress trying to head this possibility off by passing an unsolicited war resolution. "Don't your President know where the war-declaring power is lodged?" one senator asked a state department official. "Tell him by———, that if he doesn't do something, Congress will exercise the power."

The fundamental issue, as McKinley assessed it, was not simply to retain political power for himself and his party, but also to keep his administration intact by preserving the trust of a nation that seemed almost universally committed to serving the cause of freedom generally, and Cuba's in particular, by fighting Spain. The success of the latter can be measured by a comment made as America entered its "splendid little war" against Spain, when the New York *Sun* declared: "We are all jingoes now; and the head jingo is the Hon. William McKinley, the trusted and honored Chief Executive of the nation's will."

An even more striking example of presidential decision-making reflecting a central concern to maintain public trust was Harry Truman's use of the atomic bomb in August 1945. In the decades since, a fierce debate has sprung up among historians over the morality and wisdom of the attacks on Hiroshima and Nagasaki. Truman and others initially argued that since the Japanese refused to surrender, he had no choice but to use the ultimate weapon to conclude the war. Dropping the bomb persuaded the emperor that Japan faced annihilation unless it capitulated. The quick end to the fighting foreclosed a U.S. invasion of Japan's home islands, and although the atomic bombings did cost the Japanese tens of thousands of civilian casualties, defenders of the decision assert that these losses would have been far exceeded by the loss of American and Japanese lives that would have followed an invasion and prolonged fighting on the ground.

Critics of Truman's decision believe that the atomic bombings were unnecessary to bring the war to a fast conclusion. Japan had already indicated that it was receptive to surrender discussions if Washington promised to keep the emperor on the throne. In addition, had the U.S. military simply given a demonstration to the Japanese of the destructive power of the bomb, it would have been sufficient to have persuaded Tokyo to give up in a timely fashion. But, Truman's critics contend, the president and his advisers had other concerns on their agenda. They knew that military estimates of U.S. losses in an invasion were closer to 50,000 than the figure of 500,000 that Truman later cited as persuading him to use the bomb. For them, the opportunity to test the bomb against a foe as "barbarous" as the Japanese, while simultaneously intimidating the Russians was a more compelling concern than any consideration of potential losses in an amphibious attack and ground fighting. Racism and "atomic diplomacy," as Gar Alperovitz has called it, were of greater importance to the American government than its professed desire to spare Japanese lives after almost four years of total war.

Antirevisionist scholars, in turn, have disputed the conclusions denying the necessity of the attacks on Hiroshima and Nagasaki. They begin by challenging the condemnation of moral insensitivity on Truman's part as an ahistorical value judgment. In the midst of so much bloodletting, when the firebombings of Dresden and Tokyo had already taken some 135,000 lives, it is fair to conclude that the president saw little reason to back away from what then seemed like a more efficient means of attacking enemy population centers from the air.

Furthermore, the antirevisionists assert, American military planners could have no real confidence that casualties resulting from a ground assault would be relatively limited. Island-hopping combat experience in the Pacific theater had already shown that the Japanese had fought harder, and with greater losses on both sides, as the war came closer to Japan itself. The Okinawa fighting in 1945, for example, had been particularly costly. Antirevisionists quote General Marshall's later comment: "The Japanese had demonstrated in each case they would not surrender and they fight to the death. . . . It was to be expected that resistance in Japan . . . could be even more severe. We had had one hundred thousand people killed in Tokyo in one night of bombs, and it had seemingly no effect whatsoever. It destroyed the Japanese cities, yes, but their morale was affected, so far as we could tell, not at all. So it seemed quite necessary, if we could, to shock them into action. . . . We had to end the war; we had to save American lives."

No one close to the president advised him not to use the bomb, for everyone assumed that FDR would have gone ahead and deployed it, as planned. "At no time, from 1941 to 1945, did I ever hear it suggested by the president, or by any other responsible member of the government, that atomic energy should not be used in the war," Secretary of War Henry Stimson wrote later. "I know FDR would have used it in a minute to prove that he hadn't wasted two billion dollars," Admiral William D. Leahy, Roosevelt's chief of staff, commented. In fact, Truman biographer David McCullough points out, no decision was ever made about the bomb, because its use was a given. "It was never an issue," Churchill said about a Potsdam meeting on the bomb in July 1945. "There was unanimous, automatic, unquestioned agreement around the table; nor did I ever hear the slightest suggestion that we should do otherwise."

Defenders of Truman's "decision" have also argued that he could hardly have faced the public after the war if he had decided against dropping the bomb. "How could a President, or others charged with responsibility for the decision," McCullough asks, "answer to the American people if when the war was over, after the bloodbath of an invasion of Japan, it became known that a weapon sufficient to end the war had been available by midsummer and was not used?"

McCullough's question is another way of stating that a central consideration for Truman—or for any president in his circumstances—was how to maintain the trust of the American people. This is not to imply that he consciously sought to score political points with the public or felt compelled to pander to public opinion by making the decision in favor of nuclear weapons. In the midst of wartime horrors, with so many lives at stake and the fate of the world partly in his hands, Harry Truman gave no mind to how to win friends and assure his political future. His overriding concern was to end the bloodletting, to prevent the thousands of deaths that would result by any false move on his part, and to do all in his power to secure the national security and future peace of the world.

In this mission he and the people were of one mind. Since it seemed reasonable to assume that the great majority of Americans would have approved of employing a weapon that could shorten the war, Truman had no dilemma about the appropriate course of action. As an unelected president standing in the shadow of the man who had developed and almost certainly would have used the bomb, Truman was never really presented a choice between use and nonuse. His credibility as a president, as a war leader, was inextricably bound up with a weapon that apparently promised a quicker end to the fighting than by any other means. It may be that Truman erred in not promising preservation of the Japanese throne in a Potsdam declaration asking Tokyo's surrender; it may be that he should have confronted the Japanese with a display of the bomb's power as an alternative to actually bringing it into play as a weapon. But as he understood it, in using the bomb he was acting as a representative of the nation entrusted with the responsibility of carrying out its desires in a matter of the highest importance. Employing a nuclear weapon in the service of the earliest possible peace was an essential ingredient of the trust millions of Americans were placing in a man they had never assumed would become their country's political chief.

II

Holding the public's trust is a task that demands a president's constant attention. Numerous chief executives from John Adams to George Bush witnessed their credibility with the electorate dissipate and even largely disappear over the course of their terms. When their actions put them at odds with expected standards of political and/or judicial conduct, they have paid a high price in political support. John Adams, Andrew Johnson, Harding, FDR, and Ford are all cases in point.

John Adams began his presidency in 1797 with only a three-vote electoral margin of 71 to 68 over Jefferson. Under the rules then in place, Jefferson became vice president, establishing a divided administration. If this situation were not sufficient to complicate Adams's political life, divisions in the Federalist camp between himself and Alexander Hamilton further weakened his authority. However much faith the country invested in the new president as Washington's logical successor, it was still less than Washington enjoyed and required the most careful attention to assure it would not be sacrificed in the political battles of the next four years.

Although Adams initially gained standing with the public through his clashes with the French over American neutral rights and especially the X, Y, Z affair, in which he refused to pay bribes to French officials for the privilege of negotiating with them, he lost what advantages he had as a result of the undeclared war he fought against France and the events that followed from it, including the Alien and Sedition Acts of 1798. The cost of contesting French violations of American rights was considerable: new taxes, a growing national debt, fears of "monarchism," and limitations on speech and press freedoms that Republican opponents attacked by fair means and foul. "No man of any feeling," John Adams said, "is willing to renounce his home, forsake his property and profession for the sake of removing to Philadelphia [the seat of government], where he is almost sure of disgrace and ruin." Adams also complained that "under imputations of democracy, some of the ablest, most influential, and best characters in the Union" were being subjected to unmerciful criticism.

Yet however acrimonious the Republican denunciations of Adams and the Federalists, they hardly posed a clear and present danger to the United States. Criticizing Adams as "cankered by ambition and jealousy and overmastered by an ungovernable temper" was not tantamount to plotting the overthrow of the government by extra-constitutional means. Though the Republicans were vocal in their warnings against an all-powerful "consolidated government" infringing upon democratic freedoms, they were not engaged in a diabolical plan against Adams and federal authority.

In attempting to suppress Republican criticism through arbitrary use of federal power and under the protection of law provided by the Sedition Act, Adams and his party discredited themselves with the country's moderates, that "middle part," as one French traveler to the United States called it, which he calculated as "much larger" than either of the extremes. It was composed of "the most estimable men" of both parties, who loved their country more than any faction or attachment to Britain or France in the contest for world power. Because Adams could not rein in the extremism on either side, especially in his own political camp where he was vilified almost as sharply as he had been by the Republicans, he lost the mandate of the majority. In the minds of the public he was "convicted of being an advocate of monarchy, life tenure for senators, an alliance with Great Britain, and a fighting Navy." He was, in effect, seen as no friend of the people, but as an elitist who could no longer be trusted with an office he might turn against the democratic institutions that had given him power in the first place.

In the election of 1800, Adams found himself once again pitted against Jefferson, who now defeated him by eight electoral votes, 73 to 65, a reversal of eleven votes from 1796. The election demonstrated for the first time that under the 1787 compact an incumbent could be unseated peacefully or by strict constitutional means. But just as instructive for the country's long-term political practice, it showed that a sitting president who could not sustain public confidence in his commitment to basic democratic principles on which the nation had been founded was vulnerable to defeat.

Finally, the 1800 vote indicated forcefully that the rule of law and democratic governance would decide who should serve in the presidency. "By scorning the popular intelligence and behaving as though politics was a matter of preaching wisdom to the untutored masses," historian John C. Miller writes, "the Federalists condemned themselves not only to defeat in the election of 1800 but to extinction as a party."

Sixty-five years later Andrew Johnson proved that he had learned nothing from the Adams presidency—or from any other, for that matter—by undoing his public credibility in the debate over post–Civil War Reconstruction. Seeing himself as taking the high ground of conciliation as recommended by Lincoln, Johnson made return of the Confederate states to the Union a straightforward exercise. Under the leadership of provisional governors he appointed in 1865, the southern states held constitutional conventions which repealed the ordinances of secession, repudiated the debts incurred to fight the war, and approved the Thirteenth Amendment to the U.S. Constitution outlawing slavery or involuntary servitude. By early 1866, the former Confederate states had completed this process, and Johnson declared them entitled to send representatives and senators back to Congress.

But the president's almost casual solution to the problem of Reconstruction outraged the so-called Radical Republicans, some of whom urged a vindictive peace in which the southern states would be subjected to a long process of rehabilitation before they would be allowed the restoration of full rights. They also wanted rebel leaders to be punished and their property confiscated.

Prevailing sentiment in the North, however, was more moderate. It did not favor extreme punishment of the South and worried that Radical preoccupation with blacks generally and their voting rights in particular would divide the North and undermine the Republican party. "The majority of Republicans were not Radicals but moderates and conservatives," Eric Foner writes, "who resented the 'element that seem to have the negro on the brain all the time' and feared the issue of black rights would prove fatal to the party's electoral prospects."

Nevertheless, northern opinion was set against accepting the

South back into the Union without at least some solid evidence that the Confederates accepted defeat, meaning a permanent end to secession; some basic protection of black rights; and the dominance of the Republican party. By the winter of 1865–1866, northerners believed that the South had not made a commitment to such conditions. To the contrary, the Black Codes, laws passed by the provisional southern legislatures, and continuing violence against blacks, indicated that Southern whites had no intention of granting the freedmen full equality. Nor were northerners prepared to seat southern representatives and senators, who would largely be Democrats eager to take control of Congress away from the Republican party. Presidential reconstruction, one New Yorker said, "is no reconstruction at all." Or, as a West Virginia editor put it, "Abstractly the American people are not in favor of Negroes voting, but as against rebeldom ruling in Congress or even in the South, they are."

To prevent unequal treatment of blacks across the South, congressional Republicans passed in 1866 a second Freedmen's Bureau bill and a Civil Rights bill, which aimed to protect the freedmen until a Fourteenth Amendment to the Constitution guaranteeing due process and equal protection of the laws could win approval. Johnson's veto of the two bills and recommendation to the South that it not ratify the Fourteenth Amendment largely put an end to his credibility as a responsible leader whom the North could trust to reconstruct the Union. "The President has no power to control or influence anybody, and legislation will be carried on entirely regardless of his opinions or wishes," an Iowa congressman said privately in December. The struggle over the Tenure of Office Act of 1867 and Johnson's impeachment in 1868 can be viewed as further manifestations of the distrust that greeted his unacceptable plans for reconstructing the South. "He attempts to govern after he has lost the means to govern," General William T. Sherman said of Johnson. "He is like a General fighting without an army."

Blinded by personal grandiosity or a stubborn disregard for political realities, Johnson labored under the illusion that he could defeat his Republican opponents and possibly become the Democratic party nominee in 1868. But his political missteps had irredeemably weakened his hold on the majority of the electorate, who wanted no part of a leader so insensitive to public sentiment. "Why should they not take me up?" Johnson asked on the eve of the Democratic convention. "They profess to accept my measures; they say I have stood by the Constitution and made a noble struggle." Though he placed second on the first two Democratic party ballots in July 1868, Johnson was a thoroughly defeated candidate whom few in the country believed had the political wisdom to succeed at anything. His administration was an object lesson in how not to generate public trust in a president's capacity to steer the nation through perilous times, as well as a demonstration that there can be no trust without consensus, and vice versa—credibility is essential for national backing. Arguments over which comes before the other are made superfluous by the fact that effective governance depends on the simultaneous existence of both.

Warren G. Harding shares honors with Andrew Johnson as one of the least able presidents in the country's history. Although he had a better sense than Johnson of his own limits, he was unable to use that knowledge to transcend them. His administration was government by cronyism. He appointed his "God-damn friends" to all manner of high-level jobs and then proceeded to pay no attention to transgressions. "This White House is a prison," he complained. "I can't get away from the men who dog my footsteps. I am in jail." In the summer of 1923, alerted by suicides on the staffs of the Veterans' Bureau and the attorney general's office, Harding asked Secretary of Commerce Herbert Hoover what he should do if scandals were discovered in his administration. Before the unsavory dealings, which would force several resignations and send former officials to prison, including Attorney General Harry M. Daugherty, became public, however, Harding mercifully died.

Since no significant revelations about the scandals had come to light while he was alive, Harding enjoyed a substantial degree of public approval and trust as president. Even when the extent of the corruption was revealed in the years following his death, the public leveled few recriminations against a president whom they regarded as simply embodying the freewheeling unscrupulousness of businessmen and corporations out to make it big in the twenties. As historian John D. Hicks summarizes, "The abysmally low ethical standards of the businessmen who took part in the [corrupt] deals [of the Harding administration] were seemingly accepted with little resentment, both by the juries that refused to convict them and by the public at large." That such "transaction were probably a commonplace of big business worried only the liberal journalists and other professional worriers" of the time. "For the average American all this was taken for granted as just another aspect of 'normalcy.' "

Yet in time, Harding's presidency would be evaluated for what it was—a low point, along with Grant's administration, regarding respect for standards of honesty and decency. Both Grant and Harding are now seen as poor presidents who carelessly used the powers of office to appoint corruptionists or at least men without the strength of character to resist possibilities of enriching themselves and their friends by betraying the public trust.

Though Harding died before his misdeeds could be weighed by public scrutiny, he has received his comeuppance, so to speak, from history. "History will judge," political leaders under attack like to say in their defense, and indeed, sometimes it does. After the almost universal agreement among historians as to Harding's limitations as president, who would now make a case for his trustworthiness as a national chief? If for nothing else, his presidency serves the useful function of reminding aspirants to the country's highest office that their reputations during and after their terms of service greatly depend on public conviction of their integrity. To paraphrase an earlier observation about vision, when there is no trust, the president's public backing perishes.

Franklin Roosevelt represents the unusual case of a president who, although he had seriously compromised his standing with the public, was enabled by historical circumstance not only to continue his career in the oval office but to elevate his reputation for effectiveness. Though his political maneuvering during his second term compromised the electorate's confidence in him, the grave dangers of World War II eclipsed concerns about his credibility and gave him third and fourth terms. While it is doubtful, of course, that Roosevelt would even have run for another four years in 1940 without the impetus of the international crisis, had the war not intervened, widespread doubt about FDR's continuing tendency to favor personal aims over those of the public interest would surely have barred him from a third term.

The Court-packing plan had obviously sounded an alarm bell with conservatives, who criticized Roosevelt's "hunger for power," but it had also disturbed liberals, who feared that the president would weaken the courts, which they saw as the bulwark of American civil liberties. A series of sit-down strikes in 1937, which Roosevelt refused to break with federal force, added to the impression that he had lost his sense of proportion—that he was now all too ready to put his control of public policy and the programs of union radicals above traditional institutional arrangements and regard for property rights. When the country fell into a serious recession in the summer and fall of 1937, which carried over into the early months of 1938, it only corroborated the belief that Roosevelt had become a president without viable solutions to national problems. Even when the economy picked up in the following summer, the administration had no response to the continuing issue of unemployment, which stood at nine million, or about 18 percent of the work force. By the end of the year, many in the country believed that Roosevelt's New Deal was no longer relevant to current needs.

The president's credibility had suffered an additional blow during the year when congressional conservatives attacked an executive reorganization bill as "another attempt . . . to subvert democratic institutions." "You talk about dictatorship," one congressman announced. "Why, Mr. Chairman, it is here now. The advanced guard of totalitarianism had enthroned itself in the Government in Washington." Though the bill was essentially an attempt to make democratic government more efficient, the rise of totalitarianism abroad combined with deepening suspicions of the president to defeat the measure. "There wasn't a chance for anyone to become a dictator under that bill," Roosevelt asserted, but the reorganization bill had inevitably become a symbol of congressional and public concern about a president who had established himself as one of the most powerful chief executives in the country's history.

If these incidents were not sufficient to call into serious question Roosevelt's behavior in 1937–1938, his attempt to rid the Democratic party of conservative opponents confirmed the doubts of those ready to believe the worst about "that man in the White

House." The very word "purge," which became associated with this attempt of Roosevelt to fashion the Democratic party into a modern liberal instrument for advancing economic and social reforms, only helped evoke the image of an American dictator trying to build a one-party state. After the Republicans recaptured eighty-one seats in the House and eight in the Senate in the November elections, many commentators were ready to declare FDR a lame-duck leader. "Clearly, I think, that President Roosevelt could not run for a third term even if he so desired," one Washington correspondent concluded after the GOP victories.

Though bloodied, Roosevelt remained unbowed. Despite his setbacks of this period, he still enjoyed considerable popularity with the majority of Americans, who had no wish to see conservatives dismantle the principal New Deal reforms. Few wanted to return to the less humane and less regulated industrial system of the pre-Roosevelt era. Yet there was no denying that public trust in the president had suffered a serious decline during the first two years of his second term. His willingness to challenge a hallowed institution like the Supreme Court, accepted verities about the sanctity of private property, and conventional convictions about the appropriateness of presidential distance from statewide and local elections tested the willingness of middle-class Americans to believe that he was a reliable leader, dedicated first and foremost to the welfare of the nation.

No president had a harder time maintaining his credibility as a politician suited to the office than Gerald Ford. After Spiro Agnew had resigned the vice presidency in 1973 as part of a plea bargain with the Justice Department, Nixon had appointed Ford, who, as prescribed by the Twenty-Fifth Amendment, was then confirmed by a majority vote of both Houses of Congress. When he assumed the presidency after Nixon resigned in August 1974, no one other than the 120,000 people in Michigan's fifth congressional district had ever cast their ballots for him for any federal office. He acknowledged his status as an "accidental" president by telling the country: "I am acutely aware that I have received the votes of none of you."

Such becoming modesty gratified Americans, who, as after any presidential inauguration, showed themselves ready to rally round their new executive. Ford enhanced his credibility by announcing "our long national nightmare of Watergate" at an end, and declaring both that the Constitution worked and the people ruled. The country could now look forward to an "open presidency" with no "illegal tappings, eavesdropping, buggings, or break-ins." As for Nixon himself, opinion was sharply divided over whether he should be charged for the crimes he committed as president. Some felt that his resignation was punishment enough; others believed that it would be a gross injustice to prosecute Nixon's subordinates while letting him off the hook. Some urged Ford to grant Nixon clemency; others reminded him of his comment at Senate hearings regarding his fitness for the vice presidency. When asked whether he considered it possible for a new president to abort a criminal investigation of his predecessor, Ford had answered: "I do not think the public would stand for it." Moreover, at his first White House press conference, he had seemed to promise that he would not take any action on the question until and unless formal legal action was initiated against Nixon.

But Ford dissipated most of the good will he had earned during the first month of his presidency when he announced a pardon of Nixon. As he explained, he was giving his predecessor clemency for all federal crimes he had committed or may have committed as president in order to end Nixon's suffering and to spare the country from the anguish of a drawn-out criminal proceeding. Ford's unstated motive was a fear that Nixon might take his own life unless he were relieved of fears of a criminal prosecution.

Ford's decision touched off an immediate negative reaction that reverberated throughout his two-and-a-half-year presidency. Complaints that he had made a corrupt bargain with Nixon to gain the White House severely damaged his credibility as a trustworthy public official. The fact that Nixon offered no admission of guilt other than acknowledging that he had made "mistakes and misjudgments," and that he was left in control of his papers and tapes, which might allow him to effect a "final cover-up" of his misdeeds, added to the view that Ford had either sold himself to Nixon or was a man of surpassingly poor judgment. Few in the country wanted to see Nixon prosecuted, but they resented the terms of the agreement Ford had reached with him. In the atmosphere of distrust that had settled over the nation after the Johnson and Nixon presidencies, Ford's action only served to generate antagonism toward him, which crippled his presidency and all but ended his chances for an additional four-year term.

Ford's reputation for sensible leadership also suffered from his inadequate economic, social, and foreign policies. When the economy, whipsawed by rising energy costs, fell into a cycle of stagflation in 1975—falling GNP, the worst since 1929–1932; 9 percent unemployment, the highest since 1941; and rapidly rising prices, the biggest increases in twenty-five years—Ford focused only on how to keep inflation in check. In response to the worst economic downturn since the Great Depression, he urged tax increases and less government spending to reduce deficits and encouraged price restraints by handing out WIN (Whip Inflation Now) buttons. In addition, he opposed congressional efforts to stimulate the economy with a large tax cut and expanded social welfare programs by vetoing seventy-two pieces of legislation in a little over two years— nearly double the number of Nixon's vetoes in a five-and-a-half-year period and substantially more than the average in an eight-year presidential term.

Americans also doubted that Ford had the capacity to conduct a judicious foreign policy. When South Vietnam fell to the Communists in 1975, the spectacle of South Vietnamese clinging to military helicopters departing from the roof of the U.S. embassy in Saigon vividly underscored America's failure in Southeast Asia and associated Ford with a national defeat. Later that year, his credibility as commander-in-chief suffered a further setback when Cambodia's Khmer Rouge seized the *Mayaguez,* a cargo ship with thirty-eight crew members aboard. A commando raid in which forty Americans were killed after the crew had been released only added to the impression that the administration was incompetent. Even when Ford did score successes with a U.S.-Soviet Strategic Arms Limitation Treaty and a Helsinki agreement on human rights and European national boundaries, he had to face conservative attacks on détente as simply an appeasement of Moscow.

By the time of the 1976 campaign, Ford, who had an average approval rating of only 47 percent and stood thirty points behind Jimmy Carter in the initial straw polls, was a president with little hold on public confidence. Ronald Reagan and conservative Republicans did not come to his aid in a bruising nomination fight by describing his defense and foreign policies as "weak" and his management of the domestic economy as "poor." His famous gaffe during his October 1976 debate with Carter—"There is no Soviet domination of Eastern Europe"—confirmed the general opinion that he was not worthy of the presidency. One reporter dismissed Ford's comment by saying, "Oh, that was just Jerry talking about something he knows nothing about." "Yeah," nightclub comedians deadpanned, Vice President Nelson Rockefeller was "only a banana peel away from the presidency."

Although almost everyone agreed that Ford was as unassuming and amiable as Nixon had been pretentious and abrasive, the mere change in tone and style wasn't sufficient to ensure Ford's success in the presidency. His limited talents as a politician and a statesman made Americans unwilling to entrust him with a position that, for all its perceived limitations after Vietnam and Watergate, the country still believed was best held by a more effective and knowledgeable man.

III

When John Adams, Andrew Johnson, Harding, FDR, and Ford suffered a diminution in their credibility, it was largely because they had violated accepted standards or crossed political or legal lines that were generally regarded as inviolable. When Wilson, Hoover, LBJ, and Carter fell into disrepute, it was principally because they had become victims of their own overblown hopes and rhetoric about what they intended to accomplish in office. Promising more than can be delivered is a trap that snared more than one president. While it has been particularly troublesome for men like Wilson and LBJ, who were carried away by an evangelism for change beyond their reach, it has also helped ruin presidents like Hoover, Carter, and Bush who, in responding to circumstances beyond their control, made commitments they were subsequently unable to honor.

*   *   *

Wilson and LBJ are this century's most noteworthy examples of presidents who lost credibility by promising utopias at home and abroad. After leading the country into World War I, Wilson felt compelled to announce peace aims that would justify the sacrifices that had been made in human lives and resources. But the Fourteen Points were simply too idealistic, and the notion that any president or any leader anywhere in 1918 could have achieved the revolution in international affairs that Wilson envisioned now seems fantastic. An end to secret diplomacy, the realization of freedom of the seas, free trade, reduced armaments, national self-determination, diminished colonial tensions, and "a general association of nations" practicing collective security were goals any generation would comfortably endorse, and in 1918, after the most terrible bloodletting in history, people especially wanted to believe that they were attainable. When Wilson arrived in Europe in December for peace talks, millions cheered him as a savior: "Through you evil is punished," one woman wrote him. "Wilson! Wilson! Glory to you, who, like Jesus, have said: Peace on Earth and Good Will to Men!"

Yet the fulfillment of his peace program, even almost eighty years later, remains a distant hope. Of course, when Wilson first proposed it, he was also using the plan to rally his European allies, who had suffered for nearly three and a half years, and to convince enemy governments that there could be a peace beneficial to all and one without victors. Nevertheless, by formalizing such aims and promising that they would make the world safe for democracy and put an end to war, he was obligating himself to visionary designs no one could reasonably expect to achieve.

The inevitable occurred at the peace talks at Versailles in 1919. "God gave us his Ten Commandments, and we broke them," French premier Georges Clemenceau declared at the start of the conference. "Wilson gave us his Fourteen Points—we shall see." Instead of open covenants openly arrived at, the negotiations were conducted behind closed doors between the American, British, French, and Italian heads of government. Instead of granting some measure of freedom to "enemy colonies," the Allied powers became their trustees under mandates assigned by the new world organization. Instead of a peace without victors, the Big Four con-

demned Germany as responsible for the war and demanded repa-
ration payments. Instead of self-determination for peoples
everywhere, the negotiators sought only to satisfy the security
needs of the winning powers. French occupation of the Rhineland,
Italian dominance of Fiume, and Japanese control of China's Shan-
tung peninsula did not impress anyone as fulfilling Wilson's promises about national self-rule.

Yet Wilson could not or would not own up to the disappointments he met at Versailles. His speech to a joint session of Congress in July 1919, when he presented the Treaty, was in effect a
call to complete the work left undone by the conference: "The
stage is set, the destiny disclosed," he declared. "It has come about
by no plan of our conceiving, but by the hand of God who led us
into this way. We cannot turn back. . . . The light streams upon
the path ahead, and nowhere else."

Wilson misjudged the prospects for the Treaty's passage in the
United States on two counts. First, Americans had grown weary
of international crusades. Domestic economic problems, particularly inflation and industrial strikes, joined with anxieties over alien
radicals to shift national attention from foreign to internal affairs.
Second, the conviction that America could transform international
relations had all but disappeared with the publication of the Versailles Treaty. Wilson's insistence that the outcome at Versailles had
not diminished prospects for changing the world now had little
resonance in the United States. Led by Walter Lippmann and John
Maynard Keynes, who published *The Economic Consequences of the
Peace* in October 1919, critics complained that the Treaty and
League would bring disastrous results to Europe for a long time
to come.

Though a stroke in September 1919 incapacitated Wilson and
left him unable to continue his fight for the Treaty, a national belief
that the president was overly hopeful about world affairs had already settled the issue. The compromises at Versailles, coupled
with postwar upheavals in Europe had essentially put an end to
Wilson's plausibility as a convincing foreign policy leader. He was
an idealist leading a nation that had become disillusioned with utopian dreams of reforming international behavior. By now the country yearned for something Harding described as "normalcy," and
leaders whose keynote was pragmatism.

*   *   *

Lyndon Johnson rivaled Wilson in promising changes at home as revolutionary as those the Fourteen Points were supposed to produce abroad. While considerable evidence exists that the stalemate in Vietnam destroyed Johnson's presidency, there is also reason to believe that, even without a divisive policy in Vietnam, Johnson would have faced a skeptical electorate in 1968. When Louis Harris asked a cross-section of Americans in 1988 who was the greatest domestic leader among the nine presidents from Roosevelt to Reagan, only 6 percent chose LBJ. Is it really conceivable that twenty years after Johnson left the White House, his far-reaching domestic reforms were forgotten by the 94 percent choosing one of the other eight presidents as a superior domestic leader?

More likely, this survey's results indicate that a majority of Americans had lost confidence in Johnson's assessments of what the war on poverty, the Great Society, and civil rights laws could do to renew America. This skepticism did not suddenly arise in the seventies and eighties after a new conservative mood had taken hold in the country, but was rather part of the very reaction against what Johnson was attempting to accomplish in the sixties.

"Do you think poverty will ever be done away with in this country?" the Gallup poll asked Americans in March 1964, as Johnson was launching his antipoverty campaign. Only 9 percent replied yes, thoroughly outnumbered by the 83 percent who answered no. Two years later, when 80 percent of the populace had become aware of the antipoverty program, only between a third and 48 percent of those polled had a favorable opinion of the policy. In November 1966, Gallup registered only 32 percent as well disposed toward Johnson's Great Society, with 44 percent describing themselves as "unfavorable."

Similar doubts about the benefits of civil rights actions took hold during this period as well. In April 1965 a majority of Americans considered civil rights the country's most pressing problem. But after the passage of the 1964 law and the Voting Rights bill in July 1965 national sentiment reversed, as the electorate came to view the civil rights movement—or at least a significant part of its leadership—as subversive of American institutions. In November, 65 percent of respondents in a poll indicated they believed there was at least some Communist involvement behind civil rights demonstrations. By the spring of 1966, 64 percent of the country saw administration support of integration as excessive, or at just the right level; only 21 percent wanted the issue dealt with more quickly. In September of that year, a majority of whites complained that integration was being pushed too fast. In May 1969, 90 percent of Americans rejected a proposal to have churches and synagogues pay $500 million to blacks as compensation for past injustices. A year later, 62 percent of Americans opposed greater efforts in behalf of desegregation. School integration and busing were no more popular with a majority of whites.

Though Johnson pressed the case for his war on poverty, Great Society, and civil rights reforms by continually pointing to the gains made by his administration under these programs, it is clear that Americans were growing increasingly disenchanted with them. Where LBJ interpreted his antipoverty crusade as having reduced the number of Americans in want from 23 percent to 12 percent, most of the country attributed the decline in need to the swelling welfare rolls. Where Johnson celebrated the benefits of federal aid to education; universal medical insurance for the elderly and the indigent; improved Social Security benefits; more livable cities; better housing programs; cleaner air and water; safer roads, cars, tires, mines, and streets; fairer immigration restrictions; consumer protections; and public support for the arts, humanities, and public broadcasting, millions of Americans complained of a bloated government spending too much money on programs weighted down with red tape. Where the president rhapsodized over the movement toward a just nation, in which equality of treatment and opportunity for minorities and women was fulfilling the promise of American life, most of the populace decried inner-city violence and riots and accepted the Kerner Commission's conclusion that the country was split into two nations, one white and one black, separate and unequal.

By 1968 Johnson, the great reformer of 1964–1965, was seen as a true believer mesmerized by his own rhetoric but incapable of accepting harsh truths about enduring poverty or a divided America spinning out of control. Critics argued that the president's Great Society of racial harmony and contented citizens moving beyond material well-being to a higher cultural plane was merely a figment of LBJ's imagination. Along with the tragedy of the war in Vietnam, the growing divergence between the president and the public on domestic conditions arising from his programs substantially added to the belief that Johnson no longer had an accurate grasp of national concerns. Sensing that he would be overstaying his welcome if he tried for another term, Johnson reluctantly announced that he would retire from office in January 1969.

Unlike Wilson and LBJ, Hoover and Carter did not view their presidencies as vehicles for delivering unprecedented benefits to Americans. Each had hopes of advancing the national condition, as does every president, but they carried no dreams of permanent cures or of remaking America or the world in far-reaching ways. Nevertheless, after four years their respective publics had lost confidence in them, for domestic realities had given the lie to the domestic gains they did vow to achieve.

Hoover's problem, of course, was a Depression that could not be banished by encouraging words or even government actions, as FDR would learn. Hoover's great failure in the White House was his inability not only to break with an outdated vision of the country's future and respond flexibly to the changing national mood, but also his incapacity to sustain public belief in him, thanks to promises he clearly couldn't honor.

"The future is bright with hope," he announced in his 1929 inaugural speech. And so it was, especially at the New York Stock Exchange, where during the first nine months of the year the market, riding a six-year expansion, reached new highs. But in October the great reversal that preceded the depression began. Hoping that expressions of optimism could stem the downward tide, Hoover declared, "The fundamental business of the country, that is, production and distribution of commodities, is on a sound and prosperous basis." His supporters in the business community echoed that prognosis. The chairman of the board of Bethlehem Steel assured the nation that "never before has American business been as firmly entrenched for prosperity as it is today," and the president of the National Association of Manufacturers saw "little on the horizon today to give us undue or great concern."

Hoover was ready and willing to support his optimism. He com-

mitted the prestige of his office and the resources of the government to voluntary agreements with businesses and to policies that
he believed would restrict economic problems to the stock market
and keep national prosperity on course. In the first months of
1930, he predicted that the unemployment that had begun to
mount in late 1929 would begin to reverse itself within the next
sixty days. But the president's prediction proved wrong, and the
humorist Will Rogers expressed the emerging tenor of the nation
when he said: "There has been more 'optimism' talked and less
practiced than at any time during our history."

The facts did not deter Hoover from continuing to foresee rosy
times. "I am confident we have now passed the worst and with
continued unity of effort we shall rapidly recover," he said in May.
As the Depression deepened and the jobless rolls grew, Hoover
counseled the unemployed to take inspiration from "our great
manufacturers, our railways, utilities, business houses, and public
officials." He saw no reason for the government to offer direct aid
to the jobless; the country's voluntary and community organizations were entirely adequate to the task. For him and the government to mount programs of relief would undermine the
foundations of individual responsibility and self-rule. Hoover's
strongest action was to set up a President's Organization on Unemployment Relief, which launched an advertising campaign in
1931 to stimulate private charity.

The president's repeated insistence that the depression was ending or even over, that "prosperity was right around the corner,"
took on the qualities of a religious chant, which, if repeated often
enough, might have some salutary effect. He refused to look economic realities squarely in the face. "Many persons left their jobs
for the more profitable one of selling apples," he wrote after leaving the presidency, a comment that undoubtedly reflected his earlier view of the state of U.S. economic affairs. When told about an
alarming decline in public health caused by the depression, Hoover
defensively replied, "Nobody is actually starving." He believed that
if only someone could think up a good joke that would make the
country laugh or compose a song that would make them forget
their troubles or a poem that would relieve gloom, it would reverse
the nation's downward course.

The result of Hoover's willful blindness was a collapse of public faith in a man millions had admired as a model citizen at the outset of his term. The press and the president viewed each other, one journalist said in 1931, with "mutual dislike, unconcealed suspicion, and downright bitterness." Hoover soon became the object of public derision. "The very word 'Hoover,' " Arthur Schlesinger, Jr., writes, "became a prefix charged with hate: not only 'Hoovervilles,' but 'Hoover blankets' (newspapers wrapped around for warmth), 'Hoover wagons' (broken-down automobiles hauled by mules), 'Hoover flags' (empty pockets turned inside out), 'Hoover hogs' (jackrabbits)."

By 1932 Hoover's presidency was beyond redemption. His campaign for reelection was no more likely to return him to the White House than his economic policies had been equal to ending the Depression. The great majority of Americans had come to dismiss him as a man with no *good* idea of how to proceed—a man around whom the country could not possibly rally to meet its worst crisis since the Civil War. The political standing of the discredited Hoover was an all-too-apt metaphor for the national economy. But while a new leader with greater understanding of the national decline and novel ideas about how to address it could restore hope and put the economy on an upward trajectory, Hoover could never repair the damage to his political career. Once a president loses the country's trust, he serves in office on borrowed time.

Jimmy Carter's four years in the White House was another object lesson of a president's failure to sustain public confidence in his capacity to do his job. Like Hoover, Carter was a moralistic progressive with an engineer's fixation on detail and an inability to inspire the electorate. Despite these shortcomings, he had been voted to the White House under the common belief that his sense of morality, intellectual capacity, and political astuteness were compensation enough to make him a successful president.

It was not to be. For all his personal integrity, Carter's command as a moral leader was short-lived. Any question of his potential to restore morality to American political life was put to rest by the suspect financial practices of OMB director Bert Lance, who was forced to resign; by accusations that Carter's principal aide, Hamilton Jordan, was a cocaine user; by the image of brother Billy as a beer-drinking carouser; and by congressional scandals involving kickbacks and bribes that come to be known as Koreagate and ABSCAM.

Similarly, Carter's vaunted powers as a skilled manager were belied by his actual practices while in office. The impression quickly grew that the president was too focused on the details of White House business to see the larger picture and to introduce significant reform of the "bloated unmanageable bureaucracy" in Washington. Suffering from what James MacGregor Burns calls "strategic myopia," Carter found it impossible to set a sensible agenda. As Hedrick Smith has written, "Carter was an idealist, a good-government moralist, who had trouble connecting ends and means and converting his high-minded goals into politically salable programs." He "always had so many priorities that he seemed to have none. . . . Whenever I would ask White House officials for Carter's top priorities," Smith says, "the list would run past a dozen items. The focus of the Carter Presidency was not clear." Rumors that the president kept track of White House tennis court bookings was symptomatic.

Carter's unsuccessful struggle with economic problems, and particularly the country's energy crisis, did even more to raise doubts about his leadership. "Are you better off today than you were four years ago?" Reagan cannily asked voters in the 1980 campaign. With the unemployment rate only slightly lower than it had been, with inflation and interest rates in double digits, and with little prospect of a viable White House energy policy, the answer had to be a resounding no. Economic realities had joined with administration stumbling to discredit Carter as a president capable of easing, let alone solving, the country's most troublesome domestic problems.

Carter had two significant achievements abroad: the Camp David accords between Egypt and Israel, which represented a large step toward Middle East peace, and the Panama Canal treaties, which eased tensions with Panama and raised U.S. prestige in Latin America. But on balance, a deterioration in U.S.-Soviet relations produced by Communist subversion in Angola, Moscow's violations of the Helsinki agreements on human rights, the deployment of SS20 Soviet missiles against Western Europe, and an invasion of Afghanistan to support a Marxist government battling Muslim rebels raised doubts about the feasibility of Carter's policy of détente as well as about his own strength and resolve as a foreign policy leader. Stalling a Senate vote on a SALT II treaty, a commitment to deploy Pershing-2 and Cruise missiles in Europe, an embargo on grain and technology sales to the Soviets, and a boycott of the Olympic games in Moscow were steps that were finally not sufficient to restore Carter's reputation as an effective diplomat abroad.

Nothing contributed more directly to Carter's loss of credibility as an effective defender of the national security than the Iranian hostage crisis. The seizure and imprisonment of fifty-three Americans at the American embassy in Teheran, most of whom were entitled to diplomatic immunity, confronted Carter with a challenge to U.S. prestige and his administration's resourcefulness in dealing with a radical regime's defiance of American rights. The fact that negotiations for the hostages came to nothing was much less troubling than the failure of a rescue mission in which eight American troops lost their lives and equipment malfunctioned. The episode suggested a paralysis of will and an embarrassing failure of the country's power for which the hapless Jimmy Carter received the blame.

By 1980, 75 percent of Americans saw the nation as on the wrong track and Jimmy Carter as a man for no seasons. The historian Eric Goldman summed up the national mood when he said, "Carterism does not march and it does not sing; it is cautious, muted, grayish, at times even crabbed." By July, Carter's approval rating had fallen to 21 percent, the lowest ever recorded for a president in office. Carter knew that he was failing. In 1979 he had told his cabinet: "My government is not leading the country. The people have lost confidence in me, in the Congress, in themselves, and in this nation." On the eve of the 1980 election, he told CBS that his presidency deserved a B or C-plus on foreign policy, a C on domestic affairs, and "maybe a B" on overall leadership. But as James MacGregor Burns remarked, "For a president, B and C are failing grades."

When Ronald Reagan scolded Carter during a 1980 campaign debate, "There you go again," he captured succinctly the public's disdain for a politician who had been a great disappointment to his supporters and a predictable failure to his opponents. Though

Carter's patent decency in his postpresidential career would largely restore his standing with Americans, his four-year term was something of a nightmare in which a country frustrated by circumstances at home and abroad felt incapable of trusting a president who seemed unable to turn national losses into national gains.

IV

No president has served for four or more years without some erosion of his credibility. Even the most admired or best loved chiefs like the two Roosevelts, Eisenhower, and Reagan have left office against a backdrop of complaints that their poor judgment or unwise decisions on any number of matters cost the country dearly. But on balance, such missteps have been understood as largely the result of universal human failings. Far more detrimental to presidential reputation and the power to lead has been the general conviction that the president was lying to the country. "Lying" in this context does not refer to cutting political corners or self-serving seizure of political advantage; most observers of the government in action have recognized that deal-making is an unsavory if inevitable ingredient in the American political process. But outright lying or deception—however necessary the incumbent may believe it is for the national well-being—has invariably incensed Americans and turned them against the perpetrator.

Deception of the public was the most notable factor in the collapse of both the Lyndon Johnson and Nixon presidencies. Johnson's credibility gap made it impossible for him to run for another term, and as one of the most astute politicians in U.S. history, who should have recognized that betraying the public trust could spell an end to his career, it is difficult to understand his self-destructiveness in this regard.

Part of the explanation for his conduct is that he simply acted out of force of habit or of a pattern of political behavior dating from early in his career. Johnson's successful bid for national public office, first as a congressman and then a senator from Texas, partly rested on bending the rules. Hidden campaign financing and ballot-box stuffing were as common to Texas politics in the 1930s and 1940s, when Johnson was a rising star, as Democratic party dominance of state affairs. In 1937, in his first House campaign, Johnson discovered that abundant and unreported financial resources were a key to victory. In 1941, when lobbyists eager to send Governor "Pappy" O'Daniel to the U.S. Senate freely manufactured votes to cheat Johnson out of the seat, LBJ learned an unforgettable lesson about statewide Texas politics—campaign hard and count *your* votes last. In 1948 Johnson took former Governor Coke Stevenson to school when his campaign produced enough last-minute votes to gain the Senate seat he had lost because of skulduggery in 1941. When FDR called off an Internal Revenue investigation of George and Herman Brown, Johnson's supporters, in 1944, LBJ had seen that under-the-table politics reached into the White House as well.

Dubbed "Landslide Lyndon" because of his eighty-seven-vote victory over Stevenson in 1948, Johnson paid a price in public reputation for his questionable victory. But he knew that rumor was no lasting substitute for proof, and that significant accomplishments as a senator would, in time, blunt the charges against him and allow him to move on to bigger things.

Yet the machinations he had engaged in as a congressman and a senator proved untenable in the White House, though three factors encouraged him to believe he could carry on as he had earlier in his career: his view that the country's most successful politicians, from FDR to the Kennedys, had done just that; his grandiose certainty that he could manipulate the press and the public into accepting whatever he wanted them to believe; and his conviction that he was acting for the good of the country and that, even if his transgressions came to light, people would forgive what they would understand as being done on their behalf.

During the 1964 presidential campaign, Johnson had exploited the media's anxiety about Goldwater's candidacy to bend them to his will. He set up a White House working group that systematically fed information to the newspapers, radio, and television praising the president's virtues and condemning Goldwater's defects. The famous "daisy field" ad, which portrayed Goldwater as a threat to world peace or the potential instigator of a nuclear war, was perhaps the most notorious example of how Johnson played on public fears through his cunning handling of the media. The president himself held journalists in great contempt, believing, as he told the historian William E. Leuchtenburg, that they were a bunch of "whores" who would lie on the floor with any of their editors for three dollars.

Johnson's rage at the media stemmed from his growing comprehension that he could not control them on the matter of Vietnam as he had in the 1964 campaign. His expansion of the war in 1965 had been undertaken without its ever being directly acknowledged. In February, for example, as he moved toward systematic bombing of North Vietnam, LBJ was urged by national security adviser McGeorge Bundy to make clear to Americans what he was doing and that they were about to take part in a long struggle. But Johnson insisted that there be no "loud public signal of a change in policy." He took the same approach when he expanded ground forces in the summer of 1965 and doubled the number of troops in Vietnam during 1966. Instead of openly announcing the 1966 increase, he misrepresented the decision by reporting the growth of forces only a month at a time.

Johnson was well aware that he was putting himself at risk by secretly escalating the war. In February 1965, *New York Times* columnist James Reston reported that the president was "particularly sensitive to charges that he is not talking enough to the American people about the complexities and risks of the Vietnam war. He carries around in his pocket a series of private polls that purport to show that the vast majority of the people not only know what he is doing but approve what he is doing."

In guarding his decisions from close public scrutiny Johnson was convinced he was serving the national interest. He feared that if he put his commitments in Vietnam on open display, it might provoke a debate in the country and in Congress that would ultimately play havoc with Great Society laws. Likewise, he worried that conservatives would raise an effective cry against diverting funds that needed to be allocated to the war to domestic social programs. Better, he believed, to keep Vietnam quiet, despite growing commitments there, until his new domestic legislation was fully in place.

When war critics began attacking not only his policy in Vietnam but also his method of involving us in the war, he retorted, "I'm the only President you have," implying not only that he knew what was best for America, but also that active, achieving presidents have always held their cards close to their chests and acted unilaterally for the national good. Ben Bradlee of the Washington *Post* memorably described the president's attitude when he said that Johnson "was a great actor, bar fucking none the greatest. . . . He'd be trying to persuade you of something, sometimes something that he knew and I knew was not so, and there was just the trace of a little smile on his face. It was just a miraculous performance."

Where Johnson thought that the expenditure of national resources in an overseas conflict should and would rally the country to him, dissenting opinion objected that he was behaving like an imperial tsar rather than a democratic president reflecting the majority will. It was one thing to pursue a debatable policy for a short time, but a drawn-out war with uncertain ends made attacks on Johnson's covert actions inevitable.

The fact that Johnson already had a reputation for deviousness only added to the impression that he was not to be trusted on matters concerning Vietnam. Nothing had contributed to this assumption more than his public comments about the Dominican Republic in the spring of 1965. The possibility of a radical Castro-style regime arising in Santo Domingo persuaded Johnson to send in the marines as a preventive measure, but only afterward did he feel compelled to convince Americans that he had done the right thing. Though there was considerable debate about the dangers to Americans living in the Dominican Republic from the upheaval and the seriousness of the Communist threat, Johnson made it clear that these two conditions left him no choice but to intervene.

At a press conference in June he vividly portrayed the state of anarchy and panic among U.S. citizens in Santo Domingo, "pleading with their President for help to preserve their lives." But American newsmen on the scene witnessed none of what he described. Moreover, in other public statements, Johnson warned of an international Communist conspiracy, announcing, "We don't propose to sit here in our rocking chair with our hands folded and let the Communists set up any government in the Western Hemisphere." When newsmen reported that they could find no genuine radicals on a list of names the administration released to prove the existence of a Marxist threat, people began to doubt whether Johnson was capable of telling the truth.

Failure in Vietnam, overreaching himself in the war on poverty and the Great Society, and an unlovely personality that did more to alienate than attract Americans all in some measure contributed to the collapse of Johnson's presidency. But however unappealing LBJ may have been to the mass of Americans, however troubling his exaggerated promises about domestic gains, and whatever the shortfall in Vietnam, the country might have held faith with a president who understood the workings of Washington as well as he did, who was so clearly devoted to the nation's well-being, and who genuinely commanded a significant majority eager to win in Vietnam. But how could the electorate support a president who didn't trust his fellow citizens enough to tell them the truth? Better, instead, to turn to the devil they didn't know than to stay with the devil they did.

The public seemed comfortable with that view until they got a full dose of Richard Nixon as their helmsman. Nixon is the unparalleled example of a president who lost power by deceiving the country. Like Johnson, Nixon was schooled in the fine art of public deception for the sake of political gain. His campaigns for national office, his attacks on Alger Hiss, questions about his campaign finances in his 1952 vice-presidential race, and his vicious assaults on Democrats during the fifties, gave him a justified reputation as a go-for-broke politician with limited regard for the truth.

For some observers, the break-in at Democratic party headquarters in the Watergate apartment complex in the midst of Nixon's 1972 reelection campaign was simply another example of his affinity for no-holds-barred electioneering. Although Nixon's foreign policy successes in his first term and the prospect of making George McGovern, a left-wing Democrat, president gave Nixon a historic landslide victory, nagging questions about the Watergate burglary wouldn't go away. And so in the spring of 1973, when one of the burglars confessed to the connection between the break-in and the Republican Committee to Re-elect the President (CREEP), the story of White House involvement in political dirty tricks and a coverup became a topic of daily discussion in the press.

What proved to be a veritable catalogue of transgressions now shocked the country. Vice President Spiro Agnew, who had taken bribes as governor of Maryland, was forced to resign; the acting director of the FBI, L. Patrick Gray III, left office after admitting that he had destroyed Watergate documents on orders from the White House; Attorney General John Mitchell, who later went to prison, acknowledged that as head of CREEP he had discussed the break-in with the burglars; the president's principal White House aides, John D. Ehrlichman and H. R. (Bob) Haldeman, who also later went to prison, resigned in response to evidence of their participation in a coverup; and hearings before a Senate committee chaired by North Carolina conservative Democrat Sam Ervin revealed that Nixon had secretly taped his telephone and Oval Office conversations for over two years. The growing roster of bribes, buggings, burglaries, money laundering, and the details being revealed of a wide-ranging coverup left the entire country asking the inevitable question: Was Richard Nixon guilty of a crime?

Consistently denying involvement in any wrongdoing, Nixon declared at a press conference, "I am not a crook." But his every action belied his claims. The "Saturday night massacre" in October 1973, in which he fired special prosecutor Archibald Cox for demanding relevant White House tapes, as well as several justice department officials, including Attorney General Elliot Richardson, who refused to execute the president's dismissal order, only increased doubts about Nixon's honesty. An 18½-minute gap in one of the tapes that the courts compelled Nixon to release and doctored transcripts of unreleased tapes provoked calls for the president's impeachment. Only when the Supreme Court forced open additional tapes that established Nixon's clear involvement in a White House coverup did the House Judiciary Committee vote three articles of impeachment, citing his obstruction of justice, misuse of the Internal Revenue Service and other government agencies for political purposes, and his defiance of congressional subpoenas for the tapes.

On August 8, 1974, Nixon became the first president in American history to resign. Though then and later he refused to acknowledge his criminality, confessing only to "mistakes," he was thoroughly discredited and saved himself and the country from a Senate trial by leaving office.

Regardless of the likely outcome of any judicial proceeding against him in the Senate, his resignation was an admission of his incapacity to govern. For months before his departure, his immobilized administration had been unable to attend to domestic and foreign affairs. Despite a plea to the country in his State of the Union address in January 1974 to focus on public affairs other than the scandal, he could not divert attention from the questions being posed about his integrity. Indeed, as early as April 1973, Nixon knew that he had lost control of events. "It's all over, do you know that?" he told his press secretary that month. By then, Henry Kissinger says, Watergate had thrown those trying to run the government into a "panic": "I, a foreign-born American, wound up in the extraordinary position of holding together our foreign policy and reassuring our public." Stanley Kutler says that "even some Kissinger critics acknowledged that he was 'nearly the sole figure who legitimized or redeemed the government.' "

As the example of Nixon so dramatically demonstrates, once a president is suspected of legal trespass his power to govern is badly compromised. Presidents have and will continue to survive accusations of constitutional wrongdoing, but accusations alone have not been sufficient to imperil a president's capacity to rule. When, however, the public begins to believe that such accusations have some merit, then the president is faced with a crisis of confidence. Nixon's own track record and the instances of corruption in his administration made it increasingly difficult for him to sustain public trust. By the summer of 1974, even without the "smoking gun" that confirmed his involvement in the coverup, even without the threat of impeachment proceedings, his presidency had effectively come to an end, for the very appearance of impropriety had been enough to compromise his leadership. Watergate had mortally wounded him by suggesting that, even if he was not directly involved in the many crimes committed by some of the highest officials around him, he had created an administration that did not deserve the country's trust.

Matters of trust and credibility also play a part in shaping post-presidential reputations. Few presidents in American history enjoyed higher public regard while in office than Franklin Roosevelt, as his average approval rating of 75 percent during his last five years as president demonstrates. While his leadership during the war no doubt accounts for some of this popularity, it is difficult to imagine few other presidents who could have sustained so strong an appeal over a twelve-year term.

Since 1945, however, Roosevelt has been subjected to a series of attacks on his integrity, as revisionist critics have asserted that he lied the country into the war, manufactured the surprise at Pearl Harbor, and callously abandoned the Jews to Hitler's Holocaust. It is striking that none of this criticism has challenged Roosevelt's abilities as a visionary, a pragmatist, a consensus-builder, or a charismatic leader. Rather, the point of assault has been on his honesty in dealing with the public. Determined as much to lift the halo from Roosevelt's head as to recapture historical truths, revisionists have argued that the portrait of FDR as a great democratic leader is much overdrawn; that to the contrary, he was a ruthless politician whose hunger for power and self-righteous convictions moved him to lie to and mislead the country about foreign affairs. Whatever the merits of these accusations—and there seems little to recommend them—it speaks volumes about the importance of public trust in assessing presidential performance that so much has been staked on questioning this particular aspect of FDR's reputation. (It is worth noting here that the FDR antagonists have enjoyed little success for their efforts: In 1990, 75 percent of the country still saw fit to give Franklin Roosevelt high marks.)

Still, presidents and public alike should not overlook the extent to which public support for the chief executive has depended on confidence in his commitment to telling Americans the unvarnished truth. "The best leadership in a democracy will get rid of cant and hypocrisy," Schlesinger, Jr., reminds us. "Down with banality and cliché, with slogan and stereotype!" And on this point, he cedes the final word to Ralph Waldo Emerson: "Wise men pierce this rotten diction and fasten words to visible things; so that picturesque language is at once a commanding certificate that he who employs it is a man in alliance with truth and God."

AFTERWORD

How would the forty-one presidents who have served this country react to this book's assertions about what has made for effective performance in the White House? No doubt Washington, Lincoln, FDR, and a few others would nod in agreement at the high marks accorded them. But what would the many less highly rated chiefs think? *Look,* they would probably say, *you've produced a clear design for how to go about being an effective president, but you don't understand the daily realities of the office. In fact, we are the only ones who truly know the possibilities and limits of the position. And* we all agree that luck, circumstance, and chance, unforeseen events are what make the biggest difference in determining a president's fate.

The argument for chance and a certain mutability of public affairs is compelling. Presidents, after all, are not magicians or supermen capable of bending everything in their perview to their wills. Consider the track records of the greater and lesser lights in the office. For all of Washington's personal appeal and brilliance in getting the government established, he couldn't prevent the emergence of political factions or parties; for all their opposition to involvement in another European conflict, Jefferson and Madison couldn't prevent the War of 1812; for all his intelligence and wisdom in seeing the government as a vehicle for modernizing the country, John Quincy Adams couldn't put his national system in place; for all his attractiveness as a symbol for the age and the popularity of his bank war, Jackson couldn't forestall a national economic collapse in 1837; for all his effectiveness in meeting the challenge of southern secession, Lincoln couldn't avert the unprecedented bloodletting of the Civil War; for all his good intentions in trying to restore national unity during Reconstruction, Andrew Johnson failed miserably; for all their desire to extend prosperity to all classes of citizens and be remembered as dedicated chiefs who honorably served the national well-being, Grant, Hayes, Garfield, Arthur, Cleveland, and Harrison presided over a nation riven by economic strife and political corruption; for all his reluctance to fight Spain and abandon the country's anticolonial tradition, McKinley became a war president and launched the country on a course of empire.

Twentieth-century presidents fared no better. For all their determination to put U.S. foreign policy on a new plane, neither TR nor Wilson could avert the isolationism of the thirties; for all his humanitarian concerns and competence as a manager of large enterprises, Herbert Hoover couldn't develop a strategy for fighting the Depression; for all his success in transforming American domestic life, FDR couldn't end the country's economic downturn; for all his strategic good sense in meeting the Soviet challenge, Harry Truman found himself trapped in a Korean stalemate; for all his personal popularity and effectiveness in keeping the peace, Ike couldn't reach an accommodation with the Soviets or find a plausible answer to southern racial tensions; for all his determination to create greater domestic and international harmony, JFK found himself stymied at home and more of a crisis manager than a peacemaker abroad; for all his reluctance to fight an unpopular war ten thousand miles from America, LBJ couldn't head off a conflict that ended his presidency; for all his gains as a foreign policy leader and intelligence in addressing a number of domestic problems, Nixon couldn't bring himself to play by even a relaxed version of the political rules; for all his understanding of what needed doing to heal national wounds after Vietnam and Watergate, Jimmy Carter couldn't reverse the country's "malaise"; for all his conservative commitment to frugal federal spending and balanced budgets, Reagan piled up the greatest deficits and federal debt in U.S. history; and for all his eagerness to ensure decent, affordable health care for everyone, Bill Clinton failed to make even a dent in the problem.

No one can deny that presidents face a daunting task, one that no formula can simplify. Moreover, there are any number of undefinable, imprecise qualities that have contributed to presidential success. One is tempted to say simply that presidents either have that special something, which gives them an edge in addressing the problems of their day, or they don't. Like personality, which so eludes understanding, presidential effectiveness doesn't readily translate into a checklist of definable characteristics that we can look for in aspiring chiefs.

It is small wonder that we have been continually surprised at how well or how poorly our presidents have performed. No one foresaw Lincoln's greatness. Few anticipated that TR, "that damned cowboy," would prove to be an exceptionally effective leader. Who would have predicted Herbert Hoover's failure? A critic as astute as Walter Lippmann couldn't perceive that FDR was more than just a pleasant young man who wanted to be president; and certainly no one could have imagined that Harry Truman, "the little man from Missouri," would reach the heights he achieved in the White House. How many liberals expected Reagan to perform as well in office as he did? How do we explain the failure of so seasoned a politician and public official as George Bush? There are imponderables involved here that do not lend themselves to easy explanation.

The categories this book offers up are not intended to be the last, or even the first, word on how to succeed in the White House. Far from it. The preceding chapters are a historian's examination of how vision, pragmatism, consensus, charisma, and credibility have contributed to presidential performance. What seems most striking is the extent to which each of these elements has been present and absent in the leadership of the most and least effective chiefs. This is not to suggest that every well-functioning president has scored a ten in each of these categories or that the worst of our chiefs has been a zero on all five counts. Each administration has been sui generis, a presidential term distinct from all the others in the ways in which foresight, practical politics, national agreement, personal popularity, and trust have come together.

Yet however imprecise or impressionistic matters like vision and the rest may be as categories of analysis, they have been essential elements in helping presidents achieve effective leadership. While they did not guarantee presidents greatness or even consistent success, if generally and consistently applied, they would certainly have improved upon performance in the White House.

It is worth quoting here an observation of Richard Neustadt and Ernest May in their prize-winning book *Thinking in Time: The Uses of History for Decision Makers*. In response to the question of whether historical or political judgments cannot be taught to decision-makers, the authors say: "In some degree, we fear, the answer to that question is yes. No manual or course of study will make an ordinary politician an LBJ or transform an LBJ into an FDR. But . . . we work at margins. If our students were baseball players, we would not expect to turn out Ted Williamses or Sandy Koufaxes; we would be happy to see a batting average go up from .250 to .265 or an earned run average go down from 6.0 to 5.0. And we do believe that almost any continuous effort to use history routinely will improve the averages of players in the public arena."

Likewise, anyone trying to understand the components of effective presidential performance would do well to investigate the common elements that have operated across the decades in contributing to White House success. Since history never exactly repeats itself, the study of how past presidents made large gains and suffered major defeats gives us little more than a useful general guide to executive actions. There will probably never be an effective substitute for presidential intuition or innate savvy as a foundation for diplomatic and strategic skill. But presidents need every additional edge they can get in managing the world's most challenging job. Knowledge of what did and didn't work for their predecessors is worth considering. I hope this book can be a useful guide in preserving and advancing that government that still remains the last best hope of mankind.

SOURCES

I am indebted to a number of scholars and journalists for their thoughtful writings on the American presidency. The following citations will give readers a chapter by chapter listing of the books and articles on which my discussions of presidential leadership are based.

All quotations from presidential statements can be found in the series, J.D. Richardson, ed., *Compilation of the Messages and Papers of the Presidents, 1789–1897* (Washington, D.C.: U.S. Government Printing Office, 1907), and *Public Papers of the Presidents of the United States* (Washington, D.C.: U.S. Government Printing Office, 1957–).

Introduction

The introduction has benefited from Arthur M. Schlesinger, Jr., *The Cycles of American History* (Boston: Houghton Mifflin, 1986), especially chapter 11, "After the Imperial Presidency," and chapter 14, "Democracy and Leadership." Several of the quotes on the travail of the presidency are from Forrest McDonald, *The American Presidency: An Intellectual History* (Lawrence, Kan.: University Press Kansas, 1994). Also see "Presidential Bellyaches," *New York Times*, Oct. 8, 1995. The Lincoln material is from David Donald, *Lincoln Reconsidered* (New York: Knopf, 1961 ed.), ch. 4.

The Steinbeck quote is in T.D. Schellhardt, "Do We Expect Too Much?" *Wall Street Journal*, July 10, 1979. For Godfrey Hodgson, see *All Things to All Men: The False Promise of the Modern American Presidency* (New York: Simon & Schuster, 1980), 49. Wicker is quoted in Bernard J. Firestone and Robert C. Vogt, eds., *Lyndon Baines Johnson and the Uses of Power* (New York: Greenwood Press, 1988), 2–3. Taft is quoted in Schlesinger, Jr., *Cycles of American History*, 287. John Adams is quoted in Bernard Bailyn et al., *The Great Republic: A History of the American People* (Lexington, Mass: D.C. Heath and Co., 1992), I, 367. For the Schlesinger, Jr., quotes see *Cycles of American History*, 283–84, 330.

Chapter One

On the election of 1920 and Harding and Coolidge, see William E. Leuchtenburg, *The Perils of Prosperity, 1914–1932* (Chicago, University of Chicago Press, 1958); and Geoffrey Perrett, *America in the Twenties* (New York: Simon & Schuster, 1982).

On Hoover and FDR, see Arthur Schlesinger, Jr., *The Crisis of the Old Order, 1919–1933* (Boston: Houghton Mifflin, 1957); William E. Leuchtenburg, *Franklin D. Roosevelt and the New Deal, 1932–1940* (New York: Harper and Row, 1963); and Frank Freidel, *Franklin D. Roosevelt: The Triumph* (Boston: Little, Brown, 1956), and *Franklin D. Roosevelt: A Rendezvous with Destiny* (Boston: Little, Brown, 1990).

On Ike, see Stephen E. Ambrose, *Eisenhower: A Life;* Vol. One: *The Soldier and Candidate, 1890–1952* (New York: Simon & Schuster, 1983), chs. 25–27.

On Ford and Carter, see John Osborne, *White House Watch: The Ford Years* (Washington: New Republic Book Co., 1977); Elizabeth Drew, *American Journal: The Events of 1976* (New York: Random House, 1977); Betty Glad, *Jimmy Carter: In Search of the Great White House* (New York: W. W. Norton, 1980); and James MacGregor Burns, *The American Experiment,* Vol. III: *The Crosswinds of Freedom* (New York: Knopf, 1989), 521, 558, 613, 625.

Henry Adams is quoted in Schlesinger, Jr., *Cycles of American History,* 293.

On Washington, see Leonard White, "George Washington: Administrator," in *Understanding the American Past,* ed. Edward N. Saveth (Boston: Little, Brown, 1954), 143–157.

See David Donald's discussion on Lincoln in Bailyn, *The Great Republic,* I, 592, 644–54; and his books, *Lincoln Reconsidered* and *Abraham Lincoln* (New York: Simon & Schuster, 1995). Allan Nevins and Irving Stone, eds., *Lincoln: A Contemporary Portrait* (Garden City, N.Y.: Doubleday, 1962), vii–viii, 188; and Stephen B. Oates, *With Malice toward None: The Life of Abraham Lincoln* (New York: Harper and Row, 1977).

On TR, see Richard Hofstadter, "Theodore Roosevelt: The Conservative As Progressive," *The American Political Tradition* (New York: Knopf, 1948), ch. 9; John Milton Cooper, *The Warrior and the Priest: Woodrow Wilson and Theodore Roosevelt* (Cambridge, Mass.: Belknap Press, 1983).

On Wilson, see Arthur S. Link, *Wilson,* 5 vols. (Princeton, N.J.: Princeton University Press, 1947–1965); Cooper, *The Warrior and the Priest;* and August Heckscher, *Woodrow Wilson* (New York: Scribner, 1991).

On FDR, see the above references, but also see Robert Dallek, *Franklin D. Roosevelt and American Foreign Policy, 1932–1945* (New York: Oxford University Press, 1979; 2nd ed., 1995, with a new Afterword).

On LBJ, see Lyndon B. Johnson, *The Vantage Point* (New York: Holt, Rinehart and Winston, 1971); Doris Kearns, *Lyndon B. Johnson and the American Dream* (New York: Harper and Row, 1976); Richard Goodwin, *Remembering America* (Boston: Little, Brown, 1988); some of the material here is drawn from Robert Dallek, *Lone Star Rising: Lyndon Johnson and His Times, 1908–1960* (New York: Oxford University Press, 1991), and the manuscript of the second volume of my biography which will be published in 1998.

On postpresidential standing, see Adam Clymer, "Presidents Ask a Place in Posterity; Posterity Keeps Rearranging Them," *The New York Times,* Jan. 24, 1993. On Reagan, see Lou Cannon, *President Reagan: The Role of a Lifetime* (New York: Simon & Schuster, 1991).

On HST, see William E. Leuchtenburg, *In the Shadow of FDR,* (Ithaca: Cornell University Press, 1983), ch. 1, and David Mc-Cullough, *Truman* (New York: Simon & Schuster, 1992).

On JFK, see the polls in the *Los Angeles Times,* Nov. 22, 1993. Also, Theodore Sorenson, *Kennedy* (New York: Harper and Row, 1965); and Richard Reeves, *President Kennedy: Profile of Power* (New York: Simon & Schuster, 1993).

On Wilson, see the references cited above, and Robert A. Divine, *Second Chance: The Triumph of Internationalism in America During World War II* (New York: Atheneum, 1971), ch. 7.

Richard E. Neustadt, *Presidential Power and the Modern Presidents* (New York: Free Press, 1990 ed.), 153, for the quote.

For Hoover, see Hofstadter, *American Political Tradition,* ch. XI; David Burner, *Herbert Hoover: A Public Life* (New York: Knopf, 1979); Martin L. Fausold, *The Presidency of Herbert Hoover* (Lawrence, Kan.: University Press of Kansas, 1985); and William J. Barber, *From New Era to New Deal: Herbert Hoover, the Economists, and American Economic Policy, 1921–1933* (New York: Cambridge University Press, 1985).

My second LBJ volume develops these arguments about Johnson's Vietnam policy in detail. For a summary, see "Lyndon Johnson and Vietnam: The Making of a Tragedy," *Diplomatic History* (Spring 1996).

On Taft, see George Mowry, *The Era of Theodore Roosevelt, 1900–1912* (New York: Harper, 1958), chs. 11–14; and Donald E. Anderson, *William Howard Taft* (Ithaca: Cornell University Press, 1973).

On Harding, see Leuchtenburg, *Perils of Prosperity, 1914–1932;* and Robert K. Murray, *The Harding Era* (Minneapolis: University of Minnesota Press, 1969).

On Carter, see Burns, *The Crosswinds of Freedom,* 529–30, 558–60, 591–93; and Jimmy Carter, *Keeping Faith* (New York: Bantam Books, 1982); Betty Glad, *Jimmy Carter* (1980); and Clark Mollenhoff, *The President Who Failed* (New York: Macmillan, 1980).

On the 1980 election, see Elizabeth Drew, *Portrait of an Election: The 1980 Presidential Campaign* (New York: Simon & Schuster, 1981). On Bush's presidency and the 1992 election, see my discussion of his presidency in Bailyn, *The Great Republic,* II, 642–52.

The quotes on Clinton from Anthony Lewis and Maureen Dowd are in *The New York Times* for July 5 and 8, 1995. Also see Paul Richter, "Tortured Decision-Making Wounds Clinton's Standing," *Los Angeles Times,* July 15, 1995; Doyle McManus, "Tacking to Right, Clinton Borrows GOP Core Issues," *Los Angeles Times,* July 17, 1995; and Paul Richter, "Clinton Beards Lions in Their Dens in Search of Votes," *Los Angeles Times,* Aug. 9, 1995. For the Kerrey speech, see *New York Times,* Oct. 21, 1995. Also see an excellent essay on Clinton's lack of definition by political scientist Joel Aberbach, "The Federal Executive under Clinton," *The Clinton Presidency: First Appraisals* (Chatham, N.J.: Chatham House Publishers, 1995).

On Nixon, see Tom Wicker, *One of Us: Richard Nixon and the American Dream* (New York: Random House, 1991), 540–41 for the quote; Stephen E. Ambrose, *Nixon: The Triumph of a Politician, 1962–1972* (New York: Simon & Schuster, 1989); Arthur Schlesinger, Jr., *The Imperial Presidency* (Boston: Houghton Mifflin, 1973); and Stanley I. Kutler, *The Wars of Watergate: The Last Crisis of Richard Nixon* (New York: Knopf, 1990).

Chapter Two

FDR is quoted in Dallek, *FDR and American Foreign Policy,* 538. For the Schlesinger, Jr., Emerson, and Churchill quotes, see *The Cycles of American History,* x, 422, 427–28.

On Washington's leadership, see Leonard D. White, *The Federalists* (New York: Macmillan, 1948), 59–65; Marcus Cunliffe,

George Washington (Boston: Little, Brown, 1958); John C. Miller, *The Federalist Era, 1789–1801* (New York: Harper, 1960); and Forrest McDonald, *The Presidency of George Washington* (New York: Norton, 1974).

On Jefferson, see Hofstadter, "Thomas Jefferson: The Aristocrat as Democrat," *The American Political Tradition,* ch. II; Forrest McDonald, *The Presidency of Thomas Jefferson* (Lawrence, Kan.: University Press of Kansas, 1976); Alexander DeConde, *This Affair of Louisiana* (1976); and Thomas A. Bailey, *A Diplomatic History of the American People* (Englewood Cliffs; N.J.: Prentice-Hall, 1980), ch. 8.

On Lincoln, see Donald, *Lincoln Reconsidered,* chs. 4, 7; and Phillip Shaw Paludan, *The Presidency of Abraham Lincoln* (Lawrence, Kan.: University Press of Kansas, 1994), 87–88, 125–30, 133–34, 145–48, 151–58, 162–66, 185–89.

On TR and Wilson, see the above references.

On FDR, see the above references as well as James MacGregor Burns, *Roosevelt: The Soldier of Freedom* (New York: Harcourt Brace, 1970).

Truman's 1948 campaign and presidential leadership are described in McCullough's *Truman* cited above.

For the Eisenhower revisionism, see Blanche Wiesen Cook, *The Declassified Eisenhower* (Garden City, N.J.: Doubleday, 1981); Robert A. Divine, *Eisenhower and the Cold War* (New York: Oxford University Press, 1981); Robert H. Ferrell, ed., *The Eisenhower Diaries* (New York: Norton, 1981); and Fred I. Greenstein, *The Hidden-Hand Presidency: Eisenhower as Leader* (New York: Basic Books, 1982). DDE's quote about Dulles is in Cook, 151–52. For an excellent critique of this literature, see Arthur Schlesinger, Jr., "The Ike Age Revisited," *Reviews in American History* (March 1983), 1–11. Also see Stephen Ambrose, *Eisenhower: A Life,* Vol II: *The President* (New York: Simon & Schuster, 1984).

The material on Johnson rests on Ch. 4 of the manuscript of my second LBJ volume. For the quotes, see Jack Valenti, *A Very Human President* (New York: Norton, 1975), 178, 182–84; and Eric Goldman, *The Tragedy of Lyndon Johnson* (New York: Knopf, 1969), 363–64.

On Nixon and Reagan, see, Ambrose, *Nixon, 1962–72,* and Stephen E. Ambrose, *Nixon: Ruin and Recovery, 1973–1990* (New York: Simon & Schuster, 1991); and Lou Cannon, *President Reagan: The Role of a Lifetime.*

See the earlier references to Wilson as well as Thomas A. Bailey,

Woodrow Wilson and the Lost Peace (New York: The Macmillan Company, 1944); *Woodrow Wilson and the Great Betrayal* (New York: The Macmillan Company, 1945); and Edwin A. Weinstein, *Woodrow Wilson: A Medical and Psychological Biography* (Princeton, N.J.: Princeton University Press, 1981).

On FDR's Court-packing fight, see William E. Leuchtenburg, "Franklin D. Roosevelt's Supreme Court 'Packing' Plan," in *Essays on the New Deal,* ed. Harold M. Hollingsworth and William F. Holmes (Austin, Tex.: University of Texas Press, 1969). The quotes are from 69, 112, 115.

On Truman's decision to cross the parallel, see McCullough, *Truman,* 800–8.

For civil rights and Ike's caution, see Ambrose, *Eisenhower: The President;* William E. Leuchtenburg, *A Troubled Feast: American Society Since 1945* (Boston: Little, Brown, 1979), 91–103; and Burns, *Crosswinds of Freedom,* 321–23, and ch. 8.

For Nixon, see the references listed in the sources for ch. 1. See also Stephen E. Ambrose, *Nixon: The Education of a Politician, 1913–1962* (New York: Simon & Schuster, 1987); Ambrose, *Nixon: Ruin and Recovery;* and Roger Morris, *Richard Milhous Nixon: The Rise of an American Politician* (New York: Holt, 1989).

On Reagan, see Cannon, *President Reagan;* and Bailyn, *The Great Republic,* II, 627, 636–37.

Chapter Three
The Johnson material is in Goldman, *Tragedy of LBJ,* 306–9, 326–27.

For Hofstadter on FDR, see *The American Political Tradition,* 316.

On Jackson, see Hofstatder, ch. 3 of *The American Political Tradition;* Glyndon G. Van Deusen, *The Jacksonian Era, 1828–1848* (New York: Harper and Row, 1959); John William Ward, *Andrew Jackson—Symbol for an Age* (New York: Oxford University Press, 1953); and Richard B. Latner, *The Presidency of Andrew Jackson: White House Politics, 1829–1837* (Athens: University of Georgia Press, 1979).

On Wilson, see the citations in chs. 1 and 2. Also see Robert Dallek, "Woodrow Wilson, Politician," *The Wilson Quarterly* (Autumn 1991), 106–14.

On FDR, see the above citations and Harvard Sitkoff, ed., *Fifty Years Later: The New Deal Evaluated* (New York: Knopf, 1985), particularly Sitkoff's Introduction, and William E. Leuchtenburg's chapter, "The Achievements of the New Deal." Leuchtenburg's quote is on 228. For the Keynes and Berlin quotes, see Leuchtenburg, *FDR and the New Deal,* 337; and Nicholas Halasz, *Roosevelt Through Foreign Eyes* (Princeton, N.J.: Van Nostrand, 1961), 318–19.

For the polling data, see *The Gallup Poll: Public Opinion, 1935–1971,* vol. II, *1949–1958* (New York: Random House, 1972), 1011, 1016, 1051–52, 1079–80, 1082, 1089, 1106, 1118, 1121, 1130–31, 1138, 1177, 1199, 1205, 1222, 1238, 1307, 1355–56, 1399, 1407, 1427, 1457–58, 1476, 1499. For the rest, see the above citations on Eisenhower's presidency as well as Leuchtenburg, *A Troubled Feast,* 85–91.

On Adams, see Samuel F. Bemis, *John Quincy Adams and the Union* (New York: Knopf, 1956).

For Buchanan, see James M. McPherson, *Battle Cry of Freedom: The Civil War Era* (New York: Oxford University Press, 1988), 153–81; and Philip S. Klein, *President James Buchanan: A Biography* (University Park, Pa.: Pennsylvania State University Press, 1962). The expert is William E. Gienapp, who is quoted in "Buchanan, James," *The Reader's Companion to American History,* ed. Eric Foner and John A. Garraty (Boston: Houghton Mifflin, 1991), 134.

The Bonus March is reconstructed in Arthur M. Schlesinger, Jr., *The Age of Roosevelt: The Crisis of the Old Order, 1919–1933* (Boston: Houghton Mifflin, 1957), 256–65. During the last thirty years, historians have tried to rehabilitate Hoover's reputation, depicting him as a progressive, innovative leader who has been misunderstood. For a summary of these views and a fine critique, see Schlesinger, Jr., *Cycles of American History,* 374–87. The Hoover quote is on 379–80.

On Bush and national economic and political trends, see Steven Rattner, "Leaking Boats on the Rising Tide?", *New York Times,* Aug. 29, 1995; and William Schneider, "Of Independent Mind," *Los Angeles Times,* Aug. 27, 1995.

On health care reform, see Cindy Jajich-Toth and Burns W. Roper, "Americans' Views on Health Care: A Study in Contradictions," *Health Affairs* (Winter 1990), 149–57; Robert J. Blendon and Karen Donelan, "Interpreting Public Opinion Surveys," *Health Affairs* (Summer 1991), 166–69; Hilary Stout, "Seeking a Cure," *Wall Street Journal,* March 12, 1993; Robin Toner, "Polls on Changes in Health Care Finds Support Amid Skepticism," *New*

York Times, Sept. 22, 1993; Ronald Brownstein, "By 2–1 Margin, Public Backs Health Care Plan," *Los Angeles Times,* Sept. 30, 1993. Paul Starr, "What Happened to Health Care Reform?" *American Prospect* (Winter 1995), 20–31. The quote is on 25. I am indebted to Professor E. Richard Brown of the UCLA School of Public Health for sharing his knowledge of the Clinton reform plan with me.

On Lincoln, see McPherson, *Battle Cry of Freedom,* 264–75; and Paludan, *The Presidency of Abraham Lincoln,* ch. 3.

On TR, see Lewis L. Gould, *The Presidency of Theodore Roosevelt* (Lawrence, Kan.: University Press of Kansas, 1991), chs. 4 and 8.

On FDR, see Dallek, *FDR and American Foreign Policy, 1932–1945,* Parts Three and Four.

On Andrew Johnson, see Eric Foner, *Reconstruction: America's Unfinished Revolution, 1863–1877* (New York: Harper and Row, 1988), chs. 5–7; and the excellent section on Reconstruction by David H. Donald in Bailyn, *The Great Republic,* II.

On LBJ and Vietnam, see Richard E. Neustadt and Ernest R. May, *Thinking in Time: The Uses of History for Decision Makers* (New York: Free Press, 1986), ch. 5, 87 for the Humphrey quote, and 161–71; and George C. Herring, *America's Longest War: The United States and Vietnam, 1950–1975* (New York: Knopf, 1986).

Chapter Four

The quote from Barber is in James David Barber, *The Presidential Character: Predicting Performance in the White House* (Englewood Cliffs, N.J.: Prentice-Hall, 1985), 2; see also Schlesinger, Jr., *The Cycles of American History,* 284–88.

On Washington, see Garry Wills, *Cincinnatus: George Washington and the Enlightenment* (Garden City, N.J.: Doubleday, 1984). The quotes are on 23, xxi, 103–4. Also see Glenn A. Phelps, "George Washington: Precedent Setter," in *Inventing the American Presidency,* ed. Thomas E. Cronin (Lawrence, Kan.: University Press of Kansas, 1989), ch. 10.

On Jefferson, see the above references, especially Hofstadter's essay, "Thomas Jefferson: The Aristocrat as Democrat," *The American Political Tradition, ch. 2.* Also see Merrill D. Peterson, *The Jefferson Image in the American Mind* (New York: Oxford University Press, 1962); and Noble E. Cunningham, Jr., *In Pursuit of Reason: The Life of Thomas Jefferson* (Baton Rouge, La.: Louisiana State University Press, 1987).

For Jackson, see John William Ward, *Andrew Jackson: Symbol for an Age* (New York: Oxford University Press, 1962), especially 1–10, 207–13. Robert V. Remini, *Andrew Jackson and the Course of American Freedom, 1822–1832* (New York: Harper and Row, 1981). For the various quotes and paraphrases, see 1–3, 29, 31, 52, 148, 91–92, 229, 350, 369–72, 374.

On Lincoln, see the references already cited, but I have relied here particularly on Donald's essays, "Getting Right with Lincoln," and "The Folklore Lincoln," in *Lincoln Reconsidered*, especially 3–4, 18, 144, 149, 151–54; Hofstadter's essay, "Abraham Lincoln and the Self-Made Myth," in *The American Political Tradition*, especially 93–95, 129, 134–36; and Oates, *With Malice Toward None*, 45, 100, 249, 259, 389.

On TR, see Mowry, *Era of Theodore Roosevelt*, 39, 110–15, 222–23, 271–72, 294–95; and Gould, *Presidency of Theodore Roosevelt*, 9–12, 15, 19–21, 141–43, 103–4, 283, 299–301.

On FDR, see the above citations, but also James MacGregor Burns, *Roosevelt: The Lion and the Fox* (New York: Harcourt, Brace, 1956), especially 77–80, 167–68, 176, 189, 203–5, 241, 265, 317–18, 337–39, 346–47, 362, 481–87; Burns, *Roosevelt: Soldier of Freedom*, especially 26; Leuchtenburg, *FDR and the New Deal, 1932–1940*, 10, 41–42, 61–62, 115–17, 167–70, 193–94, 327–41, 346; Doris Kearns Goodwin, "Franklin D. Roosevelt, 1933–1945," in *Character Above All: Ten Presidents from FDR to George Bush* (New York: Simon & Schuster, 1996), ed. Robert A. Wilson; and the *New York Times*, Jan. 24, 1993, article on public views of past presidents.

On Eisenhower, see the above references, especially *New York Times*, Jan. 24, 1993; and Stephen E. Ambrose, "Dwight D. Eisenhower, 1953–1961," in *Character Above All*.

For Kennedy and Reagan, see the above references, and two other chapters in *Character Above All*, Richard Reeves, "John F. Kennedy, 1961–1963," and Peggy Noonan, "Ronald Reagan, 1981–1989."

On Grant, see William S. McFeely, *Grant: A Biography* (New York: Norton, 1982), 251, 265, 277, 279, 281, 381–85, 392–94, 396–98, 521–22; and Foner, *Reconstruction*, 337, 509–10.

On Truman, see *The Gallup Poll, 1935–1948*, 512, 537, 557, 587, 604, 613, 633, 739, 765–66; David McCullough, "Harry S. Truman, 1945–1953," *Character Above All*; McCullough, *Truman*; and *New York Times*, Jan. 24, 1993.

On LBJ, see Robert Dallek, the above references and "Lyndon B. Johnson, 1963–1969," in *Character Above All*.

On Nixon, see Wicker, *One of Us* and Kutler, *The Wars of Watergate,* especially xiii–xiv; and Tom Wicker, "Richard M. Nixon, 1969–1974," in *Character Above All.*

Chapter Five
For the attacks on Washington, Adams and Jefferson, see John C. Miller, *The Federalist Era, 1789–1801* (New York: Harper, 1963), 198, 262–65.

On Madison, see Irving Brant, *James Madison: Commander in Chief, 1812–1836* (Indianapolis: Bobbs-Merrill, 1961); and Ralph Ketcham, *James Madison: A Biography* (New York: Macmillan, 1971).

For McKinley and the Spanish-American War, see Bailey, *A Diplomatic History,* ch. 31.

The literature on the bomb dispute is huge. The best recent summary of the case for HST is McCullough, *Truman,* 391–96, 436–44, which includes the quotes in my text. For the best recent critical assessment of HST's decision, see Gar Alperovitz, *Atomic Diplomacy: Hiroshima and Potsdam,* 2nd ed. (London: Pluto Press, 1994).

On John Adams, see Miller, *The Federalist Era,* 198–202, 210–13, 229–35, 255–77.

See Foner, *Reconstruction,* 221–27, 271–72, 333–40, on Johnson.

On Harding, see Schlesinger, Jr., *Crisis of the Old Order, 1919–1933,* 49–53; and John D. Hicks, *Republican Ascendancy, 1921–1933* (New York: Harper, 1960), 73–78.

On FDR, see Leuchtenburg, *FDR and the New Deal, 1932–1940,* chs. 10 and 11, and 277–80.

On Ford, see Osborne, *White House Watch;* Kutler, *The Wars of Watergate,* 553–69; and Schlesinger, Jr., *The Cycles of American History,* 288–89.

For the quotes on Wilson, see Bailey, *A Diplomatic History,* 603, 608, and more generally, ch. 40; and Heckscher, *Wilson,* chs. 8–12.

On LBJ, see *The Harris Poll,* Nov. 20, 1988; and *The Gallup Poll, 1959–1971,* 1870, 2003–4, 2057, 1934, 1971, 2010, 2030–31, 2122, 2270–71, 2200, 2243–44.

On Hoover, see Schlesinger, Jr., *The Crisis of the Old Order,* 155–59, 161–65, 169–70, 172–73, 241–45.

On Carter, see Leuchtenburg, *A Troubled Feast,* 276–79; Burns, *The Crosswinds of Freedom,* 521–31, 558–60, 591–93; Hedrick

Smith, *The Power Game: How Washington Works* (New York: Random House, 1988), 337–39; McDonald, *The American Presidency*, 419, n. 57.

On LBJ, see Dallek, *Lone Star Rising, passim,* and 474 for the Bradlee quote; Leuchtenburg, *American Heritage* (May/June 1990), 58 and 62; Dallek, *Diplomatic History* (Spring 1996); *New York Times,* Feb. 27, 1965, for the Reston quote; and Goldman, *The Tragedy of LBJ,* 467–70.

For Nixon and Watergate, see Kutler, *The Wars of Watergate,* especially 319, 436, 596–97, 603.

The FDR ratings are in the *New York Times,* Jan. 24, 1993.

For Schlesinger, Jr., and Emerson, see *The Cycles of American History,* 434.

Afterword
Neustadt and May, *Thinking in Time,* 105.

INDEX

Acheson, Dean, 7, 73, 163
Adams, Henry, xiii, 10
Adams, John, xi, xviii, 47, 92, 100,
    129, 130, 149, 167, 170, 176–
    78
  credibility lacking in, 168, 176,
    177, 186
  X, Y, Z affair and, 176
Adams, John Quincy, xviii, 84, 90,
    99–101, 149, 204
  Congressional message of, 99–
    100
  election of, 99, 100
  political skills of, 99, 100
  public support and consensus
    lacked by, 99–101
  vision of, 99–100
Agnew, Spiro, 183, 200
Aiken, George, 160
Allende, Salvador, 66, 79, 80
Alperovitz, Gar, 173
Ambrose, Stephen, 145
Arbenz, Jacobo, 78
Arthur, Chester A., xvii, 3, 150,
    205

Articles of Confederation, 129
Atlantic Conference, 19–20
atomic bomb, 173–76

Babcock, Orville E., 153
Bailey, Thomas A., 172
Baker, Russell, 158
Bank of the United States (BUS;
    National Bank), 89–90,
    134
Barber, James David, 125–26
Berlin, Isaiah, 96
Black Codes, 179
Bonus march, 104–5
Bosnia, 32, 39, 40
Bradlee, Ben, 199
Bradley, Bill, 106
Brandeis, Louis D., 92
Brezhnev, Leonid, 67
Brown, George, 197
Brown, Herman, 197
Brown v. *Board of Education*, 75–
    76, 146
Bryan, William Jennings, 91, 172

219